The *Un*College Alternative

The *Un*College Alternative

YOUR GUIDE TO
INCREDIBLE CAREERS &
AMAZING ADVENTURES
OUTSIDE COLLEGE

Danielle Wood

ReganBooks
An Imprint of HarperCollins *Publishers*

 For information address HarperCollins Publishers Inc., 10 East 53rd Street, New York, NY 10022.

HarperCollins books may be purchased for educational, business, or sales promotional use. For information please write: Special Markets Department, HarperCollins Publishers Inc., 10 East 53rd Street, New York, NY 10022.

FIRST EDITION

Designed by Nancy B. Field

Printed on acid-free paper.

Library of Congress Cataloging-in-Publication Data has been applied for.

ISBN 0-06-039308-4

00 01 02 03 04 ❖/RRD 10 9 8 7 6 5 4 3 2

Contents

Acknowledgments vii
Editor's Note ix

Part 1
THE COLLEGE QUESTION

1 Just the Facts: *What Your Guidance Counselor Isn't Telling You About College* 3
2 Ask the Experts: *How to Find Your Calling or Advice for Finding Yourself* 13

Part 2
TAKING TIME OFF

3 Stepping Out: *Why Time Off Is Time Saved* 33
4 Globe-trotting: *How to Work Your Way Around the World* 37
5 Internships: *If the Shoe Fits, Work It* 62
6 Do the Right Thing: *Jobs for People Who Want Good Karma* 80

Part 3
TRAINING FOR REAL LIFE: ALTERNATIVE SCHOOLS, COURSES, AND APPRENTICESHIP PROGRAMS

7 Giving College the Kiss-off: *Training for Real Life* 105

8 Make Your Cake and Eat It, Too: *Careers in the Kitchen* 119
9 Healing Hands: *Careers in Alternative Medicine* 142
10 Busting the Blue Collar Myth 163
11 Sitting Pretty: *Breaking into Beauty* 180

Part 4
SCHOOL'S OUT FOREVER! AMAZING CAREERS WITH OR WITHOUT COLLEGE

12 Life with Mother Nature: *Jobs in the Great Outdoors* 193
13 Art Smarts: *Art Without Starvation* 215
14 How to Be a Player: *Going Hollywood* 232
15 Yes, Sir!: *Careers in Uniform* 253
16 Getting High (Tech): *How to Make It in a Brave New World* 272
17 Who's the Boss: *Starting Your Own Business* 289

Afterword 315
Appendix: Homework for Life 317

Acknowledgments

Without an essay in *Newsweek*, this book never would have come about. My thanks to the magazine for printing it and to Judith Regan for reading it and deciding to take a chance. To Vanessa Stich, whose strong opinions and unfailing insight were right on the money—you are an editing goddess. And to my agent, Gary Morris, who always managed to make me laugh, even with a honeymoon at stake . . .

A heartfelt thanks to everyone who agreed to be interviewed for this book. You made research a pleasure. And a special thank-you to Gail Blanke, whose passion is contagious.

To Nana, for interesting conversation and incredible chicken. To my parents, who have always encouraged me to dream big, and who lead by example. And to my brother Matthew, who has never found a mountain he can't climb—both literally and figuratively. To my new family: Diana, Anthony, Margaret, David, and Lauren—I'm happy to be the newest Wood's Original.

And thanks especially to Eric, for being patient enough to let me find the next big thing.

Acknowledgments

Editor's Note

When I was a high school student, I didn't think twice about going to college. The way I saw it, I could either head out to a four-year university or start scooping ice cream. Not a tough choice. What I didn't realize then is that there are hundreds of other alternatives for motivated, challenge-seeking young people that I never even heard of—from guiding bike tours through the French countryside to becoming a doctor of Chinese medicine to joining the high-tech revolution. Whatever your ambitions are, I guarantee that there is an amazing future out there for you, and that this book can help you find it.

At it heart, this book is about defying the limits of the ordinary. Don't be fooled by those that might say "You can't," "You shouldn't," or "You're too young": we are living in a time of unprecedented opportunity and its time to seize the day. As for me, I'm taking Danielle's suggestion and planning an extended trip to teach English in Thailand. Remember, it's never too late—or too early—to follow your dreams.

Part 1

The College Question

CHAPTER 1

Just the Facts: *What Your Guidance Counselor Isn't Telling You About College*

> **"You can do a lot of things if you don't know you can't."**
>
> —Sam Brownback, U.S. Congressman

YOU HAD ABOUT TEN YEARS OF BLISS. FROM SIX to sixteen almost no one asked you what you wanted to be when you grew up. Junior year of high school hits and *whammo!* Suddenly you're supposed to have all the answers. And you don't, do you?

Well frankly, if you did it would be a miracle. At sixteen it's doubtful that your work experience extends beyond the local mall. The truth is, it's a rare person who's sure what they want to do with their life at age thirty, let alone thirteen.

OK, so here's the problem. Just because *you* don't know what you should do with your life doesn't mean no one else does.

We're talking parents, grandparents, guidance counselors, the mailman . . . everybody's got an opinion. Unfortunately, your uncertainty makes you a prime target—you might as well be wearing a sandwich sign scrawled PLEASE ADVISE. In other people's eyes, you're like a fresh lump of clay, waiting to be molded. Your Uncle Morris wants you to be a lawyer. Your mom tries to convince you that accounting is making a comeback. "Plastics," your neighbor winks.

And then it comes, like a life preserver thrown over the edge of a sinking ship . . . the college option. Four heavenly years of keg parties and career postponement. A sticker from the college of your choice slapped onto the bumper of your proud parents' car.

There's no doubt about it. In this day and age, going straight to college is the obvious choice. So obvious, in fact, that few people consider doing otherwise. Before I shatter your illusions, let's get one thing straight—this book isn't meant to convince you that college is a waste of time. I spent four years behind university walls and I don't regret it for a minute. What this book *is* meant to do is open your mind to a

Percentage of High School Sophomores Who Reported Being Advised to Attend College by Various Adults: 1980 and 1990

	All Students	All Students	Lowest Test Quartile	Lowest Test Quartile
Recommended by	**1980**	**1990**	**1980**	**1990**
Father	59%	77%	40%	60%
Mother	65%	83%	48%	65%
Guidance Counselor	32%	65%	26%	56%

sea of options you may never have considered, so convinced were you that college was the only ride down the rainbow to the pot of gold. Let me throw a curveball your way—you can succeed in life without a college degree. Almost 20 percent of this year's *Fortune* "400 Richest People" did.

HISTORY LESSON

Heading straight to college may seem like a given now, but this wasn't the case for most of the century. Before World War II, only one in six Americans went on to college. Then along came a little thing called the GI Bill, meant to make it possible for former soldiers to get an education. Suddenly the college gates were thrown open and the stampede began. It's only in the past fifty years that college was transformed from the exception to the rule. Since the end of World War II, the number of entering freshmen has shot up from 15 to 65 percent. College is being touted as the new necessity.

Which would be fine if it were true. News flash: 70 percent of all jobs in the United States only require alternative education and on-the-job training. Don't get me wrong. I'm in no way trying to say that college is useless. Higher education is a wonderful thing. But be aware that it's also a two-hundred-billion-dollar industry. It's no accident that the national opinion about the necessity of a college degree has changed—it's the result of years of hard-core marketing.

Never before have so many students been told that college is the way to go. A study by the U.S. Department of Education showed that a whopping 65 percent of 1990's high school sophomores reported being told by their guidance counselors that they should apply to college—twice as many as in 1980.

Even students who scored in the lowest quarter of their high school class were being pressured to apply—never mind the fact that they showed little interest in hitting the books.

THE BIG LIE

When I was a kid, my mom would never make me peanut butter and jelly sandwiches. She told me I didn't like them. I grew up eating peanut butter sandwiches and jelly sandwiches, but never mixing the two. Truth is, I didn't try a peanut butter and jelly sandwich until I was about twenty. Strangely enough, I loved it. All those years my mom had told me that I hated PB&J. And I believed her. Turns out it was my *mother* who hated it, not me. I had been subtly brainwashed . . .

So big deal. I ate tuna fish. In this particular case, the consequences weren't drastic. But college is another story. All across America, high school students are being told that college is their admission ticket to life, as if their diploma will pave the road to certain success. The truth is that there are more college graduates than there are jobs that require a degree. According to the Bureau of Labor Statistics, there were 28,983,000 college graduates in the labor force in 1990. Twenty percent of them were "underemployed"—working in jobs that didn't require a degree. And despite the contention that college will land you a fat little paycheck, statistics from the Bureau show that more than one fifth of college graduates earn less than $23,317—the median for kids with no more than a high school diploma. It's true that college opens doors for a lot of people. But be aware that each year a large chunk of college kids graduate and wind up working behind the same Starbuck's counter as their GED brethren.

This isn't meant to depress you. It's meant to empower you. Ignorance may be bliss, but knowing that college isn't the door-opener it once was frees you to make a *conscious choice*: Is college for you?

There are many very good reasons to go to college: Your lifelong dream is to become a doctor or lawyer, you live for life in the classroom, you've got a burning desire for book learnin'. . . . There are also some not very good reasons to go to college: to get away from your hometown, to make your parents happy, or because you have no idea what else to do. Let's get two things straight. One: There are a slew of exciting, mind-blowing ways to see the world and figure out your place in it. Two: You may never make your parents happy.

CHECK, PLEASE

I don't know anyone who walks into a store, points to something, and says, "Ring it up" without even looking at the price tag. It doesn't take a genius to know that you look something

Show Me the Money

Colleges are footing part of the bill, but most families still kick in quite a bit.

In general if your family makes $100,000–124,000 a year, the guys in Financial Aid figure you can foot the entire bill for a private college—about $20,100 each September.

Families that pull in $70,000–79,000 get billed for the $12,300 a year it costs to attend a public college without aid.

And a family that makes $50,000–59,000 is expected to pay $7,400 a year, the price of a two-year public school.

over before laying down any money. But most students get on the college bandwagon without ever scrutinizing the goods. You wouldn't drop $80,000 on a pair of pants without deciding if you really needed them. Why should college be any different?

How much is that sheepskin in the window?

College may give you four years to park yourself, but the meter's running, make no mistake. The average total price to attend a private four-year college in 1995 was $20,000 a year. Even public schools don't come cheap—$10,800 a year in 1995. And things are getting worse. It's projected that hanging your hat at a private university as an entering freshman in 2005 will cost a whopping $125,000! Public school freshmen won't fare much better: $75,000 for four years.

Colleges would have you believe that inflation's to blame for these unbelievable numbers. But they're giving inflation a bad rap. The truth is, the average price of room, board, and tuition, even allowing for inflation, increased by 31 percent at private colleges and 20 percent at public ones between 1986 and 1996.

The biggest problem is, the price of college attendance has increased much faster than family incomes. Because more financial aid is being offered, more students can afford to go, but most are deep in debt come graduation. Students who get out of school in four years take with them an average debt of $13,200. That's a pretty heavy load, considering that the average starting salary for graduates with a bachelor's degree is only $22,000.

WHAT COLLEGE IS . . . AND WHAT IT ISN'T

Let's be honest. It's not hard to get into college. There are more than three thousand schools in America and the bulk of them are open-admit. The hardest part is sticking things out. According to a study by the National Center for Education Statistics, more than 30 percent of students who enter college don't return for their sophomore year. Three out of four students who enter college haven't snagged a degree five years later. These are scary numbers. Especially when you consider the debt involved. So before we go any further, how about a little homework.

Is College for You?

My strength is:

a) My head
b) My hands
c) My heart
d) My intuition

If I could be anything, I would be:

a) An artist
b) A chef
c) A craftsman
d) A professional

I would rather:

a) Do something active
b) Read a book
c) Paint a picture
d) Have a conversation

I would enjoy life as:

a) A hotshot CEO

b) A tour guide

c) An entrepreneur

d) An artist

I like:

a) To lead

b) To learn

c) To think

d) To do

I prefer to:

a) Address things as they arise

b) Live by the seat of my pants

c) Depend on others to do the nitty-gritty

d) Think things out before acting

If I won $3,000 I would:

a) Use it to travel

b) Donate it

c) Start a business

d) Take classes

If I knew college wouldn't affect my career opportunities I'd:

a) Go anyway

b) Take a break first

c) Start working right away

d) Decide in a few years whether or not to go

Give yourself the allotted number of points as follows, according to your answers.

ANSWERS:

1) a–10, b–0, c–3, d–5
2) a–5, b–0, c–3, d–10
3) a–3, b–10, c–0, d–5
4) a–10, b–0, c–5, d–3
5) a–3, b–10, c–5, d–0
6) a–3, b–0, c–5, d–10
7) a–0, b–3, c–5, d–10
8) a–10, b–5, c–0, d–3

If you scored:
0–20: It's hard for you to sit still! A hands-on learning environment might better fit your personality.
20–50: Consider college, but don't ignore your other options.
50–80: College seems like a good fit.

THE WORLD IS MY CLASSROOM

If you want to become fat, sit down and eat out of boredom. If you want to become poor, sit down and learn despite it. In other words, don't waste time and money on something if you'll get absolutely nothing out of it. If you love life in the classroom, by all means go. But if the traditional learning formula bores you, get your education somewhere else. College is only one path to a great career. For some students it can be an expensive and unnecessary delay. A culinary institute, massage therapy school, or similar vocational training might be more your style.

Don't forget: College is not a race. It's not a crime to take a few years off and do something else until you feel ready to hit the books in earnest. Three quarters of entering freshmen won't finish in four years. So why are so many people afraid to take a little break? Why not spend some time elsewhere getting something "out of your system," learning about life, or figuring out what it is you *don't* want to do so you can cross it off your list of possibilities? Truth is, there are lots of ways to expand your mind or expand yourself that have nothing to do with books.

TO COLLEGE OR NOT TO COLLEGE

College is many wonderful things, but it's not a magic compass for life. They don't hand you directions along with your diploma. You're going to have to chart your own course though the world, with or without a degree.

This book lays out some options you may not have considered. It's meant to open your eyes to what's out there. From internships to international jobs, boat-building apprenticeships to film school, there are many paths through life that enhance college or bypass it altogether.

You have plenty of years ahead of you to settle. This may be the only time in your life when you have nothing holding you back—no obligations to spouse or child, no standard of living that you need to maintain. If you're ever going to struggle, do it now. Dream big. Settle later.

CHAPTER 2

Ask the Experts: *How to Find Your Calling or Advice for Finding Yourself*

> **"The only thing to do with good advice is to pass it on. It is never of any use to oneself."**
>
> —Oscar Wilde

WHEN I WAS IN SECOND GRADE I DECIDED THAT I wanted to be a fairy godmother. Really. Too much Cinderella and not enough advice about the realities of the workday world, I guess. I was all ready for a life of scoping out pumpkins and making friends with mice. No one had the heart to tell me that "Fairy Godmother" didn't appear in your typical career guide . . .

Unfortunately, as you get older, people become less reluctant to spoil your fantasies. Your future suddenly becomes everyone else's business. And everybody's got an opinion. Even random acquaintances start asking, "What are you going to do with your life?"—and they won't take "fairy godmother" for an answer.

After high school, I used to avoid career conversations at all costs. I'd dream of walking around with a sign around my neck: DON'T ASK WHAT I'M DOING WITH MY LIFE. Sure, it would have been rude, but tact is overrated.

THIS IS YOUR LIFE

Despite the fact that people will tell you differently, there is no such thing as a one-size-fits-all career. Just like only you can make the call on college, only you can decide where you want it to take you, should you decide to go. And only you can figure out which jobs are a perfect fit, and which are less appealing than life as a McDonald's cashier.

Funny thing is, countless people will ask you *what* you want to do with your life, but almost no one will ask you *how* you want to live it. Since graduation I've tried my hand at everything from publicist to copywriter, actress to temp, movie extra to jewelry salesperson. If there's one thing I've learned, one bit of unsolicited advice that actually would have helped, one thing that no one ever told me that I wish they had, it's this: It's as important to choose the *life* you want as it is the *job* you want.

Think about all the times people have asked you *what* you want to do. Well what about the other three W's: Who,

Final Four

The U.S. Department of Labor predicts that these cities will have the most jobs in the upcoming years:

Atlanta • Dallas • Houston • Los Angeles

Where, Why? Who do you want to be? Where do you want to live? Why? These are no small potatoes. But I can't think of a single guidance counselor who ever asked. And I don't remember ever asking myself.

Thing is, a job is only as good as the life that goes with it. I have a friend who makes more money than he knows what to do with, in a field where he has gotten a lot of attention. He's thinking of quitting to go back to school. Everyone thinks he's crazy. "How can he turn his back on such a great job?!" etc. Well, easy. He's twenty-five years old and he hasn't had time to go on a date in three years.

I have another friend who's a struggling actor barely scraping by. He's so broke he doesn't even have furniture. He's good with computers. He could ditch it all for a tidy little paycheck and his very own cubicle, but he loves acting and the creativity that goes with it. He wouldn't give that up for all the furniture in the world.

YOU'RE THE BOSS

When it comes to creating a life for yourself, it's important to figure out what you value. Is it creativity and freedom? Helping others? Limitless wealth and world domination? There are no wrong answers when it comes to values, but you do have to choose. Because, like it or not, you can't have it all. If you want to become the next Warren Buffet, you'll probably have to give up a little free time. If you want to save the whales, you'll have to ditch the idea of a Park Avenue penthouse.

There are piles of personality tests you can take to figure out what you "should" be doing. You can also drop a C-note for a one-hour tête-à-tête with a private career counselor. But assuming you don't have money to burn, may I suggest the cheapskate approach to determining your values . . . you, a pen, and a piece of paper. Let's go.

Lifestyle Test

1) **On New Year's Eve I would rather:**
   a) Spend the night in a sleeping bag under the stars
   b) Stay up until dawn creating a masterpiece
   c) Take a group of friends out on the town
   d) Spend the night in a five-star hotel with room service
   e) Spend the night working in a soup kitchen
2) **My ideal job would let me:**
   a) Work in an ever-changing atmosphere, not behind a desk
   b) Constantly use my imagination
   c) Report only to myself, I don't like people looking over my shoulder
   d) Earn the big bucks
   e) Make a difference in the world
3) **Most important to me is:**
   a) Independence
   b) Feeling inspired creatively
   c) Being at the helm
   d) Money and security
   e) Helping others
4) **I am:**
   a) Easily bored—I need new challenges to keep me interested
   b) A creator—I like to pursue my own vision

c) A control freak—I like to be in charge
d) A team player—I work best with a goal in mind
e) A healer—I like to make people feel good

5) **I work best:**
a) Doing rather than thinking
b) In a creative environment
c) Under pressure
d) When there are incentives
e) Bringing out the best in others

6) **In ten years, it would bother me most not to have:**
a) The freedom to go anywhere at the drop of a hat
b) Creative fulfillment
c) Success and recognition
d) Material comfort
e) Love and commitment

7) **My secret weapon is:**
a) My curiosity
b) My intuition
c) My wit
d) My mind
e) My heart

RESULTS:

Mostly A's: You're a free spirit. You don't like to be tied down. Working behind a desk would kill you—look for a job that keeps you thinking on your feet. Live in a big city with lots to explore, or somewhere with easy access to the open road.

Mostly B's: You're a creator. You work best when you're inspired and should avoid a corporate atmosphere at all costs. Choose a job that uses your imagination. Try to live amongst other artists.

Mostly C's: You're a leader. You like to be in charge. You work best when flying by the seat of your pants. Consider starting your own business. Choose a place to live with lots of entrepreneurial potential.

Mostly D's: You're a player. You want someone to show you the money and you're willing to work within the system to get it. Don't be ashamed of your aspirations. Suit up and move somewhere with the most corporate opportunities.

Mostly E's: You're a healer. You want to make a difference in the world. Choose a job that lets you interact with more than a computer and a telephone. You have a big heart, so use it! Settle down in a small town or a laid-back city and surround yourself with close friends.

BE YOUR OWN CAREER COUNSELOR

When you have no idea what you want to do, it can be tempting to shell out money to have a professional tell you. Problem is, it's hard to separate the guys who know what they're doing from the ones who paid fifty bucks for an ad in the yellow pages and dubbed themselves "career counselors." My advice is this: Try the do-it-yourself method before heading off to a pro. Professionals may (or may not) have a slew of degrees slapped on the wall, but you know yourself better than anyone on earth. You know what you like, and what you wouldn't do in a million years. They may seem like they have all the answers, but no career counselor can look in a crystal ball and tell you where to find success. They're going to ask you some questions or have you fill out a stack of questionnaires.

So if you're feeling cheap, do it yourself. Here are variations on some of the more popular pay-to-play exercises:

EXERCISE ONE

Part A:

By some freak of nature, you have nine lives. Write one sentence describing each of them. Then pick your three favorites, or have a friend pick for you.

Part B:

If, fifty years from now, someone were to write a movie based on your life, how would it play out for each of these three options: Was there fame? Success? Fulfillment? Love? Which parts of each movie excited you? Which parts freaked you out?

EXERCISE TWO

Ask your parents and two friends to list ten things they think you're good at.

Meanwhile, write down ten things that *you* think you're good at.

Write down ten things you absolutely hate to do.

TYPE CASTING

In order to pull it all together, you need to balance your strengths and weaknesses with your dreams and aspirations. Because, let's face it, you're not going to last very long as a personal assistant if you refuse to take orders from anybody. And you may think a musician has the coolest job in the world, but you'll have a hard time making it if you're tone-deaf.

Before you set your sights on a specific job, you need to be honest with yourself—*what are you good at*? Are you a people person? A dreamer? A doer? A talker? An organizer? Because as much as I hate to pigeonhole, people generally fall into five rough categories. At least according to career counseling powerhouse Roger Birkman, and I've got to say, I think the guy's onto something.

Now I know you're looking for immediate gratification, and don't you worry, I'm going to deliver. But let me say first that my little exercise isn't going to do Birkman justice. If you want the full-out analysis, you're going to have to contact him directly or read *True Colors,* his book. . . . That said, here's an exercise to get you through in the meantime.

I'd describe myself as:

a) Assertive and direct
b) Spontaneous and talkative
c) Organized and focused
d) Imaginative and thoughtful

I'd rather be a:

a) Carpenter or architect
b) Sales rep or lawyer
c) Bookkeeper or administrator
d) Journalist or designer

My ideal work environment is:

a) Competitive, with me at the top
b) Varied and team-oriented
c) Structured
d) Cutting-edge or innovative

Personality-wise, I'm:

a) A leader

b) A people person—friendly to everyone
c) A perfectionist and a scheduler
d) Creative and sometimes shy

I'm a:

a) Problem solver
b) Team player
c) Organizer
d) Inventor

I'd describe my style as:

a) Proactive and energetic
b) Reflective and thoughtful
c) Easily excitable
d) Cautious and orderly

If a problem comes up:

a) I like to solve it immediately. I'm decisive.
b) I'll discuss it with other people and we'll decide together what to do.
c) I'm cautious and insistent.
d) I like to think about it and brainstorm ways to fix it.

How would other people describe you?

a) Full of energy
b) Friendly
c) Dependable
d) An individual

Which phrase best sums you up?

a) "That guy could lead a horse to water *and* make him drink."
b) "That guy could sell a wool sweater to someone sweating in the Sahara."
c) "That guy could whip a hurricane into shape."
d) "That guy could be the next Leonardo da Vinci or Henry Ford."

The Birkman Method is divided into two parts—interests and style. Interests are what you like to do and style is how you like to act. So even though you might have BLUE as your interest color, you might be GREEN in style. Your answers to the first five questions relate to your interests and your answers to the last four let you know your style.

Mostly A's: RED
Mostly B's: GREEN
Mostly C's: YELLOW
Mostly D's: BLUE

Red Interests: You like hands-on work that lets you see a finished product unfold. You like to build.
Green Interests: You're blessed with a golden tongue and like jobs that let you use it to sell or motivate.
Yellow Interests: You enjoy work that lets you deal with details. You run a tight ship and like to organize.
Blue Interests: You need a job that uses your imagination and creativity. You like to brainstorm.
Red Style: You're assertive, friendly, straightforward, and practical.
Green Style: You're a people magnet—social, enthusiastic, and charming.
Yellow Style: You're loyal, methodical, consistent, and organized.
Blue Style: You're intuitive and dreamy. You're kind of shy and hate confrontation.

Once you've got your colors down, you can start homing in on a career. Not that the palette's gospel, but it can at least get you moving, maybe even in the right direction. According to Birkman, if you're seeing red, you'd be a good small-business

For the real Birkman test, and someone qualified to give it, contact:

Birkman International Inc.
3040 Post Oak Blvd., Suite 1425
Houston, TX 77056
(713) 623-2760
www.birkman.com

owner. Other red careers are: producer, surgeon, aerospace engineer, architect, astronaut, private eye, and farmer. Greens tend to be good at marketing, advertising, therapy, teaching, and public relations. They also make good antiques dealers, auctioneers, and agents. If you're yellow, you might try your hand at banking, anthropology, engineering, court reporting, astronomy, or research. Yellows also do well as film editors, systems analysts, and archeologists. Are you blue? Take heart. You'd be a great composer, writer, inventor, editor, animator, child care worker, or landscape architect—basically anything creative.

ADVICE FROM THE BIG LEAGUES

Now that you've got a handle on who you are, designing a career should be a piece of cake. I say "designing" because landing in the right career is no accident. It's about consciously threading it all together—interests, goals, skills. It's about determining your dreams and then figuring out how to make them a reality.

Nella Barkley, the "Barkley" in Crystal-Barkley, gets paid big bucks to help people design their lives. The first step Barkley recommends is coming up with a mission statement—a phrase that defines who you are and what you're about. "Life and work are integral pieces," she says. Don't separate your job from the rest of your life; try to find a career that will let you explore your personal interests while still pulling in a paycheck.

First of all, Barkley warns everyone to forget the idea that other people are in charge. Choosing a career means exactly what it says: *choosing*. "There is no one perfect job for you," Barkley says, and no one has all the answers—not parents, not teachers, not even career counselors. So what keeps Barkley in business? She helps clients help themselves. And believe me, she knows what she's doing. An independent researcher at Columbia recently did a study of former Crystal-Barkley workshop participants. The average alum boosted their salary by $12,800 a year by listening to Crystal-Barkley's advice.

What's the secret? Barkley believes that every person has "unique human resources." To jump-start your life, you have to figure out what makes you special and what it is you want. The typical job candidate will fail because "she has not defined her goals. Goals provide the rationale for our lives, the reason for getting up in the morning, your 'mission,' or simply where you're headed." In other words, you can't get no satisfaction if you don't know what satisfies you.

Problem is, people get so focused on finding something to *be* that they become rigid, fixated on a word like "doctor" or "lawyer." Titles can be your biggest enemy; it's more important to figure out what your "mission" is than to figure out what to call yourself.

For example, let's say you want to help protect the environment. Thinking you don't have the skills to get hired you might send a check to the Sierra Club and apply for a job at Denny's. But in reality, you don't need to launch a nonprofit or hug trees in the rainforest to help protect the environment. You could help out in lots of capacities. "You could become a teacher, journalist, explorer, lobbyist, EPA inspector, forest ranger, or the VP of public affairs for a waste management firm. Unfortunately, many people never connect their job prospects to something they care about," says Barkley. "That's a surefire route to mediocrity and frustration."

The point is to figure out what goals are important to you, regardless of where you're pursuing them. Once you know what inspires you, you can figure out which jobs will allow you to do it. Barkley suggests a few exercises to help uncover what makes you tick:

1. Pretend that you've been given a highly visible billboard. You can put whatever message you like on it—whatever it is you want people to see. You may never have another chance like this again, so think carefully. You can use words, images, or both. Your message can announce a favorite cause, encourage or discourage behavior (like smoking or eating meat), or just declare who you are to the world.
2. Suppose you became an all-powerful ruler for a day. What in our society or in your immediate environment would you change? What do you think needs doing? Don't feel constrained by the idea that you'll have to fix it yourself, just think about what you would like *somebody* to do. You have the power to fix anything. It could be your car or the universe, your neighborhood recycling program or global pollutants. Write down exactly what needs doing in your world.
3. Now that you've listed what needs doing, which changes are you willing to participate in yourself? To what extent? For example, if you want a cure discovered for cancer,

Too nervous to do your own analyzing? Here are three Internet tests to help you out:

www.keirsey.com

It costs eight bucks but it's pretty thorough. This test, called the Keirsey self-directed search, breaks people up into six basic categories. Once they figure you out, they'll suggest careers.

www.queendom.com

Calling all test junkies! You know who you are . . . an almost obscene amount of test options for people with no clue what makes them tick. Absolutely free.

www.missouri.edu/~cppcwww/holland.shtml

Really for University of Missouri students, but up for grabs. A free version of John Holland's method. This test will help you match what you like and what you're good at, with careers that suit you.

would you: Fund research? Raise awareness? Organize a think tank of scientists to apply their efforts to the problem? Work in a hospital? In your vision, what do you see yourself actually doing, and how deeply involved are you?

WRAPPING IT UP

The problem with doing things yourself is this: You're both the client and the counselor. Don't be lazy. When time's up get it all together and take a long hard look. Where are your answers pointing you? What do the results from all the exercises so far have in common? What themes are beginning to surface?

INTERVIEW

Gail Blanke, Career Coach Extraordinaire

Gail Blanke is the author of *In My Wildest Dreams: Living the Life You Long For.* She's also a speaker, counselor, and one of the most kick-ass motivators I've ever met. I asked her to put in her two cents on the whole "What should I do with my life" dilemma.

What would you tell every twenty-something you met if you had twenty minutes alone with them?

You don't need to start with a plan. People give you the impression that you're supposed to already know who you are. You don't need to already know. Life is a constant act of becoming, not a fixed place of arrival.

One of the big things I really wish for young people to know is that *it is when you don't know that you are the most open to possibility.* So don't fall for it when people demand of you, "What are you going to do? What are you going to major in? What are you going to do with your life?" Look at them and say, "I don't know. I am open to the possibilities. I am on an adventure, and it's going to be different."

Think of it like being between trapezes. High school, or whatever, is this past life that you've been holding on to. In the mist somewhere, sailing toward you, is the trapeze of your future, whatever that is. You can't see it, but you know it's out there. The problem is, you can't hold onto two trapezes at the same time, so you have to let go of the old one, as you begin to reach out in absolute faith toward the new one.

In that time, that moment when you've let go, and you haven't connected with a new one, you're not holding on to anything. You're between trapezes. And in that moment, it's all possible. When you've already decided, then things fall into place and that path emerges for you. But when you *haven't* decided, it's *all* possible, everything is possible.

So how can people narrow down their choices?

Begin by asking yourself what your commitments are. What would make your life worth living? What do you stand for? What is your idea of a great life, completely apart from the limitations you now see on yourself?

We all have expectations—scripts for how life "should" go. I "should" make x amount of money before I'm thirty, I "should" have a car, I "should" have an apartment of my own. I call it "should-ing on yourself." One of the things you need to ask yourself repeatedly is "Who made *that* up?" Often the fixed reality that holds you back is actually somebody else's idea of reality.

My philosophy is this: There's something to be learned from every experience that will be useful. You're basically weaving a fabric, and every color counts. You're not handed a pattern, you just develop it as you go. And that's the thrill, that's the kick of it.

Why do you think so many people are afraid to take a risk?

In our culture, we like to ask our kids, "What do you want to be when you grow up?" It's a question that implies a finished destination you're supposed to reach and stay at. It teaches us to think in terms of arrival. But the idea that we become something and stay it, that we "finish" establishing an identity, is a myth. In fact, you're this ball rolling forward, like a big snowball that just keeps gathering up more stuff on the way.

Final words of wisdom?

Life is a banquet, really it is. And most of us are starving to death because we don't see that it's all there for us to take. I think the whole trick is continually exploring what you're passionate about.

Make the shift from waiting to be chosen, to choosing. If you wait for the signal, if you wait for permission, you could wait a lifetime. There is none.

Your only real job is to have a fabulous life. That's it. However you define great and fabulous. That is what you're here for. You're not here to settle. You're not here to fulfill somebody else's dream. You're not here to have an OK-mediocre-"I got through it" life. It's to thrill you. So that you can have on your tombstone, "It was beyond my wildest dreams and I wouldn't have missed it for anything in the world."

WHAT NOW?

You've listened to the experts, you've thought about what makes you unique and filled out quizzes 'til your fingers are numb. Now it's time for some concrete options. This book has a little something for everyone, but what that something is depends on who you are.

Part Two is for anyone who's considered jumping off the conveyor belt of life and taking a break. Whether you're about to apply for college, in the middle of school, or tearing your hair out at a job you hate, there's something here that could stave off that nervous breakdown. From internships to volunteer work, seasonal jobs to work around the world, this section will get you thinking about bailing out for a little while so you can figure out where you're going.

For those who have a sneaking suspicion that college isn't all it's cracked up to be, *Part Three* might be the kick in the ass you need to try something else. Truth be told, there are cheaper, faster, or just more relevant ways to learn that have nothing to do with a traditional college campus. Whether you need help figuring out how to snag a degree without leaving your living room, or want to pick up real skills you know you can use, *Part Three* will get you going.

Part Four wraps it all up with jobs that ditch the desk. This is the section for anyone who gets itchy doing the same thing day in and day out. From tips on breaking into Hollywood to starting your own business, this section highlights some of the coolest careers out there, and tells you how to get in the door.

Best Job Outlook:

website manager, military (commissioned officer), military (enlisted person), computer systems analyst, Protestant minister

Part 2

Taking Time Off

CHAPTER 3

Stepping Out: *Why Time Off Is Time Saved*

> **"Taking time off teaches you nothing, everything. I don't think there are any formulas. I don't think there are any pat things to convince anyone. All kids should take time off because for god's sake, they're going to live to be ninety. That means they have seventy years left before they die. What's the hurry?"**
>
> —Cornelius Bull, The Center for Interim Programs

AMERICANS TEND TO HAVE A VERY SILLY PHILOSOPHY called "faster is better." We rush through life, marching from grade school to high school, high school to college, college to corporate America—without ever taking a breather to be *unsure* for a little while, to honestly ask ourselves what we'd like to do if we could wave a magic wand.

But the truth is, life is not a race to the finish. You can jump off the great conveyor belt anytime, by doing a simple thing called taking time off: a few months (or years) to stop rushing and start living.

Time off is time well spent. Contrary to popular belief it will not ruin your chances for college, a job, a life. Not only will it give you a much needed break, but it may help you figure out what the hell you want to do once you're back in the game.

Taking time off lets you explore the ridiculous. It lets you try out some things you think you'd never "really" get hired to do. It can get an old dream out of your system once and for all and help you find a new one. Or it can do none of those things and just give you some time out.

If you're a high school student, taking a year or two off before college lets you check out your shaky little legs and learn to stand on your own two feet. It gets you a one-way ticket out of life as you know it—away from your parents, your friends, and all the expectations they have for you. It gives you some time to evaluate college for yourself (away from the herd), try a few jobs on for size, see the world or even fail miserably at something and move on. Your year in the real world might convince you that college isn't the right choice for you after all. Or it might help you see how college fits into your master plan. Then when you *do* decide to hit the books, you'll know why. You'll get much more out of college, because you'll know yourself that much better.

And you'll be ahead of the game. Because taking time off isn't reserved for the pre-college set. College students by the thousands are dropping their books and quitting campus for a while. And according to *U.S. News* Online, "as many as one in ten freshly minted grads postpone a 'real' job" to take some time off.

Whether you're about to leave the nest, knee deep in college, or on the brink of graduation, taking a break could save you from becoming barely legal and burnt out. And despite parental panic, most kids who take time off before or during college eventually end up on campus, and do fine.

Neal Bull has had about three thousand people in dire need of a break come through his door since he started his company, The Center for Interim Programs, twenty years ago. Things have changed a lot since he was at Princeton, when tuition was a mere four hundred and twenty bucks a year. Now he's a man on a mission to give students a chance to find whatever it is that lights their fire.

According to Bull, it's not the students who are the problem. "Most kids are very aware of their lack of readiness for college. Most do it simply because they can't think of anything else, or because their parents are hysterical they won't. It scares some parents to death. I particularly like talking to parents because A) I'm older than they are and B) I'm a lot more irreverent. I just look at the father and say, Are you financially masochistic? You just enjoy writing checks? Does it give you a good feeling to spend a thousand bucks a week to have some child of yours wasting time and then justify it in your mind by saying, 'Well, they're growing up'? Well that's a hell of an expensive way to grow up and it's a waste."

My advice to you is this: If you're not ready for college, don't go. A break is nothing to be ashamed of. Slap it right there on your résumé. It may scare parents to death, but a few years off enchants admissions officers. It may worry certain employers, but with most, it will give you something interesting to talk about during the interview. Either way, it sets you apart.

WHAT TO DO

So now that you have a year or two carved out, what do you do with it? The sky's the limit. If you're like most people your age, you don't have too many serious obligations weighing you down. Relish your freedom! Avoid conventionality at all costs. You've got your whole life to be a slave to the system.

Your year off is for a different animal altogether—jobs, internships, and opportunities that feel more like play than work. I'm talking internships where you'll be rappelling down European mountains, outdoor jobs that have you (literally) riding off into the sunset, a chance to do your part to save the world, a short stint in Paradise . . .

As far as I'm concerned, unless you've got a burning passion to do something specific, work can wait. If you're looking for adventure and sick of the classroom, you've got three other major choices: volunteering, internships, and travel. We'll talk them over in the next few chapters.

CHAPTER 4

Globe-trotting: *How to Work Your Way Around the World*

> **"I met a lot of people in Europe. I even encountered myself."**
>
> —James Baldwin

THE WORLD IS YOUR OYSTER. AND ONE OF THE best ways to figure yourself out is to lace up those traveling shoes and dive in. The good news is, you don't need a trust fund to traverse the globe. All you need's a little imagination and a willingness to work.

If you've got wanderlust, the first thing to figure out is where it's pointing you. Pull out that dusty old atlas and start daydreaming. Asia or Africa? Ireland or Iceland? Tibet or Turkey? Canada or the Caribbean? Do you see yourself trekking through the desert on a camel, or teaching soccer in the English countryside? Skiing the Alps, or sunbathing in the South Pacific? In a city, or in the middle of nowhere?

Whatever and wherever it is, there's probably someone

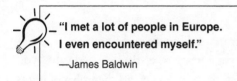

willing to hire you. Interim, for example, sends people to do everything from guiding in the jungles of Vernay to apprenticing with a blacksmith in the Netherlands. You can work with an orphanage in Jordan at King Hussein's palace or help build a boat in St. Petersburg, Russia. You can do construction work on a sixth-century monastery or help out at a wildlife sanctuary. You can teach English in the island of Falalop, Ulithi, or work for Coca Cola in Azerbaijan, near the Caspian Sea.

THE WHOLE WORLD IN YOUR HANDS

The first step to take before packing up and shipping out is figuring out what makes your heart race. Bull suggests that you start a list of where you might want to go and then a list of interests. When he meets with students he gives them a sheet with a slew of alternatives: adventure travel, agriculture, animals, anthropology, architecture, arts, bicycling, blacksmithing, business, canoe/kayaking, conservation, construction, cooking, dance, design, environment, fashion, film, foreign study, forestry, hotel management, journalism, language, Native American, marine biology, marine mammals, medical, research expedition, sailing, scuba, sculpture, skiing, spiritual, sports, theater, video/TV, wilderness, woodcraft, zoo . . .

That gets the ball rolling. Once people have circled a bunch of favorites, he begins running some options by them. For example, someone interested in medicine might like working as a courier for the Frontier Nursing Service in Kentucky, or they might prefer working with the blind. They might want to study rain forest remedies in Belize or they might want to help the handicapped.

Students taking time off have found work:

- ✔ At a castle twenty minutes outside of Prague
- ✔ At a bed-and-breakfast near Cuzco, Peru
- ✔ In Dharamsala, where the government of Tibet is exiled
- ✔ With sled dogs in a remote Native village in the Yukon
- ✔ At a national park in Mongolia
- ✔ With an Irish documentary filmmaker
- ✔ At an aboriginal school in Australia
- ✔ With street kids in Calcutta
- ✔ At a Gandhian ashram in Bali
- ✔ In Turkey's first arboretum, an hour's ferry from Istanbul

If you can't decide what to do, a program like Interim can help. They've got contacts with over two thousand employers in practically every country on the planet. They'll set you up, help with visas, even tell you what to pack. All for a tidy little sum of $1,500. It may seem like a lot, but it covers you for two years of travel advice and job hookups, in as many countries as you'd like.

If Interim's fee is too steep, you can definitely attempt a home version. Make your list and head on over to the bookstore. Pick up a copy of something like *Six Months Off* (by Hope Dlugozima, James Scott, and David Sharp), *The Backdoor Guide to Short Term Job Adventures* (by Michael Landes), or Robert Gilpin's *Time Out* (out of print, but you may be able to get it from Amazon or from the library). And remember, you don't have to pick just one thing. You can work on a ranch in Australia for four or five months and then hightail it over to the French Alps and tend the desk at a resort.

If you're willing to work hard, you can almost always convince people to give you room and board, or some sort of stipend. Your only other big expense will be plane tickets. And if you save enough money before you leave to pay for a round-the-world ticket (between $1,000 and $2,000), you'll usually get unlimited stops around the globe—as long as you keep going in the same direction.

The world's a big place. There are zillions more travel options than we've got pages. Here are some of my favorites:

EUROPE ON A SHOESTRING

Europe is outrageously expensive. Forget *Let's Go*, forget the *Lonely Planet.* You can do Europe even cheaper if you're willing to work for food: The following places will take the pain out of hunting for a job. For a small fee or a small fortune, depending on the agency, they'll do all the legwork necessary to make working abroad a piece of cake. Some, like Alliances Abroad, are direct funnels to employers countrywide. Others, like CIEE, will do your paperwork, but once you get there, finding a job is up to you. (They'll help with a list of contacts, but they're not making any promises.) With any of these programs, unless you've got some concrete skills under your hat, you'll probably end up bartending, bellhopping, or working retail. But the hours are short, the job is temporary, and housing is free or cheap.

Council on International Educational Exchange
Where: Ireland, Germany, France, Canada, New Zealand, Australia, and Costa Rica
What: For under a hundred bucks they'll take care of all the paperwork you need to work legally. The only catch? You have to have been a full-time student within the last six months, the day you get on the plane.

How Long: 3–6 months
How Much: Enough to live on.
Contact: (800) 448-9944; www.ciee.org

BUNAC USA
Where: England, Scotland, Wales, and Northern Ireland
What: Hooks students up with career-related or just plain laid-back jobs—from waiter to banker
How Long: Up to six months
How Much: $200 for help getting a Blue Card, which lets you work legally. Once you're hired, you're paid.
Contact: (203) 264-0901 or (212) 316-5312

Alliances Abroad
Where: Throughout Europe, especially Great Britain, Austria, and Germany
What: Places people at least eighteen years old in internships or "work" programs throughout Europe with at least some compensation for the hours they put in. From au pair to hotel and resort jobs.
How Long: A few weeks to a year
How Much: Usually you'll get a stipend and room and board, but there are fees. (Example: For au pair, you pay $700 for a twelve month placement but get room, board, and about $300 a month.) You won't get rich but if you stay for a while, you'll at least break even.
Contact: 888-6-ABROAD; www.alliancesabroad.com

Center for International Mobility
Where: Finland
What: Arranges jobs in farming, teaching, tourism, hotels, youth work, etc.

How Long: Up to eighteen months
How Much: About $800–1,000 per month plus help with housing.
Contact: www.cimo.fi; 358-0-7747-7033

Interexchange
Where: Austria, Czech Republic, Finland, France, Germany, Holland, Hungary, Italy, Norway, Poland, Spain, Switzerland
What: Jobs run the gamut—from picking blackberries to being a camp counselor or working at a resort.
How Long: One month to one year
How Much: $125–300 program fee but you'll make enough to support yourself
Contact: www.interexchange.org

Friendly Hotels PLC
Where: England, Scotland, France, Germany, and Denmark
What: A hotel chain with almost thirty locations, always looking for seasonal staff
How Long: Varies, with summer being the most busy time
How Much: Weekly wage, meals, and housing at some locations.
Contact: admin@friendly.u-net.com; 0171-222-8866

National Tour Foundation
Where: All over the world
What: A list of more than one hundred international jobs with tour operators, hotels, restaurants, etc.

How Long: Varies
How Much: About minimum wage
Contact: (800) 682-8886, ext. 4251

TEACHING THEM A LESSON

Teaching English abroad is one of the best free rides going. It pays well, you don't need a whole lot of experience, and it's available all over the world. All you need to know how to do is talk, and you're in. In underdeveloped countries the requirements are pretty lax. (If you're volunteering your time in a little village in Africa, do you think anyone's going to care if you have an official teaching certificate?) In other places, like Japan, you're usually hired to assist a native speaker, so you don't have to be fluent in anything but English. Korea, Taiwan, and the rest of Asia are also clamoring to get you into the classroom. Eastern Europe is a hot spot too, but they tend to be stricter about teaching credentials. Tutoring experience may be enough to get you in the door.

Teaching English?
What You Need to Ask. . .

How much will I get paid?
Do I have to pay for placement?
Who pays for the plane ticket?
Will I get housing?
Will I have a say in where I'm assigned?
Will I be working with other Americans?

One of the greatest things about teaching is it introduces you to the locals. Unlike a resort job, you won't be surrounded by other Americans. And even though teaching makes great résumé fodder, it's a pretty fun job.

From World Teach to the Peace Corps, JET to New World Teachers, agencies are lining up to get you to the chalkboard. Some pay better than others. Some actually expect *you* to pay to be placed. Before you get on a plane, make sure you find out who'll be paying for the ticket. Other questions: Do you get money for housing? Will they help you find it? Get it all out on the table before making a commitment.

A Few Places to Start:

World Teach
Where: Africa, China, Thailand, Vietnam, Lithuania, Poland, Costa Rica, Ecuador, Mexico, Paraguay
What: Finds volunteers teaching jobs in developing countries. No teaching experience needed.
How Long: Six months to one year
How Much: You pay them $3,600–4,700 for placement, training, insurance, and airfare. You'll get housing and a small salary.
Contact: (617) 495-5527; www.igc.org/worldteach

Friends of World Teaching
Where: At English-speaking schools and colleges in over one hundred countries
What: Helps North Americans find out about teaching overseas
How Long: Three months to two years

How Much: Most positions are paid
Contact: (800) 503-7436

YMCA of the USA
Where: Taiwan
What: Sends college grads to Taiwan YMCAs to teach conversational English and get involved in the community. Aside from school, you'll need to show your face at bowling parties, camp, BBQs . . .
How Long: One year
How Much: $16,000–18,000 in Taiwanese currency plus a $12,000 bonus at the end of your contract. Also housing, airfare, a week's paid vacation, and insurance.
Contact: (800) 872-9622

Considering Japan?

Stop dreaming and start planning. These two guides will help you snag a job.

Make a Mil-Yen: Teaching English in Japan by Don Best

A great guide to everything you need to know about getting a teaching job in Japan.

Costs $14.95 and can be ordered through (800) 947-7271 or www.stonebridge.com

Ohayo Sensei

A newsletter to keep you up-to-date on Japanese teaching jobs (and others), airfares, and exchange rates.

Each issue costs $1 and can be sent to you by e-mail or snail mail. Contact (415) 431-5953 or go to www.ohayosensei.com

Japan Exchange and Teaching Programme (JET)
Where: Japan
What: A program meant to foster ties between young Japanese students and foreign college grads. These are assistant language teacher positions. You'll usually team-teach with someone Japanese.
How Long: One year, renewable up to three
How Much: 3,600,000 yen per year, plus airfare
Contact: (800) 463-6538; www.infojapan.com/cgjsf

THE GOOD EARTH

If you'd rather work the land than work the bar, I've got an idea for you: WWOOF. It's a doggie salute, the sound of air seeping out of your tires, the agency that will get you around the world . . . WWOOF is Willing Workers on Organic Farms, and they've got a good thing going. The program sends young people with green thumbs to about six hundred farms scattered throughout the globe. In exchange for helping out, they get room, board, and a little spending money.

According to WWOOF Australia, the movement started life in 1972 as Working Weekends On Organic Farms in England, and it still goes by that title over there. The first Wwoofers were taking a break from their city lives by lending a hand on the BioDynamic Emerson College Farm in Sussex, and "found the experience so rewarding that they started an organization to help others do the same sort of thing." Soon WWOOF groups started popping up across the world and going Wwoofing became a popular thing to do. Over twenty countries now have national organizations, with about thirty others submitting jobs directly to the international branch.

Joining WWOOF is a breeze. Head on over to their web-

A Few Places You Can Wwoof

Australia, Austria, Canada, Denmark, Italy, the Ivory Coast, Japan, New Zealand, England, Finland, Germany, Ghana, Hungary, Ireland, Scotland, Sweden, Switzerland, Togo, Wales, Argentina, Czech Republic, France, Israel, India, Lithuania, South Africa, Portugal, Fiji, Cyprus, Indonesia, Malaysia, Nepal, Norway, Iceland, Sri Lanka, Turkey, Thailand, Spain, Pakistan, Poland, Switzerland

Check out WWOOF International
www.phdcc.com/sites/wwoof/index.html

site, find the country of your dreams, jot down their WWOOF office, and send them about twenty bucks. Badda bing, badda boom, you're registered. Soon as the post office can get it there, you'll have a list of hosts from over fifty different countries in your hot little hands. Scope out their specialties, pull out your atlas, and decide where you'd like to go first. Then contact them. Chances are, you're in.

Fact is, organic farming is pretty labor intensive—it doesn't rely on artificial fertilizers, herbicides, or pesticides. It relies on people. Most farms will gladly put you up and fill your belly for the chance to have some extra hands around. What you'll do will vary depending on the arrangement. Likely tasks, according to WWOOF International, are "sowing, making compost, gardening, planting, cutting wood, weeding, making mud-bricks, harvesting, fencing, building, typing, packing, milking, feeding." A WWOOF volunteer might shear sheep in New Zealand, plant trees in Nepal, or pick grapes for an Italian vineyard. "Many people are attracted to the romantic ideal of a small farm, self-sufficiency, or community living. WWOOF gives you a chance to sample all these lifestyles and more," according to WWOOF

Other Ways to Get Dirty

WWOOF isn't the only game in town. The International Agriculture Exchange Association sends almost a thousand eager beavers a year to farms across the world. Their scope is a little more limited (Australia, New Zealand, Japan, Denmark, Netherlands, Sweden, Norway, and Germany) but if you're willing to work, you shouldn't have too much trouble getting in.

International Agricultural Exchange Association (800) 272-4996

International. It also gives you a set of skills you can take anywhere. Lots of former volunteers have had an easy time working their way across the world with what they learned Wwoofing it.

THE KIDDIE POOL

Good with kids, bad with plants? There are plenty of jobs out there for au pairs—young people willing to do some baby-sitting (and sometimes light housework) for room, board, and a little pocket money. Your role falls somewhere between a temporary member of the family and hired help, depending on the house you're lucky enough or unlucky enough to get placed in.

Families generally like to hire people with a high school diploma, between the ages of eighteen and twenty-six. Candidates need to have an international driver's license, no criminal record, and a clean bill of health. The official word on hours is 35–40 a week, according to most agencies. The job varies. You might play with the kids, do their laundry, make their beds, drive them to school, run a few errands . . . It all depends on where you're placed. Some au pairs spend their days changing diapers and picking up toys. Others have the bulk of the day off, other than manning a few carpools.

Wherever you end up, you'll get time off each week—time that you can use to sightsee. Some placements even throw in a few weeks of paid vacation. And because visas generally go more smoothly for students than imported workers, many programs include a few classes at the local college—and you won't pay a red cent.

The application process varies. Elizabeth Elder Recruitment, an English placement agency, asks au pair hopefuls to write a "Dear Family" letter, explaining their experience and outlining their interests. Interexchange has them fill out an application and does the screening themselves. Whatever agency you go through, you'll need to send references, pictures, and a note from your doctor proclaiming your healthiness.

The jobs are usually in the U.K., France, Spain, Germany, and the Netherlands. Au Pair in Europe probably has the most options—with placements in Russia, Monaco, New Zealand, and Bermuda, in addition to the typical European cities. The jobs can last anywhere from three months to a year. String a few gigs together and you can work your way around the world by playing parent's helper.

Start by Calling

Interexchange: (800) AU PAIRS; www.interexchange.org
You pay $500 toward your airfare. If you don't quit, you'll get it back. You'll also get classes, room, board, and about $140 a week.

Elizabeth Elder Recruitment: 44 (0) 1234-352688; elizabethelder.co.uk/aupairs/apeur.htm

Room, board, and $55 a week, but you pay the airfare. They'll charge you about $64 for placement.

Au Pair in Europe: (905) 545-6305
Airfare reimbursements for the farthest-flung cities, otherwise, nada. You'll make about $75–120 a week, plus room and board.

ONE-WAY TICKET TO PARADISE

Everybody needs a break now and then. Employees in the vacation and tourist industry make it happen. People may call the jobs "seasonal," but let me tell you, these are short-term jobs you could get used to. Whether you're on a cruise ship, in a hotel, or at a resort, you'll get paid to live and work in some of the most beautiful places on earth. You may sign on for six months and never leave. It happens more than you think.

Tourism is a multi-trillion-dollar industry. Job turnover is high and openings are constant. You can find work by grabbing the guidebook of your choice and calling hotels and resorts directly. Or you can hook up with one of the big shot employers—an even easier entry into vacationland.

SLAP ON THE SUNSCREEN, YOU'RE OFF TO CLUB MED

Club Med is the worldwide leader in "vacation villages." And when they say villages, they're not kidding. These guys employ more people than your average small town. And they need everything a town would need: doctors, bakers, bartenders, receptionists, secretaries, restaurant managers, salespeople, maids, plumbers, carpenters, entertainers, teachers, child care workers, massage therapists, aerobics instructors, DJs . . . you name it. Plus, Club Med offers pretty much any sport you could think of, from golf and tennis to windsurfing and rock climbing. So basically, they're desperate for jocks.

Some positions are open from the get-go, some aren't. Some locations are, some aren't. Even though there are villages in over sixty countries throughout the world, Americans will have to pay their dues closer to home—at a Club Med based in Florida, Colorado, Mexico, the Bahamas, or the Caribbean. Poor baby.

Wherever they send you, you'll start as a Gentils Organizateur, French for "congenial host." G.O.s are the lifeblood of a Club Med village. On average, they're twenty-eight years old (the minimum age is twenty), "young, outgoing, fun-loving and open-minded, curious about other cultures and adaptable," if the official hype is to be believed. They need to be willing to relocate anywhere at a moment's notice without a whimper, and psyched to work seven days a week making guests happy. In exchange they'll get round-trip airfare, a nice room, health insurance, good grub, and access to all Club Med's facilities, plus at least $530 a month. Not much dough, but when you consider that you've got every whim taken care of—from waterskiing to scuba, Vegaslike cabarets to a fully loaded gym, who needs money?!

Should you decide to make Club Med your life, you'll eventually start moving up the ladder. One rung up from G.O. is Activity Manager (who might run, for example, all of tennis). Next comes the Department Head (who might run all of sports). And finally, the Big Guy himself, the Chef de Village (in charge of all the G.O.s in their domain).

Before you get stars in your eyes, know this: The people at

Last Resort

If Club Med isn't your calling, don't despair. There are thousands of resorts out there, and they all need employees. Love the island hideaway you stayed at with your parents last Christmas? Fax them a résumé! Just because a resort isn't advertising jobs, doesn't mean there aren't any available. Don't underestimate the power of initiative. Scope out the hotels in your favorite destination and start making phone calls.

Club Med are very picky. You need to send your application in just so, or you can forget it. If you look good on paper, you'll be called in to interview in New York, L.A., San Francisco, or Chicago. Assuming you ace the interview, you'll have between one week and one month before they tell you where you're going and ship you out. Midseason, you might get as little as forty-eight hours to throw yourself together. "A G.O. has got to be ready to go!" according to the Club Med people.

How to Join the Club

❶ Check out the website (www.clubmed.com) or call the job hot line (407)337-6660

❷ Send a resume and cover letter to:
Club Med Management Services
Elizabeth Ferguson
75 Valencia
Coral Gables, FL 33134

❸ Don't bug them. Thousands of people apply. It could take up to eight weeks for recruiters to get around to calling you.

FLOAT YOUR BOAT

Cruise ships are like floating cities. They need everyone from doctors to dancers, tennis teachers to hairdressers, receptionists to maids. Almost any job that exists on land exists at sea. If you're good at something, anything, there's no question that you have the skills you need to get shipped out. The question is, do you have the flexibility?

Cruise commitments are usually at least six months long. If you've got a girlfriend, a dog, a friend, a plant, or anything else you need to see more than that, you better think twice before setting out to sea. On the other hand, if you *do* decide to get a little salty, the payoff is big. Your every need will be taken care of—food, room, gym, sometimes even dry-cleaning. You will have absolutely no out-of-pocket expenses and you'll rake in as much as $1,000 a week.

But every line varies. It's important to do your homework. You may like a cruise ship's advertisements, but working for them is another thing entirely. Carnival, for example, is the best known ship, but according to my sources it's at the bottom end of things as far as employment is concerned. It's one of the cheapest cruises out there and those savings have to come from somewhere. I'll give you one guess where that somewhere is . . .

Everything depends on where you get on board. Cruise ships, like hotels and restaurants, are categorized—the more stars the better. The five-star lines have the best food, the best perks, and, according to Mark Landon of shipjobs.com, the best itineraries. "Most of the cruise ships will repeat the same cruise. So if you get a contract for four months, chances are you'll only get to see five or six ports in those four months. Whereas the five-star ships change itineraries constantly. So during your four-month contract you may do a month in the Caribbean, a month in the Mediterranean, a month in Asia, and a month in the South Pacific," Landon says.

The five-star ships also do round-the-world cruises once a year. Sign on for a tour of duty and you'll sail from Florida to Florida . . . the long way. Granted, you won't get to spend a lot of time in any one port, but you'll know where you'd like to come back. Think of it as a traveling tasting menu.

Cruise ships are a great way to see the world, but they do have their drawbacks. The two biggies are privacy and personal space. If you think the *passenger* cabins are small, you won't believe the size of the places they're squeezing in the crew. Most cabins are barely big enough to cram in a bed. They have a tiny bathroom and a shower just large enough to stand in. And usually, this teeny tiny shoebox isn't even your own! Most crew members share a cabin with at least one other person.

It may be tight, but close quarters bring close friendships, according to Landon. "It's a very unique situation when you live with the people that you work with, hang out with the people that you work with. In a lot of cases, the close friend you hang out with is your boss. It's an extremely high level of camaraderie. People look out for one another and it kind of reaffirms the saying, 'We're all in this boat together.'" One of the hardest things about the job, actually, is constantly saying good-bye. Everybody's on a different contract, and people leave, or quit, or get transferred all the time. And since it's not uncommon to find twenty to thirty different nationalities on a ship, it's not like you're likely to run into crewmates once you get home. "The heartbreak of the job is you really do make great friends on a ship and a lot of times you know that they're going to be gone. You never see them again," Landon says.

Most employees do only one or two cruise contracts. But a lot of people make a career of going out to sea. Once you've survived one tour, it's extremely easy to get hired for another one. Employers figure if you can make it through a full contract, it proves you're capable of handling shipboard life, especially since you're asking for another job.

Cruising is not for everyone. "A lot of people can't hack it," Landon says, "They're under the impression that they're going to go on a cruise and then they find out that they have to work seven days a week and they have to make some sacrifices that they wouldn't normally make on land."

Life on a ship is hectic. You're around people all the time. It's only at port that you might be able to get a little breathing room. Because of that, it's important to make sure you'll be allowed off the ship when it docks. And that depends on your job. The best entry-level positions, according to Landon, are the ones in the "hotel" section. That and receptionists. Because when the passengers pour into port, there's no reason for either of them to stick around.

Another gem of a job is called "cruise staff" or "activities director." They're the people in charge of keeping the passengers busy. They arrange shuffleboard tournaments, Trivial Pursuit contests, pool games, dance lessons, lectures . . . whatever will keep passengers happy while the ship is at sea. On a typical cruise, there's a lot to do. A person could see three shows in one night!

For the highest pay and the best perks, try the five-star lines:

Cunard: (800) 223-0764
Seabourn: (305) 463-3000
Silversea: (800) 697-2457

Crystal Cruises: 47-22-33-4930 (Hiring done through an agency in Norway); www.icma.nol

Check out:

How to Get a Job with a Cruise Line by Mary Fallon Miller
Cruise Ship Jobs by Richard B. Marin
www.shipjobs.com

MAKING A DIFFERENCE

If you're one of those globetrotters looking to make an impact beyond inventing a new tropical drink, there are ways to do it. Everyone and their brother wants to help you save the world. There are about a million books and articles about the Peace Corps. Here are two standouts you may not have heard of:

THE INSTITUTE FOR INTERNATIONAL COOPERATION AND DEVELOPMENT

Don't expect a free ride from IICD. It's not a huge government program or a well-funded international movement. It's just a little nonprofit trying to make a difference in the world. And as long as you're eighteen or older and looking to do the same, you're welcome to join them. You don't have to know what you're doing. You don't have to have a certain number of years of college. You just have to promise to try your best.

IICD is run completely by the funds they raise and they'll

expect you to do your part. The programs last from six months to almost two years and run anywhere from $3,800 to $5,500 dollars—meant to help offset the amount it will cost them to train you, house you, feed you, and send you to your designated country. But they'll help you figure out how to fund-raise for the money, and at these prices, it's not like they're trying to get rich.

Curently, one third of the people living in developing countries don't live to be forty. IICD is trying to tackle that problem. The purpose of the program is "building something for other people and for the future." As an IICD volunteer you "work for others—not for money or fame, but because you feel compelled to do your share in creating a better world."

What it is you'll be doing once you're there depends on which country you've signed on for. You might be building a community center in Nicaragua, teaching in a vocational school in Mozambique, working with street children in Brazil, helping out at a woman's club in Africa, launching a child care project in Angola, or teaching people in India about AIDS. Wherever you are, you'll be surrounded by people your age—you'll be working as part of a team and most of that team will be young.

The Institute for International Cooperation and Development
(413) 458-9828
www.iicd-volunteer.org
Cost: $3,800–5,500 for six months to almost two years
College Not Required

PEACE BRIGADES INTERNATIONAL

If you've always dreamed of becoming a hero, but didn't know where to sign up, you do now: Peace Brigades International. PBI sends peace teams across the world to help nonviolent groups find safe places to meet and organize. They also provide "protective accompaniment" for nonviolent local activists who are threatened or persecuted because of what they're trying to do. They escort community organizers, journalists, lawyers, witnesses, families of disappeared persons, and organizations under threat to strikes, demonstrations, and other places where violence is likely.

Volunteers are unarmed and they're not bodyguards. According to PBI, they're "walking symbols of the pressure the international human rights community is prepared to bring to bear in the event of abuse." Should something happen, they act as witnesses. They've got eyes to see, ears to hear, and cameras to document what's going on.

PBI operates in Guatemala, Colombia, Haiti, Mexico, the Philippines, East Timor, the Balkans, and in Native American communities in North America. Only problem is, for most locations, you have to be at least twenty-five to apply.

Chiapas, Mexico, is the one exception. They'll take you as soon as you're legal—the minimum age is twenty-one. Chiapas is a highly charged place, thanks to the highest rate of unemployment in Mexico and an uprising in 1994 because of ethnic discrimination. It's a hotbed. And volunteers need to be fluent in Spanish so they'll know what's going on.

Peace Brigades International
(510) 663-2362
www.igc.apc.org/pbi

Cost: Volunteers need to get themselves to the location. Once they're there, PBI covers everything.
Requirements: You must be fluent in Spanish and twenty-five plus (except in Chiapas).

CHEAP SLEEPS

If you're creative, there are millions of other ways to work your way around the world. Check out the web, raid your local bookstore, talk to friends. You'd be surprised what turns up once you start looking. But regardless of how you're getting yourself around the globe or what you're doing once you get there, there comes a time in everybody's travel life where they're low on cash but high on curiosity. When this moment arrives, you can find a place to crash with the help of two amazing organizations: SERVAS and American-International Homestays. Both are in business to promote peace, by bringing people from all over the world together in one another's homes.

For a flat $45 membership fee, SERVAS will send you a magical book with a list of possible homestays around the world. The book is divided into sections to help make your life easier—you can pick your bed based on common interests, common languages, or location. All you need to do is contact the host and see if they're up for a visit. There are people in over ninety countries willing to take you in. The one catch is this—you need to stay long enough to make a connection. The whole point of SERVAS is for foreigners to get to know each other. This isn't a hostel kind of thing. It's an idea exchange. So don't be rude.

If in-and-out is more your style, check out American-

Peace Corps?

You might think you know the Peace Corps, but a lot has changed since the Kennedy years. For one, the requirements. While it's true that most Peace Corps teaching jobs require a college degree, there are lots of other positions open to people with nothing more than some hands-on experience. If you've held landscaping or gardening jobs, helped out on the family farm, done construction, masonry, or plumbing, coached a sports team, or played an instrument, you could be eligible for the Peace Corps, even if you've never gone to college.

The Peace Corps's motto is "The toughest job you'll ever love." And it's true, this is no cakewalk. But it's definitely interesting. You might work with small farmers in Uzbekistan to increase food production, or help build schools in Africa, or teach at-risk youth about AIDS. You could be sent anywhere from Tanzania to Tonga, St. Lucia to Slovakia. They'll take your preferences into account, but they can't guarantee you'll land on the continent of your choice.

The good news is, you'll return with work experience, confidence, and a foreign language under your belt. The Peace Corps will also sport you a $6,075 readjustment allowance, career counseling, and preferential treatment when applying for government jobs. And you'll get scholarships and reduced tuition at more than fifty colleges across the country, should you decide to go.

Pay: A monthly living allowance, housing, and health care

Perks: Free round-trip airfare and 24 vacation days a year

Length: Two years, plus three months of training

Pro: Nine out of ten peace corps returnees would make the same decision

Con: Possibility of getting placed in an extremely isolated location

International Homestays. Same idea, but this company lets you eat and run. *What* you'll eat depends on your host, who'll cook up something authentic, then take you around town for a personal tour. It's potluck travel—some hosts are retirees, some are college kids. The only thing these people have in common is that they're brave enough to open their doors to strangers for a mere $49 per night—food, bed, and tour included.

Two ways to give your wallet a rest:

SERVAS: (212) 267-0252
American-International Homestays: (800) 876-2048; www.spectravel.com/homes

CHAPTER 5

Internships: *If the Shoe Fits, Work It*

> **"All genuine knowledge originates from direct experience."**
>
> —Mao Tse-tung

OK, SO MAO WASN'T TALKING ABOUT INTERNSHIPS. But he could have been. Truth is, internships are one of quickest ways to go from "inexperienced" to hiring-desirable without paying someone off.

Think of the internship as the ultimate career litmus test. You wouldn't buy a car without taking it for a test drive. Why choose a career before trying it out? Jobs, like cars, all look pretty good when you're peering through the window. You've got to get in the door to see if the experience actually lives up to the image. An internship is the perfect way to cut through the hype and see what a company is really like from the inside.

So what's in it for them? Cheap labor, to put it bluntly. Corporate downsizing has managed to create a nice little niche for the young and willing—a place in most companies where you can get a bird's-eye view of what it's like to work there, without making a long-term commitment.

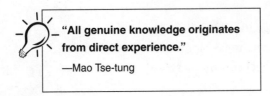

Make no mistake, while you're checking them out, they're looking you over, too. Companies sponsor internships because they allow them, for a very small investment, to get a preview of what it'd be like to have you on board. Anyone can finesse a résumé. Internships take potential employees off the page and into the office for a dry run, without the promise that goes with an official job offer.

That said, the rate at which companies hire their former interns is out of control. Take places like *The Late Show with David Letterman*, where, according to *The Internship Bible* by Mark Oldman and Samer Hamadeh, 90 percent of the staff were once interns, or Eastman Kodak (70 percent), or the Atlanta Hawks (60 percent). In a recent survey by the College Placement Council, employers reported that three out of ten new hires were former interns. According to the Lindquist-

The Ten Best Internships, According to *America's Top Internships* by Oldman and Hamadeh

Academy of Television Arts and Sciences
Elite Model Management
Ford Motor Company
Georgetown Criminal Justice Clinic
Hewlett-Packard
Inroads
Lucasfilm/Lucas Digital
Northwestern Mutual Life
TBWA/Chiat Day
The Washington Post

Tip

Most companies offer internships all year long, but the bulk of candidates apply for summer positions. Improve your chances for the internship of your dreams by sending your résumé off-season.

Endicott Report, put out by Northwestern University, 33 percent of new hires in 1994–95 served in their company's internship program.

The trick to turning a short stint as an intern into a permanent spot at the water cooler is simple: Become invaluable. Make the most of your days as a peon. Offer to do more than you're asked. Be impossibly useful. It's easy to say good-bye to an intern who merely did what was expected. It's terrifying to say good-bye to the one who reorganized the computer system. Your goal as an intern is to make life with you so much easier that life without you is inconceivable.

TAKE IT FROM A PRO

I've had more internships than Elizabeth Taylor has had husbands. None have been particularly generous as far as pay is concerned. But they were worth their weight in gold. Some taught me something about the particular business they were in. Some were even more useful—they helped me figure out what I *didn't* want to do. When you're looking for an internship, remember that money isn't everything: Sometimes the best experiences pay the worst.

Case in point: My internship at a New York talent agency

paid twenty-five dollars a day, almost enough to cover the rent for the cheapo Times Square pit I'd managed to sublet. I worked one day a week as a temp at a publishing company to make up the difference, and a little extra. It had me in a windowless office for eight hours a day, next to a life-sized cardboard cutout of Fabio, typing index cards for their library's card catalog. Not fun, but useful résumé fodder.

I once auditioned against several hundred people to land an internship that paid a whopping forty dollars a week. Not much moolah, but they gave us room and board. They also worked us too hard to have any time to spend the little we were making.

I spent a summer working in a fly-infested kitchen as a dishwasher, to help me float an internship at Berkshire Theatre Festival. Hard, disgusting work, but I lost a lot of weight.

The thing is, people who pay you next to nothing know that working for peanuts sucks. They feel like they owe you and they do. Milk that guilt for everything it's worth—freebies, knowledge, and especially recommendations. A strong recommendation letter can make all the difference in getting your next job, or in getting into the school of your choice.

While you're there, make the most of it. Watch your coworkers like a hawk. Figure out which jobs look interesting. Ask for career advice. Start a Rolodex of all the great contacts you're making and collect business cards like they're going out of style.

GET WHAT YOU PAY FOR

The most important thing to realize about an internship is that you're essentially paying to learn. Maybe not with money, but with your time and energy. You wouldn't pay to take a

Spanish class and let the teacher turn it into a study hall. So don't let your company shuttle you off to a summer in the copy room where looking on is impossible. Internships may force you to work for free, but they also entitle you to learn for free. Remember: You are bartering your time for knowledge here—don't work cheap.

Making the Most of It: 5 Ways to Improve Your Internship

1. Read everything that comes through your hands: faxes, copies, files . . .
2. Ask your boss if you can sit in on a few meetings.
3. Make sure you get at least one assignment you find interesting.
4. Take advantage of industry perks: company discounts, free tickets to events, box seats to games, conferences . . .
5. Come up with an independent project and ask your boss for feedback.

IF THE SHOE FITS, WORK IT

In 1976, internships were barely a blip on the radar. Only one out of every thirty-six companies offered some kind of internship, according to vaultreports.com. Now, it's up to one in three. There are barely enough candidates to fill all the positions. The question isn't, can you get one, the question is, which one do you want.

With so many choices out there, it's hard to separate the good from the downright delicious. But no matter what turns you on, I guarantee there's something, somewhere, worth your time. Here are just a few picks from the pile. Figure out which type of internship piques your interest, then put your best foot forward.

THE BIRKENSTOCK: *Internships for Nature Lovers*

You're as granola as they come. You'd rather be out in the middle of nowhere, watching the bees buzz, than in the middle of Manhattan, front row center at a Broadway play. These jobs will have you hanging out with Mom Nature and teaching people how to treat her right.

1) **Fernwood Nature Center**—Welcome to your playground: one hundred and five acres, a fifty-five-acre nature preserve, five acres of reconstructed prairie, eight acres of gardens, a forty-acre naturalistic Arboretum, and three miles of hiking trails. This outdoor heaven in the southwest corner of Michigan offers nature walks, bird-watching, natural science classes, and canoeing on the St. Joseph river to kids preschool through high school. As an intern, you'll help out by maintaining trails, writing articles, caring for animals, and conducting programs for families. You'll make $5.50 an hour and get cheap housing ($100 a month) and some great hands-on training.
Contact: (616) 695-6491;
landtrust.org/fernwood/fernwood.htm
Location: Michigan

2) **Slide Ranch**—Your ticket to a stay in the Bay, this place teaches people to make ecologically friendly choices about how they live and what they buy. The basic idea is to show

guests where their food and clothing come from, so they'll understand how dependent they are on natural resources, and how it's in their best interest to help preserve them. Interns get training in outdoor education and teaching, and lead groups in activities. They also help out with chores—whether composting, gardening, or taking care of the goats, sheep, chickens, rabbits, and other animals on the ranch. Stints last either three and a half or seven months. You'll get $200 a month, good food, and your own room.
Contact: (415) 381-6155; www.igc.org/slideranch
Location: California

3) **Trees for Tomorrow**—You'll work side-by-side with professional foresters and naturalists at a sort of conservation camp, teaching people (mostly kids) how to manage natural resources. We're talking hands-on learning. During the winter you'll lead ski tours that blend in natural resource education. In the spring you'll lead bog studies, teach tree identification, and run wildlife programs about wolves, beavers, and bats. You'll also learn how to keep a class perky, write for *Northbound* (an environmental magazine), and network your little tail off. Interns get room, board, and $500 a month.
Contact: (800) TFT-WISC; www.treesfortomorrow.com
Location: Wisconsin

4) **Vermont Raptor Center**—Every year, more than six hundred ill or injured birds of prey come here for a little TLC. Most have been hurt as a direct result of human stupidity—toxic spills, power lines, car collisions, and illegal hunting and trapping. A team of staff, vets, and volunteers take them in, fix them up, and do their best to get them back into the wild.

They also introduce visitors to the over twenty-six species of eagles, owls, and hawks housed in the Center's flight habitats. Life at the Center is maybe 75 percent rehabilitation, 25 percent education, and interns will focus on one of these areas. Don't do this for the money, do it for the experience. This is one of the only internships around that gives hands-on rehabilitation training to volunteers. The housing and small stipend that interns used to receive has been temporarily suspended. It may or may not return.
Contact: (802) 457-2779
Location: Vermont

5) **Garden in the Woods**—This "living museum" has more than 1,600 different kinds of wildflowers, many of them rare or endangered. They've been offering internships in horticulture and conservation for over twenty years now and lots of grads have gone on to careers in landscape architecture, plant conservation, ecological restoration, or at botanical gardens. The forty-five-acre site has an endangered species garden and a native plant nursery that produces over 30,000 plants a year. Interns usually work Tuesday through Saturday and take home about $200 a week. They also get housing.
Contact: (508) 877-7630, ext. 3403;
www.newfs.org/volunteers.html
Location: Massachusetts

Make sure to check out the list of over 650 paid environmental internships put out by the Environmental Careers Organization: Visit www.eco.org or call (617) 423-0998

THE DOC MARTEN: *Internships for Artists*

You like black turtlenecks, Clove cigarettes, and the throaty groan of a good Billie Holiday song. You've got creativity coming out of your ears. Here are five places that can teach you to produce cutting-edge art and still manage to stay in the black.

1) **Arena Stage**—The granddaddy of resident theaters, this is the place to be if you want to submerge yourself in the life of the stage. There are internships in everything from costume design to casting. Interns work under one of four umbrellas: artistic production, technical production, art administration, or The Living Stage—Arena's social outreach theater. They work their fingers to the bone for a small stipend and some help with housing, but they get seminars with some of the biggest directors, designers, and administrators working in the theater today. Duties could include anything from drafting grant proposals to helping plan a jazz series, arranging artist transportation to working on a show as a design assistant. With three theaters (an 800-seat, a 500-seat, and a 150-seat) there's plenty of work to go around.
Contact: (202) 554-9066; www.arena-stage.org
Location: Washington, D.C.

2) **Jacob's Pillow**—America's oldest dance festival, now in its sixty-seventh season. Past artists have included the Mark Morris Dance Group, Trisha Brown, the Paul Taylor Dance Company, David Parsons, Mark Dendy, and other dance greats. Summer is the hottest time—with over thirty productions in about three months—but there are intern positions open all year long. You'll work a six-day week, for housing,

meals, and a $300 a week stipend. Most of the openings are in production, where interns work as running crew for shows put on by visiting and resident artists, and try their hand at lighting, sound, stage management, wardrobe, and most other areas needed to get a show up and running. Other intern positions are in operations, development, marketing, box office, education, programming, archives/preservation, the business office, or documentation.
Contact: (413) 637-1322, ext. 18; www.jacobs-pillow.com
Location: Massachusetts

3) **The Kennedy Center**—This place is no joke. Part memorial, part performing arts mecca, the Kennedy Center is mandated by Congress to present and produce the finest productions in the world. Each year, over two million people attend more than 3,200 music, dance, theater, and opera performances on the Center's seven stages. Internships last three to four months and are available in everything from public relations, to work with the National Symphony Orchestra. Interns get workshops with various artistic gurus, free tickets to events, and $650 a month to cover housing and other expenses.
Contact: (202) 416-8821;
www.kennedy-center.org/internships
Location: Washington, D.C.

4) **Metropolitan Museum of Art**—Think you're the next Picasso? How about an internship with one of the most respected museums in the world? Summer or six-month internships are available in nineteen curatorial departments, plus The Cloisters, a Met baby devoted to the art of medieval Europe. Interns will do things like conduct gallery workshops with kids, work at the visitor information center, and prepare and eventu-

ally present a gallery talk. A summer stint carries a $2,250 honorarium and a six-month internship pays $8,000. So make sure you come with a nest-egg. You'll never survive on that in New York.
Contact: (212) 879-5500; www.metmuseum.org
Location: New York

5) **Spoleto Festival USA**—From chamber music to jazz, Spoleto's got it covered. This Charleston whirlwind presents over one hundred and twenty events in seventeen days for more than 75,000 people. And not just any old thing—world-class stuff. The *Washington Post* dubbed it "The most varied arts festival given on this continent." And it needs about seventy interns to make it run. You could be a lucky little rehearsal assistant or just some kind of general production or administrative underling. They'll need you from May to June and pay you about $225 a week for your trouble. They'll also sport you housing and free tickets to any and all events.
Contact: (843) 722-2764; www.spoletofestivalusa.org
Location: South Carolina

THE HIKING BOOT: *Internships for Explorers*

Monotony for you is out of the question. Every day has to bring surprises; otherwise, why bother getting out of bed. You need a gig where curiosity is the key to success. Here are a few places to get excited about.

1) **National Marine Fisheries Observer Program**—Ready for an adventure? Sign up with these guys and you'll be placed on an American fishing boat operating off the Alaskan coast. Your mission: to collect information for fisheries management

enforcement. You'll be out to sea for a maximum of ninety days. This is a temporary job, not an internship, so you'll get a salary and benefits, just like you would in the real world. You'll also get housing.
Contact: (206) 526-4191; www.refm.noaa.gov
Location: Alaska

2) **California Institute for Peruvian Studies**—Your chance to join an archaeological expedition. No experience required, but you must be at least eighteen. You'll learn how to identify artifacts, find lost ruins, and document it all for posterity. And you'll be on the Peruvian coast—not a bad place to spend a few months living out the Indiana Jones fantasy. There is a drawback—cost. A month with the mummies doesn't come cheap: $1,500–3,000 for room, at least one meal a day, a two week dig, some transportation, and "a week or two of tourism."
Contact: (760) 373-1171; www.inkatrail.org
Location: Peru

3) **Center for Investigative Reporting**—A starting point for journalists in search of the hidden stories that most of the press miss or gloss over. The Center helps public interest groups and the media dig for information. Stories sparked by their help have caught the interest of Congress, the courts, and the UN and spurred change. They've also forced certain corporations to change the way they do business. Interns are paired with senior journalists and conduct interviews, gather information, search public records, and contribute to final stories. They get $150 per month, plus a byline on any story they've helped create. The Center is a staple for the *Los Angeles Times*, *20/20*, *Frontline*, and a score of other heavy hitters. The money may stink, but the contacts are priceless.

Contact: (415) 543-1200; www.muckraker.org
Location: California

4) **American Orient Express**—All aboard! A deluxe private train made up of restored antique cars from the forties and fifties, making six incredible trips across North America. This ain't no Amtrak. We're talking grand pianos, meals served on good china, and compartments done up in mahogany and brass. You'll work seven days a week, ten hours a day, as a porter or in the dining room. You'll get room, board, tips, pay, and the chance to see some of the most beautiful places on the continent.
Contact: (303) 534-2233.
Location: Travels all over North America
(office based in Missouri)

5) **Green Mountain Club**—For those listening for a call of the wild, this could be it. Work Vermont's 440-mile trail system. You could be a caretaker in the backcountry or at the summit. Or you might do trail patrol or be part of a trail crew. Either way, you'll get about $50–180 a week, room, board, and all the fresh mountain air you can stand.
Contact: (802) 244-7037
Location: Vermont

THE HIGH-TOP: *Internships for Good Sports*

You've got a lifetime subscription to *Sports Illustrated* and a serious addiction to ESPN. If you own anything but sneakers, no one's ever seen them. You burn more calories in a weekend than most people do in a month. Here are a few jobs that could use a little muscle.

1) **U.S. Olympic Committee**—Feeling particularly patriotic? How about an internship with an American staple: the U.S. Olympic Committee. Despite the scandals and intrigues, this is a pretty cool job. You'll be sent to their headquarters in Colorado Springs, Lake Placid, or Chula Vista and focus on broadcasting, journalism, sports science, or sports administration. Life here is a jock's dream, with some of the nicest pools, gyms, and recreational facilities you'll ever lay your eyes on, all at your disposal. Other than that you'll get room, board, and $45 a week.
Contact: (719) 632-5551
Location: Colorado Springs, Colorado; Lake Placid, New York; or Chula Vista, California

2) **Women's Sports Foundation**—Billie Jean King was one of the best tennis players ever. And she was no slacker off the court either. Sick and tired of the lack of opportunity and funding for women in sports, she and a group of other elite athletes founded the Women's Sports Foundation. These people do whatever they can think of to level the playing field—fund conferences, put out information, coordinate events . . . Interns will help out wherever they're needed and get paid $350–1,000 a month.
Contact: (800) 227-3988
Location: New York State

3) **PGL Young Adventure Ltd.**—Sailing, canoeing, rafting, surfing, swimming, pony trekking, judo, fencing, climbing, caving, rappelling. . . . Whatever a European kid has their heart set on learning, PGL has an instructor capable of teaching it. If you decide to work for them, you'll get your very own group of kids to lead. Put up with their whining and

you'll score food, housing, and about thirty to a hundred English pounds a week. If you start early in the season, you may even get a bonus.
Contact: 011-989767833
Location: Britain, France, and Spain

4) **Rose Resnick Lighthouse for the Blind**—A camplike haven for the blind and visually impaired, this place offers everything from rehabilitation to pure recreation. Interns teach horseback riding, swimming, arts and crafts, music and drama, sports, and outdoor education to help build visitors' confidence. The program demands at least six months of commitment. You'll get room and board.
Contact: (415) 431-1481
Location: California

THE PENNY LOAFER: *Internships for Brainy Types*

You're like Clark Kent without the phone booth. Even if you *had* a phone booth, you'd be too busy devouring the yellow pages to bother changing clothes. Might as well accept your fate as a serious noodle and take a job capable of challenging you for more than five minutes. Forget busy work and pick something with some meat to it, something like this:

1) **Interns for Peace**—Trying to succeed where politicians have failed, this training program attempts to strengthen relations between Jewish and Arab communities. Interns are the lifeblood of this organization and they do real, in-depth work. They're trained and then shipped off to Israel to work in paired Arab and Jewish neighborhoods for two years. Once there they develop community projects that Arabs and Jews

can work on together. Interns get room, board, a weekly stipend, and one of the hardest, coolest life experiences around.
Contact: (212) 870-2226
Location: Israel

2) **Library of Congress**—This is no ordinary library. They've got over ninety million books, maps, photos, manuscripts, and films, and not nearly enough hands to deal with them. As an intern, you'll find yourself in one of many departments: Geography and Maps, Broadcasting, Motion Pictures, the Africa and Middle East division, Music, Recording, Rare Books . . . just to name a few. You'll attack the never-ending stream of material that needs to be researched, organized, and eventually catalogued. The Library of Congress has some amazing stuff and you'll be able to touch, see, or listen to it well before it's open to the public. Interns get help with housing and $300 a week.
Contact: (202) 707-8253
Location: Washington, D.C.

3) **Florissant Fossil Beds National Monument**—If you liked *Jurassic Park*, this place will blow your mind. They've got fossils and geological evidence dating back thirty-five million years. You'll get up close and personal with petrified redwood trees and carbon impressions from some really old plants and insects. Depending on your internship area you might help with excavation, monitor sites, work on a geology project, or help with museum curating. You'll have 6,000 acres to explore, housing, and a minuscule stipend.
Contact: (719) 748-3253
Location: Colorado

4) **Hopewell Furnace National Historic Site**—This site is a history buff's dream. It's a restored iron plantation, complete with mansion, workshops, and a blast furnace that churned out stoves during peacetime and ammunition during the Revolutionary War. The furnace is in great shape. But better yet, there's a crew of workers dressed up as servants, blacksmiths, housewives, and other people, re-creating life in the old days. Interns might help out at the museum, staff the desk at the visitor center, do a sheep-shearing demonstration, or pop on a costume and get to work. There's shared housing and some money for living expenses.
Contact: (610) 582-8773
Location: Pennsylvania

5) **Legacy International**—A Global Youth Village with people from almost eighty countries all trying to get along. The point of this place is to get people from different backgrounds and cultures together in order to help eat away at prejudice and conflicts based on ethnic, social, or religious differences. The site is beautiful—there's nothing like the Blue Ridge Mountains to make people feel peaceful. Housing, meals, and a stipend are included for most internships.
Contact: (540) 297-5982; www.legacyintl.org
Location: Virginia

This list of internships is just the beginning. There are literally thousands of amazing positions out there, just waiting to be snatched up. Here are some additional resources to help you out:

America's Top Internships: Mark Oldman, Princeton Review

The Internship Bible: Mark Oldman, Princeton Review
Yale Daily News Guide to Internships: Staff of *Yale Daily News*

Websites:

www.internshipprograms.com
www.rsinternships.com
www.jobtrack.com

CHAPTER 6

Do the Right Thing: *Jobs for People Who Want Good Karma*

> **"The difference between what we do and what we are capable of doing would suffice to solve most of the world's problems."**
> —Mahatma Gandhi

GENERATION X. GENERATION Y. THE ME Generation. Regardless of what people call us, they can all agree on one thing: We're too damn greedy. In one sense they're right: You'd be hard pressed to find any of us in the streets, flowers in our hair, waving a sign that says LOVE. And when it comes to picking a job, most of us are looking out for ourselves.

But there are those among us hell-bent on saving the world. If you're one of these altruistic souls, don't worry. You can look out for others while looking out for Number One. The U.S. government and a whole host of private organizations sponsor service programs that let you help the world while helping yourself, and the majority of them *don't require a college degree.* Truth is, putting on those goody-two-shoes, whether for a year or for a lifetime, has never been so easy. Here are a few ways to do it:

AMERICORPS

Uncle Sam wants *you.* And not just for the military. Since 1993, a program called Americorps, funded by the feds, has been recruiting people just like you for a "full-time volunteer force" forty thousand people strong, pledged to "get things done" for America. Problem is, you've probably never heard of it. Americorps may do a good job getting things done, but they do a pretty crappy job getting the word out. Don't let the lack of buzz stop you. This is one of *the* primo ways to spend a few years figuring out what you want to be when you grow up.

So what is it? Think of Americorps as a warm and fuzzy version of the military—an *un*-armed forces. It may sound weird, but they've got a lot in common: You can get your foot in the door from the day you turn eighteen, you're given a place to report for duty each and every morning, and you'll have a temporary resting place while you try to figure out what to do with your life.

Let's get one thing straight. All Americorps programs are not created equal. Some offer nothing more than an educational award. Others give you room, board, health insurance, pocket money . . . even uniforms. There are almost six hundred state and national programs under the Americorps umbrella to choose from. Choose right.

WHAT'S OUT THERE

Basically, Americorps programs fall under three categories: Americorps State/National, Americorps VISTA, and Americorps NCCC. The distinction stems from a bunch of different things—some job description, some funding. Don't get bogged down in the intricacies. In a nutshell, this is what you need to know:

Americorps funds all kinds of programs from hundreds of nonprofit agencies. The kinds of positions and perks nonprofits give the Americorps volunteers who land on their doorstep is up to them. The *average* pay for all Americorps programs is a stipend of between $8,000 and $15,000 a year, plus an educational award of almost $5,000. The highest paid Americorps program is Teach for America—their volunteers get a starting teacher's salary of between $20,000 and $30,000, plus the educational award. The lowest paid Americorps programs are well-entrenched organizations like the Jesuit Volunteer Corps, which gives Americorps volunteers a whopping $75 a month, plus housing and the educational award. If you've got your heart set on chilling with the Jesuits despite the poverty factor, go for it. Otherwise, look before you leap.

AMERICORPS STATE/NATIONAL

The Americorps State/National route is the least defined. Everyone from the American Red Cross, to Habitat for Humanity, to Big Brothers Big Sisters has an Americorps program in place. Americorps State/National volunteers are knee-deep in "direct service"—hands-on work. They might tutor elementary school kids or clean up a park, knock on people's doors to remind them to get their children immunized, or

How Direct Are You?

Americorps gigs fall under one of two umbrellas: direct service or indirect service. To see which is a better fit, take this handy-dandy quiz:

Which set of things sounds more exciting?

List A:

Recruiting doctors to provide free health care to families without insurance

Raising funds to set up a community center in inner-city Chicago

Developing a computer skills training program at a community employment center

Scrounging up book donations for a bilingual library

Writing a grant proposal for a high school dropout prevention program

List B:

Teaching a kid to read

Installing drywall for a low-income housing project

Cleaning up trash from a beautiful beach

Planting a community garden in a vacant lot

Handing out food to hurricane victims

Answers:

If you prefer List A: You're a big-picture kind of person. You'd like indirect service—check out VISTA.

If you prefer List B: You're a hands-on kind of helper. You'd thrive doing direct service. Apply for Americorps State/National or NCCC.

man the phones for a health care referral service in an underserved community.

Unlike VISTA and NCCC, to get a position you'll need

to decide which nonprofit you want to work for and then *apply to them directly*. To get an idea of what's out there, call Americorps (1-800-942-2677) and ask for some brochures or, even better, visit their website (www.americorps.org). The site has listings of nonprofits in each state in need of volunteers. Each entry includes a short description of what you'd be doing there and how to apply. Opportunity abounds. So whether you're a city boy looking forward to a few years in the sticks, or heart set on a job in a bursting metropolis, you should have no problem finding something that fits the bill.

VISTA

The official word on VISTA, Volunteers in Service to America, is this: "VISTA places individuals in disadvantaged communities to help residents become more self-sufficient." VISTAs live in the places they serve, creating programs that will last long after they've hit the road. The program has been around since 1965—sort of a domestic Peace Corps.

Like Americorps State/National, VISTAs choose one nonprofit agency to work with. Unlike Americorps State/National, which does "direct service," VISTAs work behind the scenes doing "indirect service"—things that benefit the community as a whole rather than just one individual.

VISTAs are trailblazers. They're leaders. They're like community service entrepreneurs—brainstorming start-up programs that will benefit the community. They network, organize, fundraise, recruit. . . . Whereas in Americorps State/ National an education project might involve tutoring a child, a VISTA project might be *starting* a tutoring program—everything from polling the community to see what people want, to writing grants, to creating a board of directors to run the program, to finding and training the volunteers, to publicizing the program to let the community know it's available.

VISTA has more projects than Imelda Marcos had shoes. They run the gamut, but basically fall into four major categories: education, public safety, the environment, and human needs. Projects could be anything from fund-raising to creating computer labs in low-income neighborhoods, to launching a prenatal care outreach program. VISTAs might help communities get safe drinking water and indoor plumbing. They might create a peer lending program or a link between the community and entrepreneur mentors. They might start a shelter for families facing domestic violence and organize counseling, food, and activities for people who come there.

One little-known VISTA perk worth considering: Unlike Americorps State/National, VISTA gives volunteers relocation expenses. You can tell your recruiter, "I want to go to Alaska" or "Show me what you've got in Hawaii" and they'll hook you up. One recruiter warns, "We're not a travel agent, but we do look at what projects we have available, we look at geographically where they'd like to be, and we'll work with them." If you know what you want to do, but don't care where you do it, recruiters can also tell you what they have available throughout the country in your area of interest.

A word of warning—if you're high-maintenance, VISTA is your worst nightmare. The pay is a mere $600–800 a month, plus the educational award. It's not a lot to live on. But according to Monica Gugel, head of California recruiting, people rise to the challenge. Some live with families, some with relatives or friends, some do it as a couple and save money by sharing a small apartment.

"I've heard all different stories. I know one girl in D.C. who has a house rented from somebody who went overseas with the State Department. He rented her the house for $175 a month . . . It's a seven-bedroom mansion. I know someone who lived in a private room in a homeless shelter and she had to cook pancakes every morning, so she got free rent. I know a young man who lived in a convent. The nuns had a certain housing area that they rented out, similar to the YMCA. He paid fifty dollars a month. There are a lot of opportunities out there if you're creative." Gugel suggests picking the brains of the VISTAs serving where you want to work and asking them how they've managed to swing it.

Just to let you know, the low pay isn't meant to torture you; it has a purpose. VISTAs are there to make a difference in poor neighborhoods, but also to become part of those communities. That means living like the people they serve.

Gugel cheerfully told me that money was not a major issue. "VISTAs are very resourceful people. Especially by the end of their year. They'll know where all the free food is. They'll go to ceremonies to get food. That's just part of the fun of it. Making it work."

NCCC

For people with no idea what floats their boat, the National Civilian Community Corps (dubbed "N-triple-C") is golden. It's the perfect gig for someone who loves to dabble. Take it from Gugel, who did the program herself: "The NCCC is the smorgasbord of community service." Volunteers get a mix of environmental, education, public safety, and other community projects.

NCCC is like college without the homework: dorm rooms, cafeteria food, and a group of ready-made friends all twenty-four and under. Volunteers live at one of five cam-

INTERVIEW

Robert Nagel,
Americorps volunteer, California

Tell me about your transformation into a do-good.

After I graduated I did an internship with a production company. I was doing weddings and bar mitzvahs and birthday parties—learning the editing and the filming of it. I got to the point where if I saw people do the limbo one more time I was going to jump out a window. If I heard one more Elton John song. . . . And they tell you, "One day, you could be the head camera guy, the head editor!" And I'm thinking, "What a life—living in New Jersey and taping bar mitzvahs. Can't wait for the next ten years."

I was at a party and I saw this guy I'd known in college and he said that he was doing Americorps. He told me how exciting it was—that he was actually doing real work—that he was writing grants, working on disaster relief, developing all kinds of interesting projects.

I looked into it. It was Memorial Day four years ago and I just knew that it was time to go. That if I stayed I'd just get used to things and caught up in the mundane despair of New Jersey.

How did you end up on the West Coast?

I wanted to live in California. So I came out to L.A. and started talking to people who were doing VISTA. They took my girlfriend and me on some site visits in South Central and East L.A. They were working with kids there. And coming from New Jersey, I was like, "Whoa! I don't know if I can do this. There's no *way* I'm going to do this in South Central or East L.A. because, you know, I saw *Boys in the Hood*—I don't want anybody shooting at me.

But I went a few more times and the vibe was amazing. There were these really incredible people coming together and focusing on the project, and the people, and the community. And it was really something I'd never had the opportunity to experience. I decided to do it.

What's a VISTA's typical day like?

It was really interesting. I worked for the 4-H Afterschool Program, which was dedicated to helping kids ages seven to thirteen living in the public housing communities in East L.A. Every day it varied what you were going to do—sometimes you'd be writing grants, sometimes you'd be out making presentations, sometimes at a community meeting, sometimes recruiting volunteers, sometimes teaching kids all day. The main focus was to get out in the community.

With our programs, we'd try to get kids from different neighborhoods together at least six times a year. We brought kids together from twenty-three communities and planned different events for them to help open their minds to diversity. Because as they get older, it becomes very separate and very segregated. Kids from different cultures don't always interact.

Honestly, I think I learned more during that one year than I learned during those four years of college. It was just real life experience: working and interacting with people from diverse cultures, being able to focus on project goals, being able to take initiative in getting things done, living on a low income allowance and being able to survive on so little money.

It's not much of a paycheck. How did you survive?

It's amazing what you can do with so few resources. I worked with fifteen other VISTAs. We'd have barbecues, we'd have parties instead of going out. You'd go to the matinee or you'd rent a movie. You pooled your resources. Money, surprisingly, is not really a major issue. It's not the focus of your year because you're focused on the community and the experience. I even did it a second year.

We have people in New York and San Francisco and the cost of living is outrageous, but there's a network there and people are able to hook in and get help finding reasonable housing. It's part of the adventure to be able to survive on nine thousand dollars a year. You really utilize your resources and your know-how. If you can survive, you're ready for anything.

Why did you pick VISTA over the other Americorps programs?

I liked the idea of VISTA because it was behind the scenes and I liked the idea of developing sustainable resources for communities. Tutoring, mentoring, teaching, and building houses are all important. But I like the idea of putting things in place that the community can take over, so it's more than just a Band-Aid, it's a solution.

What would you tell someone who's on the fence as to whether to sign up?

Jobs are always going to be there. But VISTA gives you the opportunity to go into a new community and take a leadership role at such a young age. It makes you so much more flexible, you're able to listen and communicate with people more effectively because you've had experience assessing the needs of a diverse group of people. It's very motivating. I met amazing people and it's inspired me. I was clueless and it's given me a real direction.

It's amazing what people go on to do. Doing VISTA shows commitment and dedication to complete something you've started. It shows focus and vision. It really opens the doors to anything. As far as college, you've learned so much doing this program that you're ready. You do one of these programs and you're prepared for anything that life can throw you.

puses: Charleston, South Carolina; Denver, Colorado; Perry Point, Maryland; San Diego, California; or Washington, D.C. They go from project to project, state to state, with most jobs lasting between six and eight weeks.

Some of these jobs are more glamorous than others. Since they're a residential program, available at a moment's notice, the Red Cross has the NCCC on call for disaster relief. "The Red Cross can call us and say, 'We need two hundred people to go to Puerto Rico. We just had a huge hurricane there,'" according to Gugel, and a set of corps members pack their bags and get on a plane.

NCCC is also a favorite of the U.S. Forest Service. They train volunteers who've passed a hard-core physical fitness exam in fighting forest fires. "Volunteers don't jump out of helicopters or anything," Gugel explains. "Usually they start pretty small, rather than doing something a hotshot crew would be called in to do." But a lot of members go on to do the crazy stuff—many get hired on with the U.S. Forest Service once their NCCC stint is over.

Each of the NCCC campuses covers about a ten-state region. And volunteers get to see a lot of it. For example, a Denver campus corps member might spend their first two months working at Denver's Boys and Girls Club, implementing after-school programs. Their next project might be creating hiking trails in a state park in Wisconsin. The next, going to Montana and doing a water sanitation project or working to stop soil erosion. Then they're off to build a community garden in an urban area or to create a school dropout prevention program. If Habitat for Humanity calls, they could be pouring concrete or sanding wood floors. If there's a natural disaster, members might be brought in to hand out supplies.

Not only does the NCCC tend to help people figure out what they want to do, but it's also a real résumé builder. "When I finished the program I could say 'I've worked for the U.S. Forest Service' when applying for an environmental job, or 'I've worked in several health programs' when I applied for a job in health," Gugel says. It may not be a lot of experience, but it's a foot in the door. And lots of volunteers get hired directly by the nonprofits they've worked with during their time in NCCC.

WHO'S JOINING?

Most people who do Americorps are under the age of thirty. In NCCC, a third are right out of high school, a third have completed at least one college class, and a third are college grads. If you're not planning on going to college, Americorps can give you a jump start on all kinds of amazing careers. If college is on your agenda, it can help you figure out what you might want to learn once you get there.

Everybody has their own reasons for joining. Some people want to do something "good," others are looking to bulk up their résumés. "Some people are making a transition in life—whether it's right out of college, right after a job ends, a divorce. We get a lot of phone calls from attorneys and accountants and they say, 'I've been doing this for five years, since college, and I'm sick of it. I just think there's more to life and I want to do something different,'" says Gugel.

It's obvious no one's doing it for the money. But Americorps is a great way to test out the world and figure out where you fit into it. If nothing else, it can help you eliminate some options—you may realize you hate working outdoors. You might find you love working with kids. Who knows? A parting shot from Gugel: "It really opens people's eyes and broadens their world. It exposes them to things they've never experienced before. I hear some of our members saying, 'I learned more in this program than I learned in four years of college.' And when I think about that, I think, we pay a *lot* of money to go to college and gain skills in this country. This is somebody paying you a *little* bit to get all this experience."

Straight Up: Cliff Notes on What You Need and What You Get

Americorps State/National

Direct service with one nonprofit agency, chosen from over 600

Must be at least 17 years old

NO COLLEGE REQUIRED

Full time for one year

Pay varies, anywhere from $75 a month plus housing, to $30,000 a year

Usually need to find own room and board

No relocation expenses

Projects in all 50 states, Washington, D.C., Guam, Puerto Rico, and the Virgin Islands

Apply directly to the program you want. For a list, call (800) 942-2677 or check out www.americorps.org

VISTA

Indirect service with one nonprofit agency

Must be at least 18 years old

College degree preferred; otherwise 3 years of volunteer/job experience

Full time for one year

Pay varies, usually $600–800 a month

Need to find own room and board

Can choose $1,200 cash instead of education voucher

Relocation expenses

Projects in all 50 states, Washington, D.C., Guam, Puerto Rico, and the Virgin Islands

Send application to the recruiter in your state

NCCC

Direct service with a slew of different places

Live with a team of 12–15 in a campus environment

Must be 18–24 years old

NO COLLEGE REQUIRED

Full-time for ten months

Room, board, uniforms, and $4,000 in pocket money

Transportation to and from your campus

Campuses in Charleston, S.C.; Denver, Co.; Perry Point, Md.; San Diego, Cal.; and Washington, D.C.

Send application to Americorps NCCC centralized recruitment in Washington, D.C.

Note: All the programs give members a $4,725 education award voucher. It can be used to pay for college or vocational school (within seven years) or to pay off loans (which, by the way, can be postponed during service).

A DIFFERENT WAY TO MAKE A DIFFERENCE

If you are looking for a particular type of community service opportunity, odds are that Americorps can hook you up. But that doesn't mean that Americorps is your only option. Take a look around. Explore the nonprofit organizations in your area. You'd be surprised how many opportunities there are on the local level. Need evidence? Check out these programs:

HARD CORPS

Youth Corps are often confused with Americorps, but while some of them get Americorps funding, most "have a broader scope," according to the National Association of Youth Service Community Corps, a clearinghouse for over a hundred programs across the country. Today's youth corps trace their roots to Franklin Roosevelt's Civilian Conservation Corps, set up during the Depression to keep teenagers and twenty-somethings busy. "Idle hands . . ." and all that. In general, corps employ people between the ages of sixteen and twenty-five. Over twenty-six thousand people each year, to be exact. They're meant to "harness the energy and idealism of young people to meet the needs of communities, states, and the nation" by giving them paid, full-time, useful work. They operate in nearly every state, plus Washington, D.C.

Projects run the gamut, with corps doing everything from park projects and forestry to building renovations and human services. They might run classes for kids living in neighborhoods where drugs and gangs are popular or help out after a hurricane.

Most corps will go in and do anything that needs doing, but a few specialize. The California Conservation Corps, for example, focuses on the environment and emergency response. They can be on the scene for floods, fires, oil spills, earthquakes, and almost any other kind of natural disaster within a few hours. The corps puts in over three million hours a year in conservation work, emergency assistance, and environmental cleanup. From planting trees, to building trails, clearing streams to responding to major oil spill disasters, the CCC's motto: "Hard work, low pay, miserable conditions. . . and more!" hasn't stopped more than seventy thousand 18- to 23-year olds from joining its ranks in the twenty plus years since it started.

LIFE IN THE CITY

Another popular Youth Corps program is City Year, a high clout, highly competitive program with nine hundred volunteers putting in more than one million hours of service each year, in ten cities across the country. Unlike most other youth corps, City Year focuses on education. The majority of their work is in schools, with young kids.

A major City Year goal is to "better the ratio of adults to students in the classroom," according to Kristin Thalheimer of City Year's national headquarters. Corps members work in teams, and Monday through Thursday most teams head off to their assigned school and fan out into separate classrooms. "Each corps member is assigned a classroom and works directly with the students and the teacher tutoring and mentoring. They may help kids who aren't quite getting it, or help the kids who are a little bit accelerated," Thalheimer says.

Although City Year volunteers play a key role in the classroom, they don't have to be college grads themselves. City Year values diversity, motivation, and talent more than a bunch of degrees on the wall. "You can be a corps member and have graduated from an Ivy League school. You can also be a corps member and not yet have graduated from high school but be working on your GED. It can be a little scary for members who feel like they haven't done all that well in school to go into a classroom and be in a leadership position," Thalheimer admits, "but by the time they get into the classroom, they're ready, even if it is a challenge for them."

City Year is all about challenge. And to get in, you have to show you're up for it. Candidates "have to know that they will be pushed beyond their comfort zones and they have to want that. When people go into the Peace Corps and they're sent somewhere like Uganda, they know they're going to be pushed. Well, the same is true of City Year," Thalheimer says. You have to be prepared to tough it out, because it will get tough.

Because the City Year day goes from eight to six and most schools run from eight to two, corps members often run after-school programs when the school day is done. They might also get sent to do service elsewhere—in a homeless shelter, a senior citizens' home, or some other nonprofit organization.

"A lot of kids come to City Year and don't know what they want to do with their lives," Thalheimer says. "They have such a variety of experiences over the course of their service that their ideas become crystallized. People have come to City Year and found they have a knack for computers—because they need to work on them and they never have before. Or people come in thinking they want to be teachers, and they go into the classroom and realize they don't want to be teachers, they'd much rather work in a nonprofit atmosphere or work in the corporate world, because they had the chance to shadow one of our corporate sponsors," Thalheimer says. Some corps members end up getting hired by their service sites. Some leave service pointed in a different direction altogether. And some end up working for City Year. The executive directors of City Year Philadelphia and City Year Rhode Island, for example, are alums. A new program, City Year Detroit, is being launched by a former corps member.

City Year

Motto: "Young enough to want to change the world—old enough to do it."

Timeline: Lasts ten months, usually September–June
Pay: About $150 a week, plus $4,725 from Americorps if you do a full stint
Makeup: In 1998 16 percent of corps members were getting their GED, 42 percent had graduated from high school but had no college, 25 percent had some college, and 16 percent were college grads.
NO COLLEGE REQUIRED
Contact: www.city-year.org

The thing that sets City Year apart, according to Thalheimer, is its focus on diversity. "It's the only service organization, as far as I know, that makes this such a priority. And it's an incredible role model when a team like that walks into a school and you've got a white kid and a black kid and a Latino and an Asian and they're all getting along, they're all working together," she says. "It sets an incredible example."

Wired to Serve

If you're over eighteen but under twenty-five, able to live on a shoestring budget, and ready for an adventure, a youth corps could be the ticket. These websites will get you started:

www.city-year.org
www.servenet.org
www.nascc.org

THE VILLAGE PEOPLE

There's a movement brewing all over the world—in more than ninety locations and over sixteen countries. It's working its way around the globe, but I doubt you've ever heard of it.

They're so busy doing good stuff, they haven't really set aside time for advertising. Too bad, because Camphill is a pretty great place to spend some time.

Camphill communities are mini-villages throughout the world. Life there is a mix of hard work and utopia. To call them cooperatives for people with developmental disabilities doesn't do them justice, but in a nutshell, that's what they are. They were created to help mentally and physically challenged kids and adults reach their true potential—well beyond what society in general thinks they're capable of.

That's the philosophy. But what they really are is a camp-like atmosphere of people from all kinds of backgrounds and dozens of countries, working together. Camphill villages range in size—some communities have fifty members, some have over two hundred.

Most Camphill locations have farms or gardens. Some have well equipped artist craft shops. A few do beekeeping or baking. On the one hand, they teach usable vocational skills. On the other hand, they give each person a job to help keep the community afloat—from cooking to child care.

Basically, Camphill focuses on the *abilities* of each person, not the disabilities. Everyone in the village contributes what they're capable of, and what that is varies. For the "villagers," the people in the community with special needs, it might be learning how to sand a wood plank or pushing around a baby carriage. For the "coworkers," or residents, that may mean running the community garden or working in the bakery.

"You get pretty much thrown into the deep end when you arrive and it's interesting, because you could pretty much end up doing anything—from being in the house cooking for fourteen to twenty people, to house cleaning," Lael Kretschmer, a coworker, says. "There's the garden and the farm, obviously.

There's a small organic food co-op: Someone might work there. There's also a candle-making workshop for those villagers who want to be more focused. There's a weavery, a glass workshop, a wood workshop . . . There's also a bakery that bakes all our bread for us and supplies eggs and cookies. You become integrated into one of those things."

At Camphill, everyone works as equals. Although Camphill residents hail from a wide array of cultures and countries, they all need to work together in the village. "It's great to have men from India, say, who in their culture have never learned to cook. Suddenly they're seen as equals and most women do the same kind of work. So they're immediately thrust into having to learn how to do housecleaning and cooking," Kretschmer says.

Many people who work at Camphill point out that it's not a normal job. In fact, it's not a job at all. It's a lifestyle. There are no shifts, really. Officially, work goes from nine to twelve. There's a rest until 2:30 P.M. Then it's back to work until five, unless you're working on the farm or in the garden, where the hours may be a little bit longer. But aside from your official "job," there's a lot more that needs doing. Coworkers and villagers live mixed together in a bunch of cheerful houses strewn about the villages, and everyone pitches in with cooking, cleaning, and organizing. If villagers need help brushing their teeth or getting dressed, coworkers help with things like that, too. They do what's needed, when it's needed. There's no set free time.

It may sound like a lot of work, and it is, but everyone I talked to said they got at least as much out of Camphill as they put in. "It's hard to describe. I come from London and I went to a private English school. There was a lot of stress and pressure to do this and do this. And here, there's lots of work to do, it's not a nine-to-five job, but I find that it's a very accepting place. I feel at home here. And it's allowed me to grow up a bit. I mean, I'm only nineteen now, I came here when I was eighteen. And I feel I've matured here and that this place has allowed me to be more myself than I was before," Kathy Dale, a coworker, says.

Coworkers put in a lot of hours, but they're surrounded by a huge group of interesting, supportive people. "It really is a village. I mean, you come to a place with two hundred and twenty people and you have two hundred and twenty new friends. People are so friendly. You can't walk down a road, even for a few minutes, and not stop and talk along the way. There are friends all around you," Dale says.

There's lots to do at night and on the weekends—concerts, lectures, dances, swimming . . . Many times a house will plan a trip to the movies. Someone just finished organizing a folk festival. And because of Camphill's connections to some pretty famous artists, visits from acclaimed pianist Andre Watts, or the equivalent, aren't at all unusual.

"One thing I'd say about it: This is the most luscious, highest standard of living I've ever lived. Higher than I'm comfortable with," says Colin Corby, a coworker at Camphill who's doing an internship in biodynamic farming. "We have so much money. We can get whatever food we want. We have our own co-op, each house has a car. . . . It's pretty amazing."

It's true, no one at Camphill is exactly roughing it. Villagers' families contribute a certain amount for them to live there, and private donations are plentiful. The villages are far from threadbare. They have beautiful common rooms and up-to-date equipment. Each coworker has their own room and everybody's well fed. Plus, Camphill's villages are on some of the most gorgeous land in the world—from Ireland to

South Africa. Many are old estates that have been donated, with renovated mansions and several hundred acres.

Coworkers planning to stay for a while will have lots of opportunities to travel. Because the work is so intense, Camphill encourages all long-term volunteers to take four weeks off each year—all paid for by the community. It's done on what they refer to as a need basis. "So if one year I decide I need to go to India, someone else may say, 'OK, I'll go to New Hampshire.' And next year maybe they'll have to go further away," Kretschmer explains. Moreover, once you've worked at one village, it's easy to do a stint at another location in a different part of the world. They're all based on the same philosophy.

What that philosophy is, is anthroposophy—a worldview developed by an Austrian educator named Rudolf Steiner. According to Camphill's brochure, "Anthroposophy embraces a spiritual view of the human being and the world. It's a path of self knowledge which encourages us to develop in a balanced way the capacities of our head (thinking), our heart (feeling), and our hands (action)." Camphill's aim is to create communities where the arts, education, and the care of the earth are all key elements in the life of the community. The Camphill movement was founded in Scotland in 1939 by physician Karl Koenig and a group of young artists, doctors, and teachers who'd fled from Nazi-occupied Austria.

Whatever your reasons for going there, you can learn a lot at Camphill, for free. And I'm not just talking learning a lot about yourself, and all that foo-foo stuff. I mean hard skills—farming, woodworking, office administration. . . . The villages vary in what they offer, but a lot of them have long-term training programs. Some have apprenticeships in biodynamic agriculture (an offspring of organic farming), others have three- or four-year training programs in social therapy or curative education. And because many of the villages have incredible art equipment, you can flex your creative muscles in copper-making, batiking, toy-making, weaving, glass blowing, and a whole batch of other things. When you leave Camphill you'll have more than a full heart. You'll have marketable skills.

Camphill can be an incredible experience, but it's not something to do on a lark. "One would have to be serious about giving oneself over to people with special needs. If you're ready for that, it's an amazing place to go. But if you're not ready for it, it could be overwhelming, I'm sure. They'll take every bit of energy that you put out there. It's all up to you to provide your own boundaries," Corby says.

Camphill Villages

Villages for the developmentally disabled in ninety locations across the world.

Where: Sixteen countries, including the U.S. and Canada

Cost: None. You'll get room, board, and your basic needs covered, plus vacation.

NO COLLEGE REQUIRED

Contact: (518) 329-7288; www.camphillassociation.org

Part 3

Training for Real Life: Alternative Schools, Courses, and Apprenticeship Programs

CHAPTER 7

Giving College the Kiss-Off: *Training for Real Life*

> **"A child educated only at school is an uneducated child."**
>
> —George Santayana

THERE'S AN "ALL YOU CAN EAT" SUSHI PLACE near my apartment. Thirty bucks for all the sushi you can manage. My friends love to go there. It's "a good deal." Or it would be if I liked sushi, which I don't. On me, the place is wasted—thirty dollars blown to eat a few California rolls and stare wistfully out the window at the Italian restaurant across the street.

In a way, college is just like an all you can eat sushi bar. For those hungry for what they serve, there's no better bargain. But for students hungry for something else, or just not ready to sit down and eat, college can be a waste—too much money shelled out to pick at a bowl of rice.

If you're someone who's been pushed toward college your

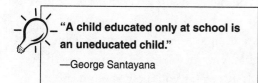

whole life, a four-year liberal arts education may seem like the only option. But it's not. There are cheaper, quicker, and just plain more practical ways to prime yourself for a great career. The programs run the gamut—from trade school to long-distance learning, apprenticeships to co-op education. Now with everyone you know pushing the sushi bar, it can be difficult to head off to the Italian restaurant. You may not even *know* about the Italian restaurant. But just because your guidance counselor hasn't told you about it, doesn't mean it's not worth considering.

People talk a lot of trash about trade school and other types of vocational training. And some schools deserve it. But alternative education is a broad umbrella. And some of the options it includes will make you more marketable than almost any college diploma out there. So humor me. Before you write them all off as not for you, how about a short tour through some of the alternatives to the four-year liberal arts degree.

APPRENTICESHIPS AND ON-THE-JOB TRAINING

Before running water, before central air, when transportation was by foot or horse and America was a brand-spanking-new nation, education was a different thing altogether. It wasn't uncommon for parents to deliver their ten-year-old boy to a craftsman's doorstep and deposit him there. To make a living, you had to be a specialist—a blacksmith, a builder, a cobbler. . . . And knowledge was passed down the old-fashioned way—on the job, at the knee of a master.

In exchange for hands-on instruction, apprentices agreed to about five to seven years of grunt work. They cleaned the tools, swept the shop, started the fire in the morning—whatever needed to be done. They basically swallowed their pride and sucked it up for the chance to pick somebody's brain and learn a marketable skill.

Then along came something called the Industrial Revolution. Hand-made was abandoned for mass-made. The machine was business's new best friend and the assembly line was king. The desire for things built by a master craftsman was replaced with the desire for things people could actually afford.

Mass production dramatically reduced the popularity of apprenticeships, but that doesn't mean they disappeared entirely. Many chefs, carpenters, actors, electricians, and a slew of other professionals still pay their dues the old-fashioned way. The major benefit of this type of learning is that it's hands-on. Instead of talking about how to do something, students actually do it. They graduate with practical, usable experience. They can dive right into work because they don't need on-the-job training.

Famous Apprentices

Ben Franklin, inventor and American forefather: at a printer's shop

Christopher Reeve, actor: at Williamstown Theatre Festival

Thomas Hardy, author: with an architect

How Do I Get One?

To keep things on the up and up, apprenticeships are regulated by the U.S. Department of Labor. According to Uncle Sam, there are exactly 825 "apprenticeable occupations," from accordian maker to X-ray equipment tester. To see what's out there, look in the blue pages for your State Apprenticeship Council, or contact your closest affiliate from the Bureau of Apprenticeships and Training:

Denver: (303) 844-4791
San Francisco: (415) 975-4007
Atlanta: (404) 562-2335
Chicago: (312) 353-7205
Boston: (617) 565-2288
Kansas City: (816) 426-3856
New York: (212) 337-2313
Philadelphia: (215) 596-6417
Dallas: (214) 767-4993
Seattle: (206) 553-5286

TRADE SCHOOLS

When most people hear the words "trade school," they think auto mechanics. But trade schools, sometimes dubbed "vocational education," get a bad rep, mostly because they're often the final resting place for students that high schools have given up on. A lot of vocational *high schools* deserve their image problem—U.S. government studies show that more than half of the students who take high school vocational classes graduate with useless, obsolete skills.

But there's a world of trade schools out there that give students just the opposite—modern, expert-level skills that have employers banging down their doors before they've even graduated. According to the National Commission on Co-op Education, 84 percent of students who go to technical institutions find work.

If you decide trade school is the way to go, you'll have no problem finding a place to enroll. There are almost seven thousand vocational schools in the U.S. According to the National Center for Educational Statistics, the biggest areas are health care (33 percent), business and management (27 percent), engineering technologies (15 percent), protective services (6 percent), and visual and performing arts (6 percent). But people go to trade schools to learn how to be everything from massage therapists to advertising executives, dental technicians to midwives.

CO-OP

Let's face it, the phrase "trade school" makes most parents nervous. If your parents fall into this category, you've got your work cut out for you. Sure, it'd be great if their opinion didn't matter. But chances are, you're hoping that they'll foot at least part of the bill for your education. In other words, you've got some convincing to do.

May I present co-op education. . . . This could just be the olive branch you've been looking for. Co-op programs mix work with school—giving students the opportunity to graduate with a résumé that has some meat to it. But more than an olive branch, co-op is sort of the best of both worlds. You can have a bit of the traditional college experience—at least two thirds of your school days will be spent in the classroom—but work off some of your tuition (and learn some concrete skills) with a job at a local company. Some colleges have exclusive relationships with a certain company. Others are polygamists—spreading their love around. But about three quarters of community colleges have partnerships with at least one company.

The co-op option was introduced by a University of Cincinnati engineering professor in 1906. In those days, he was a renegade. Today, about one thousand two- and four-year colleges have bitten the bullet and developed programs that combine hitting the books with pounding the pavement. Some send students into the workforce part-time, with the rest of their day spent on campus. These are called "parallel" programs because work and school happen side by side. Other colleges opt for "alternating" programs, where students alternate between semesters in the classroom and semesters at work. They typically graduate in four years with two or three years of work experience to crow about. The only downside is, they usually work summers.

The statistics for co-op programs are incredible. According to the National Commission for Co-op Education, about 80 percent of students have an extremely easy time snagging their first job—half with their co-op company and half with another company using skills they picked up during their co-op assignment. Plus, they're usually less in debt. Unlike internships, almost 100 percent of co-ops pay (typically about $7,000 a year) and over two thirds also give college credit. Plus, co-op programs help you yank open doors that may be harder to open post-graduation. More than 85 percent of the top one hundred Fortune 500 companies have co-op programs—a great way to make yourself known before a rush of senior résumés land on the boss's desk.

THE CHEAP SEATS: OUTSTANDING COMMUNITY COLLEGES

Community college isn't what it used to be. Once considered a second-rate option for kids not smart enough to get into a "real" college, community colleges have become the first choice of the smartest cookies around. With college costs rising faster than the temperature in Chicago on a summer day, community college is emerging as a way to slash the price tag of higher ed in half. More and more students are deciding to stay local for their first two years and then transfer to a four-year college for the second half of their college stint. Come graduation, they've got a regular diploma from the four-year college and a lot less debt on their plate.

In addition to price, community colleges have a few other things going for them. Students can use the two years to plump up their GPA. Classes are usually small, so there's a chance for individual attention. In Florida, California, and a few other states, community college transfers are given first priority for admission. And some community colleges have better job placement than their four-year counterparts.

Case in point: Cuyahoga Community College, where 92 percent of vocational graduates get jobs. The Cleveland-based college offers programs in everything from engineering to plant and landscape technology. Its music program, offered in partnership with the Rock and Roll Hall of Fame, was recently showered with an eight-million-dollar gift from the state. When students get tired of cracking open the books they can head on over to the studio and produce a CD for Cuyahoga's own record label. Kids with absolutely no rhythm can do well here, too—Cuyahoga is a magnet for recruiters at the Environmental Protection Agency and one of the best schools in the nation for job training in health care.

Santa Monica College, within walking distance of the beach, gives artists a leg up for a drop in the bucket. Tuition is a mere four hundred dollars a year. Santa Monica's Arts Mentor Program provides advanced students with one-on-one instruction with professionals in their field. Movie buffs can enroll in Santa Monica's Academy of Entertainment and Technology and get up to speed on digital animation, interactive media, and special effects before shopping their résumés around Hollywood. The college has an award-winning radio station and its nursing program has a job-placement rate of almost 100 percent. Pretty good odds for such a small investment.

As for the skeptics who say that community college doesn't provide the "name" grads need to land a high-paying job, take a look at Florida's Miami-Dade Community College or Washington's Bellevue Community College—both of whose graduates average starting salaries above $30,000 a year, well above the average for your typical liberal arts grad.

Community colleges are cheap. But more than that, there's one out there specializing in anything you can think of. De Anza College in Silicon Valley can hook you up with Apple (Steve Jobs and Steve Wozniak are alums), Hewlett-Packard, IBM, or a slew of other tech companies. Bellevue is an unofficial funnel to Microsoft and Nintendo. Miami-Dade is known for kick-ass performing arts classes. Nassau Community College trains budding fashion designers and Brookhaven College in Texas places 99 percent of its automotive tech grads in jobs—sometimes with starting salaries above $50,000 a year.

Even if you've got the grades to get into a four-year college, why not look local first. Who knows what your nearest CC's got going. . . .

The Top Ten According to *Rolling Stone* Magazine

Bellevue Community College, Washington; Brookhaven College, Texas; Cuyahoga Community College, Ohio; De Anza College, California; John A. Logan College, Illinois; Johnson County Community College, Kansas; Miami-Dade Community College, Florida; Nassau Community College, New York; Northern Virginia Community College, Virginia; Santa Monica College, California

THE WAITING GAME

About three quarters of students who decide to go to college go straight after high school. But sometimes procrastination can be a good thing. For one, by waiting a few years to start college, you can shed your "dependent" status and become an "independent"—increasing the chance of a free ride if you're broke, and saving your parents from having to mortgage the house to help put you through school. Who knows, if you're motivated enough to take a few community college or continuing education classes, you might even boost your high school GPA enough to be a real contender.

If good grades or old age aren't enough to get your bill taken care of, there's another option: getting your company to pay for your enlightenment. In 1978, the U.S. government did a beautiful thing. They introduced legislation that lets companies deduct employee education assistance costs as a business expense. In other words, you're a company write-off, baby!

Don't think the mom and pop drugstore that pays you six dollars an hour is going to send you to Yale. There's got to be some serious cash coming in for a write-off to be an option. The bigger the company, the better your chances. According to the National Institute for Work and Learning, over 80 percent of companies with between five hundred and one thousand employees offer tuition programs. Once the company roster is between one thousand and ten thousand, the percentage shoots up to 92 percent. And since few workers realize that help is out there, few take advantage, making competition slim.

FROM A DISTANCE

When most people think of college, they think of a physical place—buildings, campus, parking lot—the glossy college brochure. Well, you get what you pay for. One of the reasons college costs so much is the appearance—it's not cheap to keep all the buildings painted, the campus lawn mowed. . . . Students with a computer and an imagination at the ready can save a bundle if they're willing to toss the image aside and pop a copy of *School Ties* or *Love Story* into the VCR should the yearning for a campus strike.

Because the truth is, these days you can earn a college degree without ever leaving the comfort of your couch. Correspondence courses have entered the modern age. And with so many colleges struggling with overcrowded classrooms, it just might be the wave of the future. Over a hundred universities and colleges now offer correspondence courses in everything from auto mechanics to poetry. You can set your sights on any of more than twelve thousand classes offered through correspondence and have those credits count at almost any college in the country.

Leading the pack with the most college-level courses are Brigham Young University, Louisiana State, Ohio University, Penn State, the University of Alabama, the University of California, the University of Iowa, the University of Oklahoma, the University of Wisconsin, the University of North Carolina, and the University of Tennessee. There is one catch, though. While dozens of colleges will let you take *some* of your courses from your kitchen table, most limit the number to around 50 percent. Truth is, as "modern" as they like to think of themselves, colleges still want you on campus spending money in the bookstore, paying rent for a dorm bed, and storing up nostalgic moments so you'll give generously as an alumnus.

There is no typical correspondence course. But if there were, if would be worth about three units, cost around two hundred and fifty dollars, and span about eighty hours spread out over five to twenty lessons. There would be a small written paper due at each session and questions to be answered. And when it was all over, you'd have to haul your butt on over to a local college to take a supervised final under the watchful eyes of an official proctor.

Correspondence courses can rustle up anywhere from one

Schools with the Most Choices for College-Level Correspondence Courses:

University of the State of New York, Western Illinois University, Thomas Edison College of New Jersey to six semester hours of credit. They can be as cheap as forty dollars per semester hour or as much as one hundred and fifty. Some do things the old-fashioned way—through the mail.

What to Ask Admissions

- Is the school accredited by the U.S. Department of Education or the Commission on Recognition of Postsecondary Accreditation (CORPA)?
- Can I talk to a graduate?
- What's the average age of students taking this class?
- Is there a class size limit?
- How will I get my course work? (fax, mail, web . . .)
- Can I take a test run to see if that works for me?
- How often will I hear from my teacher?
- Are there any group projects? Will I work with or talk to other people in the class?
- Will I have access to a library or a computer database?
- Are there any extra costs for mailings, being out of state, etc.?
- What will happen if I need to go out of town or work late unexpectedly?
- Will I need to take a certain number of credits on-campus to get a degree?
- On average, how long does it take to graduate?
- Will my transcript say my credits were earned at a distance or just the name of the college?
- Are credits transferable?
- Is there any financial aid?
- Is there job placement or career counseling?

Some send videotapes, faxes, e-mail, or a combination. But most take advantage of that new-fangled invention called the Internet. You can listen to your professor live—through audio fed through your computer's speakers or you can type in your question and watch the answer pop up on your computer screen in "real time." If the course sets up an online bulletin board, you can even bitch to the other people in your class.

The upside of taking a correspondence course is the flexibility. You can learn on your own time, from your own place—part-time, full-time, it's your gig. There's no commuting, no psycho roommate, no cafeteria food. And if money's tight, there's no beating long distance. Take Regent's College, the biggest correspondence school in the country—an entire bachelor's degree will only set you back "about $2,500–3,000, plus the cost of study materials," according to their admissions department.

The downside to distance is you're often working in a vacuum. There's no adviser breathing down your neck. It's easier to procrastinate. And if you choose the wrong course, you can be stuck in the stone ages—mailing lengthy assignments through the U.S. Postal Service, with no real interaction with anyone else taking the class. Five million people a year take classes through virtual colleges, but you may never meet any of them.

Now that you've gotten the crash course in alternative education, let's get down and dirty. The next few chapters will get specific on cool careers where a college diploma doesn't carry much water. To get hired, you'll need hands-on training. In other words, you'll need to have gone alternative. . . .

RESOURCES

Bear's Guide to Earning College Degrees Untraditionally by John B. Bear

Virtual College by Pam Dixon

National Commission for Cooperative Education: www.co-op.edu; (617) 373-3770

Council for Adult and Experiential Learning: www.cael.org (312) 922-5909

Regents College—largest in U.S. for long distance learning: (518) 464-8500; www.regents.edu

Distance Education and Training Council—lists accredited colleges: www.detc.org

Online Education: www.caso.com

CHAPTER 8

Make Your Cake and Eat It, Too: *Careers in the Kitchen*

> **"There is no love sincerer than the love of food."**
>
> —George Bernard Shaw

WHEN I WAS A KID, LIFE REVOLVED AROUND the kitchen. My mom was an amazing cook and she was always stirring something on the stove and putting a spoon up to my mouth to let me have a taste. Once a week, my brother and I were in charge of cooking dinner for ourselves. We made some pretty weird stuff. I remember a particularly harrowing incident with food coloring . . .

I had a slow start, but I eventually learned how to boil water, scramble an egg, bake cookies. Mom gave us free range in the kitchen, license to make a mess. And we did. You never knew in my house just how delicious or disgusting the food we made was going to be. Every week was an adventure—good or bad.

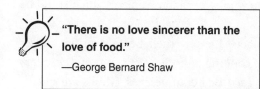

Some people never get over that feeling of peering into a pot, waiting for magic. The kitchen is a playground long after they get tall enough to reach the counter. If you're one of the few creative enough to make spices bow to your every whim, and disciplined enough not to become a glutton, a culinary career could be your calling. You can turn your taste buds into cold, hard cash.

And while you might not get rich doing it, you won't be standing on the unemployment line, either. Fact is, the Bureau of Labor Statistics predicts that the food industry will be one of the fastest growing professions around. We're talking about 200,000 new jobs a year, any one of which could be yours.

Why? Face the facts. Despite their best intentions, fewer and fewer people are cooking at home. We're out of *Leave It to Beaver* and into the Taco Bell commercials. Moms are spending less time in the kitchen and more in the boardroom. And since lots of households have two people working, there's more eating out and more money to be spent on it.

Even dinner at home isn't what it used to be. People are just too tired to cook. So they pick up prepared food at the local supermarket, deli, or gourmet store. They grab a loaf of fresh baked bread to put on the table next to the just-like-homemade lasagna. Well guess what—somebody's got to take care of the "prepare" in "prepared foods." Somebody's got to do the "bake" in "fresh baked bread" and put the "home" into "just like homemade." Chefs, cooks, and other kitchen workers held over three million jobs in 1996 and those numbers are growing fast.

GET COOKING

There's more than one way to skin an onion, just like there's more than one way to skin a cat. People become culinarians in all kinds of ways. Some learn to cook by trial and error—testing spices one by one in their own kitchen, whipping out a knife and practicing until they can slice like a pro. Some learn about food by eating—less precise but more fun. But typically, pros learn their trade in one of two ways: apprenticeship or culinary school.

The Guide to Cooking Schools, put out by Shaw Guides, lists 358 professional cooking programs around the world. Double that number if you're not looking for a degree. Pretty amazing when you consider the fact that a professional culinary school is a pretty new concept. The Culinary Institute of America was the trailblazer, opening its doors on the Yale campus, in 1946.

History Lesson

- In 1877 Fannie Farmer entered the Boston Cooking School. She eventually published a cookbook that did away with handfuls and pinches and introduced accurate measuring into cooking recipes.
- 1946 was a kick-ass year for cooks: James Beard tried his hand at that brand-spanking-new medium, television, and the Culinary Institute of America started up.
- In 1976 the American Culinary Federation found a sugar daddy in the U.S. government. They got a grant to start an apprenticeship program which is now the seventh biggest in the U.S.

THE LOWDOWN ON CULINARY SCHOOL

Every culinary school has its own way of doing things. At the French Culinary Institute, you can go from kitchen klutz to certified chef in six months flat. The bread baking program is even quicker—a mere six weeks and you're ready to throw that bun in the oven. Why so short? FCI is a total immersion program. It was created by four extremely famous chefs: Jacques Pepin, Andre Soltner, Jacques Torres, and Elain Sailhac. Just to give you an idea of their culinary credentials—Pepin alone has eighteen cookbooks under his belt. He's been a private chef to three French heads of state, the head of a four-star restaurant, host of a TV cooking show, and a *New York Times* food columnist.

The difference between FCI and most of the other biggies is time. Culinary schools usually take two to four years, with three being the average. They teach you everything from how to cook the perfect crème brûlée to how to keep track of the business end of things. At FCI it's only cooking, which is great if you have a good head for numbers, but could be disastrous if you don't.

No guide officially ranks culinary schools, but there's an *unofficial* Ivy League of cooking, and it's generally thought to be: The Culinary Institute of America, Johnson and Wales, The New England Culinary Institute, The French Culinary Institute, Baltimore International Culinary Arts Institute, California Culinary Academy, and Pennsylvania Culinary.

Prestige doesn't come cheap. A graduate ready to hit the streets after four years at the Culinary Institute of America (CIA) usually has about $52,000 in debt weighing her down. Even if she was the next Julia Child, it would probably take her five to ten years to work her way up to head chef at a restaurant. And according to the National Restaurant Association, she'd only rake in an average of $41,000 a year.

Three Schools Duke It Out: Culinary School Costs Compared

Adapted from the October 25, 1998, issue of the *New York Times*

Culinary Institute of America:
Program takes four years for a bachelor's degree.
Costs $52,400 but most students are on financial aid. Includes two meals a day.
Average salary for grads: Entry level: $22,400. After ten years: $50,000.

French Culinary Institute:
Program lasts only six months.
Costs $22,760, including uniforms, tools, and books.
Average salary for grads: Entry level: $21,000. After ten years: $65,000.

New England Culinary Institute:
Program takes three-and-a-half years and includes three paid internships.
Costs $63,180 but students are paid an average of $6,000 for each six-month internship. Includes uniforms, health insurance, and health club membership.
Average salary for grads: Entry level: $23,000. After ten years: $41,000.

THE APPRENTICESHIP OPTION

For cooks with big dreams and small bank balances, there's always the apprenticeship route. And a lot of would-be cooks choose apprenticeship because they can't afford to go to a hot-shot culinary school. But according to Arlene Weber, the program coordinator for the American Culinary Federation's Apprenticeship Program, cheap training isn't the only reason. Sure, the three-year program allows you to work full-time, which helps cut costs, but it also gives you three years of work experience to put on your résumé, come graduation. "When college grads go to their first job, it's a rude awakening. And it can be the same for people who've graduated culinary school and had lots of classroom cooking study, but not enough on-the-job training. That's not to say culinary schools don't give a wonderful education, but here we're making sure students fit a strict set of criteria. Some restaurants will *only* hire apprenticeship grads, because they know they're prepared," Weber says.

Apprentices train under the watchful eye of a qualified chef—one of dozens spread out all over the country, willing to take a student under their wing. The program is coordinated through local chapters of the American Culinary Federation—they do the networking and the placement. You can see what's available in your state by checking out ACF's website (www.acfchefs.org). If you've got your heart set on a certain chef or a certain location, apply early. Some places have room for a truckload of apprentices, others are limited by the size of their kitchen. For instance, New Orleans is teeming with opportunity because it's jam-packed with restaurants who need help. But smaller places may have fewer slots to fill.

Apprentices spend about 6,000 hours of their three years in the kitchen and 192 in the classroom. There are almost two thousand flitting through the ACF's various apprenticeship locations at any one time. They start at the bottom (steward) and work their way up to lead chef. It's not all sauces and sautés. They also get an earful on sanitation, nutrition, and menu planning, and a host of other subjects. Classroom commitments are pretty slim, "usually only once a week at a local community college," according to Weber, "a little more if an associate's degree is being given, too." On-the-job training is full-time, with typical chef hours—apprentices will need to be in the kitchen and ready to work the lunch, dinner, and sometimes breakfast crowd.

Costs vary, but apprentices should expect to shell out an average of $1,000 to $4,000 a year—about what it costs to fulfill the necessary classroom hours at a local community college. Then again, some programs only ask apprentices to pay for books. And some cost nothing at all.

IF YOU CAN'T STAND THE HEAT . . .

Cooking isn't all chef hats and rave reviews. It has its dark side. For one, it's high pressured. Vitaly Paley, owner and head chef of Portland's hot restaurant Paley's Place, warns students, "Think twice before embarking on a career as a cook. There's no glamour in it. You cook for real people. If you don't please them, they don't give you a C on your report card—they just won't come back." Then there's the hours—late nights every week, or up in the morning at the crack of dawn. Culinarians work when everyone's out playing and get off work long after most people have gone to bed.

People always dream about the cooking. More than half of the students at culinary schools are former ad executives, brokers, lawyers, doctors, and other guys sick of the daily grind and hoping to turn their hobby into a full-fledged career. They dream about the stiff hat and the wooden spoons. Few think about the heavy pots they'll have to lift, small kitchens with too many people, or how tired their feet will feel after standing all day.

THE RESTAURANT LADDER

Should you decide that restaurant chefing is your calling, you'll start at the bottom—probably as a line cook, making, at most, $25,000 a year. The line cook prepares all the food for a specific department. For example the vegetable station line cook dices all the veggies, while the meat station line cook trims the fat off the steaks. A dish is put together sort of like your car was probably built—it goes down an assembly line. In a top restaurant of decent size, there might be fifteen to twenty people in the kitchen. There are line cooks for each major dish type—fish, meat, pasta, vegetable—getting the dirty work done, each making about $7.43 an hour. A small step up are the cooks at each of those stations, making about the same pay. Tournants, or floaters, fill in wherever they're needed. Meanwhile, the saucier makes all the sauces. The sous chef supplies all the creativity and inspiration, standing at the stove all day creating masterpieces. The executive chef, who originally created the menu and each dish, merely checks everything as it goes out the door, making sure things look as good as they taste.

On the sweet side, there are pastry assistants, a pastry sous chef, and an executive pastry chef, all climbing a similar ladder.

Moving up a rung can take years and it depends on more than just your cooking. A good chef has to be able to take charge of all the peons below her. She's more than a cook, she's a boss. Restaurants also want a tightwad—someone who can estimate what will be used each week and only buy enough food to go around. A bunch of extra fruit just sitting in the pantry rotting isn't good for the restaurant.

Show Me the Money

Culinary salaries are hard to pin down. A lot depends on how much the restaurant you work for is raking in each day. But here are some rough numbers, care of the National Restaurant Association.

Executive Chef:
Median pay at a restaurant making less than $500,000 a year: $35,000 (plus a $3,500 bonus)
Median pay at a restaurant making over $2,000,000 a year: $50,000 (plus a $5,000 bonus)

Sous Chef:
Median pay at a restaurant making less than $500,000 a year: $21,000 (plus a $1,500 bonus)
Median pay at a restaurant making over $2,000,000 a year: $30,000 (plus a $2,000 bonus)

Cook:
Median pay: $7.75 an hour

Line Cook:
Median pay: $7.43 an hour

Bread and Pastry Bakers:
$6.00–7.75 an hour

BEYOND THE RESTAURANT WORLD

Restaurants may be the obvious choice, but they're not for everyone. Chefs with a good head on their shoulders sometimes decide to ditch the restaurant route all together and strike out on their own. Usually, they do one of three things: Start a catering company, launch a personal chef service, or work as a private chef. All three options toss them off the restaurant ladder and into a world ruled by referrals. They basically become foodie entrepreneurs.

CATERING

When Tracy Callahan and David Saltzman started the company Rhubarb, they had their reasons. And it had nothing to do with lack of choice—fresh out of the California Culinary Academy and the Cordon Bleu, Tracy could have had her pick of jobs behind the stove. David had a good head for business so they'd tossed around the idea of starting their own restaurant. A short stint at a catering company changed their minds. "We saw how you could start with nothing," David says. The tables, the chairs, even the dishes and tablecloths can be rented. "There's overhead because you have to rent a kitchen and pay for your staff and all that, but at a restaurant you have to have your chef and your sous chef and your waiters and your dishwashers there every night, whether there's two customers or a hundred and twenty. With catering, if we have a big party then we have a lot of people in here, if we don't have a big party we have fewer people. There's less waste," David explains.

Money was also a motivator. "The restaurant business just doesn't pay very well," David warns. "I mean people are coming out of culinary school in debt $26,000 or something and getting a job that pays them ten dollars an hour."

That's not to say that catering is a moneymaker from the get-go. Before things get rolling you should expect to do almost everything yourself—from cutting the vegetables to setting the tables. "At the beginning we did everything," Tracy says. "Everything. You just have to. You can't afford anyone. I used to prep everything myself, cook everything, take it to the site . . . I mean, just recently we got towel service, which is one of the most wonderful things in my life, because we would have to wash the towels every week."

The hours are a mix of crazy and lazy. At the beginning of the week, if there's a party, ordering the food begins on Tuesday, things come in on Wednesday, and the food is prepped on Thursday and Friday. On Saturday, all hell breaks loose. A typical party day is sixteen hours long. If the party's at five, "we get to the kitchen at nine, finish off whatever needs to be finished off, load the van, drive to the site, unload the van, set everything up, set all the tables, cook the food, serve the party, break everything down, load the truck, bring it back, unload the truck, and wash all the dishes," Tracy says. Even though Monday and Tuesday may be a breeze, Saturdays are a nightmare.

The biggest difference between cooking at a restaurant and cooking for a party is timing. At a restaurant they prepare all the food during the day and cook it that night. Caterers set up a kitchen *two hours* before they have to serve two hundred people, so they have to come with everything already prepped—the sauces already made, the garnishes already cut. There's no time once they get there to be peeling potatoes. Things are usually partially cooked before caterers get to a party and then finished off there so they'll be hot.

Caterers have to be superhumanly patient. This is the

biggest party most of their clients will ever throw. If you think about how nervous you are before a little get-together in your apartment, you can only imagine how nervous these people are on D-day. "They're spending a ton of money and they're freaking out to begin with and you have to be sensitive to their needs of being coddled and tell them 'It's OK. We're going to take care of everything. Don't worry.' But at the same time, you can't let people push you around and you can't take in their nervousness," Tracy says. "I've had people try to bully me and say, 'I'm not going to pay for this.' So you have to be able to turn on a dime. It's a weird little psychological game that you have to play with your clients." It's a strange back and forth between sweetness and backbone.

Just Add Water: Ideas for Instant Catering Careers

1. Gourmet picnic baskets sold at concerts or in the park
2. Lunch box feasts for busy bachelors
3. Cooking classes for kids—perfect for parents looking for a few hours of child care
4. A Dessert-of-the-Month Club: people pay for a one-year membership and each month you deliver some sweet treat to their door
5. Edible airline meals for private planes
6. Handmade chocolates to rival the big guys on Valentine's Day
7. A catering company for childrens' birthday parties with a menu of fun, kooky food
8. Handpainted tins with fresh Christmas cookies for the holidays
9. A home-based microbrewery
10. Gourmet care packages to send kids at college (or camp)

Money Matters

The pay at restaurants may suck, but at least it's steady. Because caterers are basically running their own show, there's not as much stability. In catering, when you get jobs you have money; when you don't get jobs, you're broke. On the other hand, you can head off to the beach on your birthday or go on a two-month vacation if you feel like it. You're the guy granting permission. You're the only one you have to convince.

Rhubarb is a high-end caterer. They rake in about six to eight thousand dollars for a typical wedding. Of that, David estimates that they take home about two thousand—once everyone who works for them has been paid and they've shelled out money for all the food and rentals. They figure they need to average about one party a week to stay firmly in the black.

Caterers need to be creative in thinking up ways to keep themselves afloat during the slow times. Not every month is as party-friendly as another. Some weeks there are eight shindigs and some weeks there are none. A few years ago, Rhubarb started making chi-chi Christmas cookie baskets. They were "totally amazed" at the response. Entertainment companies started buying them up like they were going out of style—Tracy could barely keep up with the demand. Last year they decided to ditch Christmas parties altogether and churn out baskets all season long. They made enough dough to last them three months.

Catering isn't for everyone. More than creativity, more than business sense, and even more than passion, you have to look yourself squarely in the face and figure out if you're cut out for the lifestyle. "It's a massive amount of work," Tracy warns. "Either you have the aptitude for it or not. Either you can stand being up for sixteen hours at a time and not sitting down, or not. And you just have to know that about yourself. I think there's a set of people who are very suited for catering and there's a set of people who are very suited to working in a restaurant. You have to figure out which person you are."

Caterer

Pro: You don't need a lot of cash to start your own business.
Con: Say good-bye to your weekends.
Average Hours: 50/wk
Average Pay: $19,000–50,000

PRIVATE CHEF

Let's say you figure out that you're not either person. You don't like having to cook the same dishes day in and day out. You don't like cooking for so many damn people.

Believe it or not, the big money's in going back to the basics, doing what your mother did all those years—cooking for just one family. Not just any family, mind you. A super setup, superrich, superstar family. I'm talking politicians, movie stars, royalty. . . . You think these people have the time or the energy to cook for themselves? Think again. Enter the private chef.

Cooking for a family may seem easy. But these are special families. They're used to eating the best, but because of who they are, they don't like to go out. (It's hard to enjoy dinner when people are swarming the table for an autograph.) So they want to have restaurantlike food served to them at their own dining room table.

Variety is everything. Just because your clients don't want to go out doesn't mean they don't want their pick of the litter.

Christian Paier, whose company, Private Chefs Incorporated, places chefs in rich and famous homes all around the world, explains, "It's just like the restaurants you pick for yourself. Sometimes you feel like this and sometimes you feel like that. You need to be a jack-of-all-trades. If you worked in an Italian restaurant, then you're going to know how to cook pasta. But one day these people are going to say, 'Cook us an Indian dinner' or 'Make sushi.' So you have to be well rounded." People pay big bucks to have their very own chef slaving away in the kitchen. They expect them to be able to make a great midnight snack or a dinner for fifteen people with five courses on short notice.

When a dinner party comes up, the pressure is on. Every client likes to feel like their chef is the best. They're in show-off mode. And these guests aren't just anyone. At the last party thrown in the home where Paier is a private chef, the guest list included everyone from Nancy Reagan to Michael Caine, Johnny Mathis to Barbra Streisand. Sherry Lansing, head of Paramount, and Rupert Murdoch, head of Fox, were at the table. So was Sean Connery. "You should have seen the security!" Paier laughs. "Everybody brings their own bodyguards!"

The dinner party is a pretty big occasion because it's the only kind of place where celebrities can relax. No one's going to bother them. No one's going to snap their picture—everybody there is famous, too.

People become private chefs in strange ways. For Victoria Fond, it all started with a muffin. After working her way up the ranks at a bunch of restaurants, Fond decided it wasn't for her. So she started a kind of gourmet delivery service to some of L.A.'s big law firms and talent agencies. "I was twenty-three at the time. And I realized how much these guys were paying for lunch. And I thought I'd try my hand at a business.

Basically, I started looking at it as cooking practice. I was getting all this experience and loving it." Fond was pounding the pavement with her executive lunch business and working part-time at the Pritikin Diet Center. She decided to test out some of her muffins on Pritikin clients. "It was a healthy muffin. And this thing, I swear, if it was about four hours old you could play baseball with it. It was great until about noon."

Despite its performance after twelve, it must have been some muffin. One of the women who bought one liked it so much that she referred Fond to her friend Barbra Streisand . . .

According to Fond, the main thing a private chef needs is flexibility. In Hollywood, for example, everybody wants egg whites, less carbs, fruit sugars instead of cane. "So you have to learn a whole new way of baking. You experiment and because of lack of ingredients you try something new, you learn by trial and error." People want to eat well, even if they're on a

Feeding Sigourney

Stars are notoriously picky eaters. They like things just so. And a PC has to accommodate. Here's a typical day in food for Sigourney Weaver, as cooked by Victoria Fond.

Breakfast: Egg-white frittata

Midmorning Snack: 3 small celery sticks with peanut butter

Lunch: Steamed artichoke stuffed with 4 ounces of Italian-style tuna

Afternoon Snack: Asian pear or 4 ounces steamed Edamame soybeans

Dinner: 8 oz. fresh nondairy asparagus soup; 4 oz. marinated skirt steak; 3 petite red rose potatoes with fresh lemon, rosemary, and garlic; steamed yellow wax beans

Dessert: Homemade tapioca pudding

strict diet. "When I worked for Sigourney Weaver she was working on *Aliens 4*," Fond says. "I got up at five-thirty and I basically had to make breakfast, lunch, dinner, and snacks for the whole day." Weaver's driver would come at ten-thirty to pick up all the food and deliver it to her on the set. "I was following the guidelines of her trainer, so I was really careful about portion control and protein," Fond says. To succeed as a private chef, you need to be willing to bend. Fond's not a morning person, but she had no choice. "That was her schedule because she was at the studio all day long. And that was how we fit her schedule."

You'll get paid well for grinning and bearing it. The chefs PCI places make a minimum of $1,000 a week. That's the *minimum.* Salaries can easily go into the hundred thousands with a few more years under your belt. And there are perks beyond the money—travel, vacation, generous time off. If your client goes to a spa for a month to relax, you still draw a paycheck. If he goes on location to Hawaii, you'll probably go with him. You'll land on the same private helipad and stay in the same five-star hotel.

Sometimes chefs become pretty tight with the people they work for. "Some clients may spend more time with their chef than with their spouse. Because let's say that it's a movie star," Paier explains, "the chef is with them on location. The spouse is not most of the time." Jack Nicholson, for example, and his chef are thick as thieves. "When he's in the trailer and in a bad mood, the director sends the chef to go get him, because they're buddies. No one else will dare go in there!" Chefs walk a fine line, though, between friend and employee. Even if the people you work for tell you you're family, and many will, no one's truly family if they're drawing a paycheck.

One really amazing thing about being a private chef is the

budget. There is none. In other words, go crazy. The recipe calls for a teaspoon of pumpkinseed oil and they only sell it by the quart? Who cares! The point isn't to bargain shop, the point is to drive these people out of their minds with the stuff on their plates. And as a private chef, you have a big advantage over the guys slaving away in a restaurant—those poor suckers need to churn out eighty or ninety plates a night. You have all day to cook the perfect meal for two. If there's a party that night, maybe the perfect meal for ten. Either way, time is on your side. And after dinner you'll see how you did. Most bosses will bring the chef out after the meal to tell them what they thought and introduce them to the dinner guests.

All that mingling means you've got to have a personality. When someone's eating in a restaurant, they could care less if the cook is a jerk. But in a home, there's a lot of contact between the hand and the mouth. Finding a chef is like finding a date. Pick the wrong person and table talk could be a drag. Paier considers himself a matchmaker. Each time he places someone, he's looking for the perfect fit. And it's more than just cooking style. It can be everything from religion, to background, to temperament. There's a lot that comes into play. "These clients lead very stressful lives. The chef's job is to figure them out completely, like they are their own mother. She knows what you liked as a kid, she knows what you like now, when you want your favorite dish. That's the chef's job, to read you like a book so you can sit down, be happy after a meal and not even know why."

If you're good at putting a smile on those stressed-out faces, you'll have no trouble finding work. A private chef is a luxury item and the U.S. economy is on a hot streak. In the past ten years the number of millionaires has almost doubled.

And lots of these people are too busy to boil water, let alone cook themselves a meal.

Sounds great? Where do you sign up? Well, here's the one and only problem with this job—it's usually by referral. Even when it's not, to get into a prime position, you need to know how to cook absolutely anything your boss could desire. Anything. And if you don't know how to cook it, you need to know how to wing it—whether it's dim sum or samosas, filet mignon or mac and cheese.

That means a lot of experience. Paier likes to place people with at least seven years of sweat behind the stove. Not there yet? Paier recommends starting a kitchen tour—making the rounds at a string of restaurants. "The main mistake everybody makes is that they get stuck in one place because it's kind of comfortable, they know the place inside out. But what they forget is that you stop learning after three months if you're in a small restaurant. You need to move a lot. Every year." And not just anywhere, according to Paier, somewhere great. Somewhere where you can watch the chef like a hawk and learn at his knee. Make no mistake, the pay at these places stinks. But don't let pay be your guide. "You need to work with chefs that inspire you to want to do something extraordinary," Paier says. "You'll make more money of course if you go and work at some little diner or something, but you'll be flipping hamburgers. You're never going to be a chef."

Private Chef

Pro: The budget and the time to create extraordinary meals
Con: Hard to break in without lots of experience.
Average Hours: depends on the client's schedule
Average Salary: $25,000–130,000

PERSONAL CHEF

The rich and famous aren't the only ones starving for some attention. One of the hottest businesses in the country, according to *Entrepreneur* magazine, is the *personal* chef. Unlike private chefs, who only cook for one family, personal chefs spread their love around among a few—usually about ten. They don't come in to cook every day. Instead they make a house call about once or twice a month and cook enough food to last until they come back.

Personal chefs ring in at about $250–300 a visit, according to the United States Personal Chef Association. There are about two thousand of them in the U.S. as we speak, but that number is on the rise. Why? Do the math. The only real certification is a home study course that lasts about thirty days, but personal chefs can rake in $50,000 a year. They make their own hours and usually only put in four hours at a time. The work is done in whoever's kitchen they're cooking for—so they don't have to invest in a commercial kitchen or any fancy equipment. In general, all they have to pay for is a good set of knives.

As you read this, fifteen to twenty thousand American families are chowing down on meals made by a personal chef. Chefs spend a few hours at each client's home, cook enough main and side dishes to last about two weeks, label them with cooking instructions, and stick them in the fridge or freezer. Meals cost about eight dollars per person, including food, which the personal chef shops for themselves.

Why is it so popular? Consider this. According to *Cook's Illustrated*, three out of four Americans have no idea, by four o'clock, what they're going to have for dinner that night. Of all meals eaten at home, 41 percent come from fast food joints, 21 percent are restaurant takeout, and 22 percent supermarket takeout. Less than one in six are actually home-cooked meals. Good-bye June Cleaver, hello Ronald McDonald.

It's no wonder Americans are fatter than they've ever been in history. But who can blame us? We're working longer hours than we ever have before. And most houses have both parents working. The last thing mom wants to do when she comes home from a tough day of work is cook a meal for four. And why should she? At two to three hundred dollars a pop, personal chefs are a bargain. The typical family might spend that on a few restaurant meals, so why not get fourteen for the same price and cut out the trip to the supermarket?

Personal Chef

Pro: You can work as much or as little as you want.

Con: You need to hustle to make a lot of money.

Average Hours: Eight hours a day (for those who make a living)

Average Salary: $250–350 a visit. Successful entrepreneurs can make up to $55,000.

FINAL WORD OF MOUTH

All the people I talked to had one thing in common—they agreed you had to be a "people person" to survive in the culinary business, and strike a balance between being nice and being a doormat. As for training, they were split. Lots of roads will take you to culinary success and everyone has their favorite highway.

Ninety percent of Paier's chefs aren't culinary school grads. He thinks would-be chefs should hightail it to Europe, find an apprenticeship at a good restaurant or resort, and come back in three or four years. Not only will the European connection give you clout, but over there they'll pay you to learn, in addition to taking care of room and board if you're sweating it out at a resort. He thinks culinary school is a waste: "It costs you fifty thousand dollars and you're coming out not that good."

The guys at Rhubarb disagree. Culinary school "is like boot camp" and you'll be a ready little soldier when you hit the streets after a few years in the classroom. Susanna Donato of the French Culinary Institute says students who go to one of the big names will never have trouble finding work. Graduating FCI students typically get about five job offers.

Even TV can help. Victoria Fond got the hang of things by watching cable cooking shows and trying out the recipes. "I learned a lot, just by practicing and practicing and practicing," she says. Because to make things really well it helps to have made them at least once really badly.

Whatever way you decide to go about it, learning to cook is time well spent. It's not as though the jobs will ever go away. People eat. Someone's got to cook. David says it best: "It's like learning to be a plumber or learning to be a bartender or learning to be an auto mechanic. You have a job that you can do and everyone in the world needs somebody to do that job. So you can go anywhere."

RESOURCES

Chefs Collaborative 2000: (617) 621-3000 Network of 1,500 chefs

International Association of Culinary Professionals: (800) 928-IACP; www.iacp-online.org

National Restaurant Association—research and info on the restaurant industry: www.restaurant.org

Women Chefs and Restaurateurs: wcr@hqtrs.com

Rhubarb—Tracy Callahan and David Saltzman: 6511 1/4 Sepulveda Blvd., Los Angeles

American Culinary Federation Apprenticeship: (800) 624-9458; www.acfchefs.org

Shaw Guide to Culinary Schools: www.shawguides.com

United States Personal Chef Association: (800) 995-2138; uspca.com

Private Chefs Inc.: (310) 278-4707; www.privatechefsinc.com

Becoming a Chef by Andrew Dornenburg and Karen Page

The Guide to Cooking Schools by Shaw Guides

CHAPTER 9

Healing Hands: *Careers in Alternative Medicine*

> **"Nothing is too small to know, and nothing too big to attempt."**
>
> —William Van Horne

AMERICANS ARE PRETTY DAMN COCKY. WESTERN medicine is barely out of puberty but it waves its magic wand and declares all other healing methods "alternative," even though some of them have been around practically since the dawn of civilization. Not only that, but it lumps them all together. Everything from massage therapy to Reiki, acupuncture to ayurveda, is labeled "alternative."

It wasn't always that way. Once upon a time in America, herbs were the medicine of choice, naturopaths were respected, and homeopathy wasn't a dirty word. So what happened? A little thing called the microscope. Suddenly anything that couldn't be seen, touched, or ID'd under the lens was dismissed.

They say beauty's in the eyes of the beholder. Well, so's "alternative." According to the *New England Journal of Medicine*, one out of three Americans uses some sort of alternative medicine on a regular basis. Americans made 629 million visits to alternative healers last year, compared to a mere 386 visits to "regular" doctors. So just who's alternative, hmmm?

No use bickering, it doesn't really matter. What matters is that this field is on the rise in a big way and you should think about getting in on the ground floor. The number of alternative medical schools is growing, and many will let you in *without* four years of college under your belt. Even traditional med schools are getting on board—over half now have classes in alternative medicine—including Yale, Stanford, Harvard, and Johns Hopkins.

Between 1990 and 1997, visits to alternative practitioners jumped 47 percent. In 1994, only four health plans covered alternative medicine. Four years later, it was fifty. There's no question that the field is on the upswing. The question is, are you a swinger?

Modern Medicine

In August 1998 the *Los Angeles Times* surveyed Americans to see if their opinion of alternative medicine had changed over the past five years.

40% were more positive

58% were the same

2% were less positive

WHAT IS IT?

First things first. "Alternative medicine" is a pretty vague term. It means different things to different people. It can cover everything from massage therapy to acupuncture, gnarled Chinese roots dished out by a naturopath to a bottle of echinacea picked up at the local pharmacy.

So before we go any further, let's get to the basics: a speedy guide to some of the most popular alternative treatments out there, a.k.a. what you'd be doing if you went into the field.

> ***Traditional Oriental Medicine:***
> Over five thousand years old, TOM is grounded in the principle of yin (the feminine) and yang (the masculine). They're both aspects of qi (life force energy), which flows through the body and when blocked, can cause health problems. TOM doctors have lots of tools in the toolbox—acupuncture, herbal medicine, massage, exercise, and diet.
>
> ***Acupuncture:***
> Acupuncturists believe that the body has channels, or meridians, running through it. Basically, pain and illness come from blocked channels. Practitioners insert tiny needles into specific points along the meridians in order to remove these blocks.
>
> ***Acupressure:***
> Same concept, no needles. Acupressurists clear the blocks by applying pressure with their hands, elbows, sometimes even feet, to certain points along the meridians. Similar

to shiatsu (which was invented in Japan and uses mostly finger pressure), acupressure helps balance yin and yang. It was developed in China.

Chiropractic:

Chiropractors try to alleviate back pain and other problems by "adjusting" and manipulating the spine. They must be doing *something* right—more than fifteen million people visit chiropractors each year.

Homeopathy:

The skinny on homeopathy is the principle that "like cures like." Homeopaths try to *increase* symptoms a patient already has, instead of suppressing them, because they believe the symptoms represent the body's effort to heal itself. They give the patient tiny doses of substances that produce a symptom overdose and stimulate the body's natural defenses. Homeopathy first come into vogue in the 1800s when it was shown to heal scarlet fever, cholera, and yellow fever. It's very popular in Europe.

Herbal Medicine:

Herbal medicine has been around since the beginning of civilization. Herbalists take extracts from a variety of plants and flowers and use them to cure what ails you. Eighty percent of the world's population use herbs for some aspect of primary health care. Four billion people can't be wrong.

Aromatherapy:

An offshoot of herbal medicine, aromatherapy is gaining ground, especially in combination with massage. It helps the body relax through scent.

Naturopathy:
Naturopaths are doctors. They go to med school and the whole deal. Like your typical Western doctor, they analyze a patient's complaints and prescribe treatments. Unlike a typical Western doctor, they use a combination of herbal medicine, homeopathy, massage, Ayurvedic Medicine, Traditional Oriental Medicine, and nutrition. There are about nine hundred licensed naturopaths in the U.S.

Massage Therapy and Bodywork:
You may think you know massage, but there are a whole slew of treatments you've probably never heard of. All attempt to do the same basic things—release toxins, remove tension, and improve blood circulation—they just do it in different ways. Aside from Swedish massage, there are oriental methods (like acupressure and shiatsu), energetic methods (like therapeutic touch, polarity therapy, and Reiki), and movement integration (like Rolfing, Hellerwork, and Trager), just to name a few.

Ayurvedic Medicine:
An ancient Indian healing method that uses massage, herbs, detoxification, aromatherapy, diet, meditation, yoga, and other methods to help the body fight illness and come back into balance. Ayurvedic practitioners get a glimpse into what's up with a patient's internal organs by checking out their eyes, nails, pulse, and tongue.

TRADITIONAL ORIENTAL MEDICINE (TOM)

First put to paper 2,300 years ago, Traditional Chinese Medicine (TCM) has been around at least five thousand years. Its theories were first laid out in the *Huang Di Nei Ching* (*The Yellow Emperor's Classic of Internal Medicine*) and then spread throughout Asia about a thousand years later. As each culture gained access to TCM, they changed it to suit their needs—adding their own techniques and changing herbal recipes to use what they could get locally. Because of their contributions, TCM became TOM—Traditional Oriental Medicine.

TOM is a melting pot of techniques—from acupuncture to herbal medicine, bodywork to diet. Unlike Western medicine, it focuses on prevention. It has techniques to heal illness or injury, but it tries to prevent them before they happen by bolstering the body's natural defenses. When ailments do arise, Eastern doctors take a very different approach than their Western counterparts.

Let's say someone comes into the office with tremors in her hands. According to TOM practitioner Al Stone, "The Western doctor might perform tests to determine if there is a problem in the brain giving rise to Parkinson's disease. Perhaps they would look at the spinal column to explain the neuromuscular problem, or a brain lesion might be sought out with an MRI. However, a practitioner of Chinese medicine would quickly know the problem is that there is 'wind' blowing around the acupuncture channels. Then, they would seek to determine the cause of internal wind, which could be a deficiency of blood, body fluids, qi energy, or perhaps a high fever. The practitioner of Chinese medicine would feel the pulse on the wrist and look to the color and shape of the tongue to determine what is deficient. . . ." Same patient, same symptoms, totally different way of looking at things.

What's Up, Doc?

You can become a doctor without signing half your life away. Doctors of Oriental Medicine spend a mere three to four years in med school, and only need an average of sixty college credits to apply (about two years' worth of classes). You'll have a better chance if some of those credits are in science.

But the degree isn't a cakewalk. Karrel Burgess, a student at Dongguk Royal University's School of Oriental Medicine and Acupuncture warns: "You'll be studying your tail off. You won't have time to get sidetracked, believe me." As things stand now, you'll need to put in about 2,500 hours of classroom and hands-on study. Rumor is that the number may rise to 4,000 hours soon. Costs vary, with the typical program taking four years and ringing in at about $20,000. Karrel urges, "My advice is to go somewhere close, that's inexpensive, and get out as quickly as you can. You can take science requirements at a local junior college to cut down on your costs."

Programs cover a variety of healing methods. In order to pass the state certification exam you have to know at least three hundred oriental herbs and more than sixty formulas. You have to pass a notoriously difficult hands-on acupuncture exam, plus a written test. While at school you'll also get your fill of pathology, physiology, anatomy, Western internal medicine, pharmacology, physics, gynecology, pediatrics, nutrition, tui-na massage, and tai chi and chi gong exercise. Programs usually have a clinical component, where students test their skills on patients willing to be guinea pigs in exchange for a price break.

Karrel Burgess got into TOM because he saw an industry on the rise. "People are sick out there and Western medicine isn't helping them." If he had any doubts before entering the program, those doubts are long gone. "We had a patient come in with a cyst the size of a golf ball. His doctors were unable to reduce it. We shrunk it down to the size of a pea. We had a man come in after a back surgery that put him in a wheelchair. By the time treatment was finished, he was up and walking." When asked what he thinks caused these medical miracles, Karrel explains, "It's qi stagnation. It acts like a dam in a river. If the water backs up, it gets dirty. Qi needs to flow freely."

It may sound loopy, but it works. Research shows that oriental medicine often succeeds where Western medicine draws a blank. TOM doctors can build up the white blood cells to fight fatigue by inserting needles in the elbow. They can give you a nonsurgical facelift by inserting needles along your forehead wrinkles. They can fight chronic fatigue syndrome with a change in nutrition and tonics for the kidneys.

TOM Training

Requirements: Usually two years' worth of college, some of which should be science.

Cost: About $20,000 for the entire degree (3–4 years).

Time: Typically 2,500 hours of hands-on and classroom training. But rumors are flying that the bar will soon be raised to 4,000 hours.

ACUPUNCTURE

One of Oriental Medicine's key weapons is acupuncture. It's based on the principle that there are twelve major pathways in the body along which qi can travel. Just like cars, sometimes qi gets stuck on the road. Acupuncturists insert hair-thin needles along these bodily highways to get the body's energy moving again. Every organ is connected to a major channel and symptoms often appear in other places along that channel. For example, Dr. Dimitris Efstatthiou, a professor at Dongguk Royal University, recently explained at an acupuncture demonstration, "If you have lower back pain, I'm pretty sure that you have kidney weakness."

According to the Food and Drug Administration, about nine to twelve million Americans use acupuncture. Each week, about ten thousand procedures are performed to treat a whole range of health problems, from minor disorders like muscle aches, sinus infections, and baldness to major ailments such as infertility, AIDS, and cancer. Drug addicts use it to reduce their cravings and chemotherapy patients use it to alleviate their nausea.

One of the things that's so appealing about acupuncture is its cost. You can get a basic treatment at a school clinic for under twenty bucks. Even very expensive Western procedures often have cheaper Eastern counterparts. For example, acupuncturists can prevent a breech birth if they catch it two or three weeks before delivery. Turning the baby around during labor "would cost about $18,000. We can do it by inserting a needle into UB67, a point on your little toe, for about $1,000," Karrel says. Acupuncture can also stimulate an overdue mother to go into labor, or ease chronic migraines.

How does it work? Depends on who you ask. Eastern doctors believe acupuncture rebalances the body's energy. The Western take is that acupuncture stimulates the nervous system to release endorphins, the body's natural pain killers.

Whatever the explanation, the financial rewards can be huge—if you're willing to work hard. "It's a business," says

Nuts for Needles

In Germany 77 percent of pain clinics use acupuncture.

In Belgium 74 percent of acupuncture treatments are performed by regular doctors.

—*British Medical Journal*

Karrel Burgess. "You need to know how to sell yourself. Go to parties with your business cards in hand." It's tough work, he says, "but the money potential is unbelievable." How unbelievable? "I know acupuncturists who have a little herb store and between the two, they make more than a million bucks a year," he says.

Acupuncture

Cost: Sessions can cost as little as $20 (at a school clinic) and as much as $1,000 (for a major, specialized problem).
Training: 3 years
Pro: 9–12 million people a year visit acupuncturists
Con: Only 38 states license practitioners
Resources: www.acupuncture.com; Accreditation Commission for Acupuncture and Oriental Medicine: (301) 608-9680

MASSAGE

Massage therapy has come a long way from the kneading, chopping, and pummeling we inherited from the Swedes.

Sure, the traditional Swedish massage is still popular, but it's feeling the heat from shiatsu, reflexology, and a whole bunch of other treatments. The number of massage therapists is growing, but so are the number of people who want massaging. According to the American Massage Therapy Association, almost one quarter of the adult population have had a massage within the past five years.

Ready to rub? Careful. There are over eight hundred massage schools clamoring for your savings, up from only fifteen in 1969. And all schools are not created equal. Before forking over your money and signing on the dotted line, make sure they'll give you what you'll need to play with the big boys. In order to get certified and hired at the best spas and hotels, you'll need a minimum of five hundred hours of training, plus a passing grade on a licensing exam.

Even with all that preparation, you may not get respect. In this country, massage therapy is still trying to shed its image as cousin to the facial and manicure. Try not to lose your temper if your family acts less than thrilled about your career choice. Despite the research, the government's been slow on the upswing—massage therapists are only licensed by twenty-five states, plus Washington, D.C.

But who cares what the government says. Money talks. And consumers spend between four and six billion dollars on massage each year. Customers who visit a *licensed* therapist average about seven visits a year. It's a habit that's hard to kick, but a healthy habit for a change.

Why? It's common knowledge that massage reduces stress and can help with muscle pain. But recent studies have proven it does much more. It's been shown to boost the immune systems of patients with HIV and help premature babies gain weight more quickly. It battles everything from insomnia to

All You Knead to Know

Swedish Massage:

The grand dame of Western rubdowns, it's been around for more than one hundred and fifty years. It's the massage you know and love. Swedish uses kneading and long strokes in the direction of the heart to release toxins and get the blood flowing.

Rolfing:

So deep it makes some clients yelp. Named for Ida Rolf, its originator, Rolfing's specialty is releasing the deep-down tissue and membrane that covers the muscles, organs, and joints. It's great for slouchers and is known to boost energy and improve posture.

Sports Massage:

Focuses on muscles strained by a specific sport. Has been shown to improve performance in professional athletes. Sometimes used before a competition to help athletes warm up or afterwards to help sore muscles heal faster.

Shiatsu:

A rhythmic Japanese technique that uses pressure points along the body's meridians, instead of strokes and kneading. Studies show that it may release endorphins.

Watsu:

Shiatsu in a pool. Watsu uses warm water to support the body and take pressure off the spine. The patient is swept through the water while the therapist applies pressure-point therapy. The result? Relaxation like you've never known on land.

Reflexology:

A mix of East and West. Focuses on the feet, where the meridians end. Each section of the foot is thought to correspond to a different organ or part of the body. Reflexologists apply pressure to the appropriate foot area to relieve stress or illness.

Trager:

Especially good for back, neck, and shoulder pain, Trager uses rocking and shaking motions to remove tension and rigidity in the body. It was developed about fifty years ago by a doctor named Milton Trager.

Craniosacral:

Releases tension and pain by balancing the rhythms and movements of the nervous system. Hands are usually placed on the skull and moved slightly in and out, in synch with qi energy. Helps banish deep-seated stress, get rid of headaches, and put the body back in synch.

Jin Shin Jyutsu:

A gentle Japanese method where energy blocks are identified by feeling the pulse. The practitioner holds two (of twenty-six) major energy points at a time to unlock them and harmonize the body.

Feldenkrais:

Meant to reeducate the nervous system through movement patterns and massage. Feldenkrais improves flexibility, coordination, and posture. It also helps the body release stress and muscle pain.

Myofascial Release:

Helps the heart as well as the muscles. This method uses stretching and movement to get rid of both physical and emotional problems. It's based on the notion that the mind and body are one and the same. Great for healing deep wounds and for your garden variety self-awareness.

Biofield Therapeutics:

At least two thousand years old, biofield techniques come in a variety of forms: Healing Touch, Therapeutic Touch, Reiki, Polarity, and SHEN therapy are some of the more popular versions. The method is based on the theory that every body has a biofield surrounding it and extending out several inches from the skin. Healers place their hands directly on or over the patient's body for anywhere from twenty minutes to an hour to create a deep sense of relaxation and help the body heal. There are about 50,000 practitioners in the U.S.

And Don't Forget . . .

Animals get sore, too. And while your typical pet won't sign himself up for a week at the spa, there are things owners can do to help their four-legged friends. Massage, for example. Go ahead and scoff, but pet massage is big business. Whether it's acupressure, craniosacral, Swedish, jun shin jyutsu, or sports massage, it's probably being used on some animal somewhere right now. Why? Massage has been shown to help animals with stress, muscle tension, cramping, and injuries. It also increases their flexibility and helps correct behavioral problems.

It may sound like a passing fad, but animal massage has been around since the Roman Empire, when soldiers' horses were given a little rubdown to prevent injuries. It's used today on racing greyhounds, Grand Prix champions, and your lucky everyday house pet.

The most renowned program is called Tellington Touch. At the heart of the technique is a series of small, randomly placed circles "drawn" on animals to soothe both their aches and pain, and their emotional stress. It works. Zoos, wildlife rehabilitation centers, breeders, and animal shelters send employees in droves.

TTOUCH certification takes two years, but it's very spread out. There are six sessions of about a week long each. Students practice on abandoned animals from shelters and attempt to cure them of nasty habits like biting, chewing, and barking. You can also bring your own pooch or puss.

Contact: Tellington Touch (800) 854-8326. Courses offered in almost every state and in over 30 countries

depression. In Canada, basic health care covers a certain number of massage sessions a year. It's only a matter of time before the trend sneaks across the border, making careers in massage an even better bet.

Massage

Cost: Sessions usually cost between \$45 and \$150 an hour.
Training: 500 hours, minimum
Pro: Watching people turn to Jello.
Con: The work is physically exhausting.
Resource: The American Massage Therapists Association www.amtamassage.org

There's the Rub

Massage therapy may be relaxing for the guy on the table, but for the therapist, it's hard work. According to Anthony McMorran, who runs Westview Massage Therapy, massage "is physically and emotionally demanding." Some therapists develop

Advice from Anthony

1 Try It Out: Get massages from a variety of therapists. If you like their work find out where they trained and what techniques or approaches they use. Ask them what they like about the work and what they dislike.

2 Do Some Reading: Find out what textbooks are used in the programs you're considering and check them out. I'd also recommend:

The Anatomy Coloring Book by Wynn Kapit & Lawrence M. Elson

Job's Body: A Handbook for Bodywork by Deane Juhan

Complementary Therapies in Rehabilitation by Carol M. Davis

3 Work the Web: Check out the American Massage Therapist Association's website at www.amtamassage.org for research and tips on getting started.

pulled muscles themselves while trying to work the kinks out of their patients. Wrists and hands can take the biggest beating. And severely sore hands can put a therapist out of commission for a while. McMorran makes it a habit to stretch, ice, or do self-massage on his arms and hands after each treatment, to prevent injuries.

Massage has other possible drawbacks as well. For one, you have to be nice, even when you're having a bad day. It's not always easy. McMorran warns, "Honestly evaluate if you will thrive in a profession with such a high level of personal contact with the public and if you are willing to make the lifestyle choices that would make you a role model for the people who choose you as a health professional." In other words, you're not going to make a good therapist if you're more stressed out than your clients. Obviously no one's perfect. But you have to be able to urge your patients to take better care of themselves without looking like a hypocrite. "You shouldn't bother getting into the health care field if you don't have a commitment to your own health and well-being," McMorran says.

BIRTH OF THE COOL

Don't mess with a pregnant lady. Her hormones are so out of whack, you never know what she might do. Pregnancy does strange things to women: makes them crave bizarre food combos at 3 A.M., cry for no apparent reason, and, sometimes, decide to brave birth au naturel.

When women make the decision to forego doctors and hospitals and do things their own way, they usually depend on two types of people to see them through the process: the midwife and the doula.

Both offer an alternative for women looking for a warm and fuzzy kind of birth. In a nutshell, doulas are the coaches and midwives are the deliverers. Both jobs are held almost exclusively by women.

STAND AND DELIVER: THE LIFE OF A MIDWIFE

Midwifery goes back a hell of a long way. Long before obstetricians entered the picture, midwives were helping women all over the world deliver babies. Midwifery slipped out of the mainstream in America earlier this century, but in Europe midwives still handle about 70 percent of all births. In the U.S., it's only about 10 percent, but those numbers are on the rise.

Midwives do more than just deliver. They monitor how the mom is doing—both physically and emotionally. And, like regular doctors, they provide moms-to-be with prenatal and postpartum care. But midwifery is all about nurturing and the typical midwife is willing to spend as much time as necessary with a patient, much more than the average doctor.

In general, midwives try to handle births with as little technology as possible. Most will deliver the baby in the patient's home or someplace similarly unclinical. But they'll do it in a hospital if they're asked, or if they think a patient might have complications. They also refer women to an obstetrician if necessary.

There are two major paths to becoming a licensed midwife: apprenticeship and school. Either way, candidates have to attend at least forty births and perform a slew of exams to get certified: at least seventy prenatal, twenty newborn, and forty postpartum. They need to pass a written test and prove their skills in a hands-on examination in front of a qualified examiner. Midwives also need to get a stack of recommendations and master CPR. Only ten states currently license midwives, even with all the hoops.

Midwife
Salary: Up to $3,000 a birth.
Training: Certification through apprenticeship or midwifery school and exams
Pro: Helping women give birth more naturally
Con: Only ten states currently license midwives.
Resource: North American Registry of Midwives (888) 84-BIRTH

I DOULA

A doula is a pregnant woman's temporary best friend. She (99 percent of doulas are women) does everything from preparing a woman for labor to helping her get through it when she's cursing at the guy who put her there in the first place.

The Greek word "doula," pronounced *doo-lah,* means "in service of." In the old days, the doula was the most important slave in the Greek household. Today, the doula is still "in service"—soothing, coaching, and supporting women in labor. A doula isn't a medical or clinical specialist. She's more of a birth assistant. While the doctor is worrying about the baby, the doula is focused on the mother. Doulas encourage moms-to-be when they want to give up, and look out for their interests within the hospital.

The doula's job starts long before their patient gets wheeled into the delivery room. They work with the couple before labor, getting to know them and helping them prepare a "birth plan" describing what they hope the birth will be like.

They're on call twenty-four hours a day. When a mother feels her first contractions, she calls her doula well before she calls her doctor.

Labor can really freak people out, no matter how prepared they are. In addition to encouraging the mother, the doula takes the pressure of primary support off of the mom's partner. She helps the mom with breathing patterns, lets her know how she's progressing, puts her into more comfortable positions, and walks her around the room. Other doula techniques are massage, cradling, pelvic rocking, and Jacuzzi. But perhaps most important, the doula lets the woman in labor know that everything's okay. With the average first-time labor taking about eighteen to twenty-four hours, that's a big deal.

It may seem very flighty and new age, but numbers don't lie. According to a widely circulated research study by Marshall Klaus, women who used a doula had half as many cesareans, a 25 percent shorter labor, a 40 percent reduction in forceps delivery, and were 60 percent less likely to ask for an epidural. Even HMOs are beginning to see the light and starting to pay for doulas.

You might think they go together, but most women choose either a doula *or* a midwife. "Women who're having a midwife usually don't think that they'll need a doula. Whereas women who are planning to give birth in a hospital are often a little bit uncomfortable about being in the hospital, realizing that they're not sick and they're not patients. They don't want to be treated either as a sick person or in a routine way. Every woman wants to be treated uniquely," says Kelli Way, a doula.

There's no one path to becoming a doula. Licensing is available, but not required. Certification through DONA (Doulas of North America) is easy. You just take a childbirth education course, like a Lamaze series or a Bradley series, as if you were pregnant. It's usually a six- to twelve- week course meeting once a week. Then you take a three-day training class "where you learn a little more in depth how to really help a woman in birth as well as the business of being a doula," according to Way.

The training may be a breeze but the job isn't. The hours are pretty difficult—you have to be willing to leave what you're doing at a moment's notice for much longer than your typical nine-to-five gig. It's hard to be spontaneous because you're on call all the time. "You end up leaving family dinners, getting up in the middle of the night. . . . If your partner says, 'Oh, let's go away for the weekend!' you can't. That's probably the major drawback," Way says. "But, you get to witness the miracle of birth all the time."

Another difficult thing about being a doula is finding work. Doulas are basically entrepreneurs. Most are hired by referral, but they have to be able to toot their own horn. The good news is, you'll earn good money for every successful toot: Doulas typically make between two and eight hundred dollars per birth.

Doula

Salary: Between $200 and $800 per birth
Training: None required, but certification is available.
Pro: No requirements to enter the field so it's easy to get in.
Con: Easy for other people to get in, too.
Resource: Doulas of North America (206) 324-5440;
www.dona.com

RESOURCES:

Doulas of North America: (206) 324-5440
www.dona.com
North American Registry of Midwives: (888) 84-BIRTH
Homeopathic Educational Services:
www.homeopathic.com
Acupuncture.com
Accreditation Commission for Acupuncture and Oriental Medicine: (301) 608-9680 or National Acupuncture Foundation: (202) 332-5794
Council on Naturopathic Medical Education:
(503) 484-6028
American Massage Therapists Association:
www.amtamassage.org

CHAPTER 10

Busting the Blue Collar Myth

> **"Any jackass can kick down a barn, but it takes a good carpenter to build one."**
>
> —Sam Rayburn

EVEN IN THE EARLY DAYS, THERE WERE CRAFTSMEN. Any old Neanderthal may have known how to find a cave, but not just anyone could spruce it up with some cave paintings or invent the wheel.

Everybody's got hands. Some people are just better at using them. They're the ones who don't need to read the directions that come with the stereo, the ones who can fix the door when it goes off its hinges. They're the tinkerers.

Well, we're way past the cave days, but there's still a place for people willing to get a little dirty. And just because you want to use your hands, doesn't mean you don't have a good head on your shoulders. Blue collar employment is one of those fields shrouded in misconception. It can be a lot more creative, and lucrative, than you'd think.

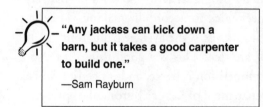

TRAINING FOR THE TRADES

The best way to learn is still by doing, and there are tons of programs out there that will *pay you* to learn hundreds of skilled trades. Eight hundred and thirty to be exact. Ever since 1937, the U.S. Department of Labor has been on a mission to establish apprenticeship programs across the country in everything from auto mechanics to accordion making. They last anywhere from one to six years, the average being four.

Apprenticeships are free. This is a good thing. It's also a bad thing. Why? Competition is fierce, and it's getting worse. According to the Department of Labor's Bureau of Apprenticeship and Training, the number of applications is on the rise: "Unable to find suitable jobs in their own fields, college graduates have turned increasingly to the skilled trades for work." For some programs, a diploma will help you; for others, experience means a lot more than a piece of paper.

Either way, applying for an apprenticeship is a long haul. Filling out the application is only the beginning. There are requirements to satisfy, tests to pass, and interviews to ace. Once you've jumped through all the initial hoops, you'll be ranked based on how you did and put on a waiting list until a spot opens up. Should an opening arise, it goes to the person with the highest ranking. Moving up the list can take months, even years. It all depends on the number of openings and the number of good people who want them. According to the Bureau of Apprenticeship and Training, each year about a hundred thousand new apprentices join the ranks.

Old habits die hard. Just like the military, some apprentices are women, but not many. Right now, chicks make up only 7 percent of the ranks. No worries—the government is

Things to Think About Before Choosing an Apprenticeship

- Is the job monotonous?
- Is it safe?
- Is it clean (like electrical work) or dirty (like mechanics)?
- Does it take a lot of stamina?
- Will you have to move from job to job?
- What's the work environment like?
- Will you have to join the union?

on it. They've started outreach programs to help women and minorities get in the door. They tutor them, teach them how to beat the test, even prepare them for the interview. They're sort of like coaches for the underdog.

BECOMING A BIG KAHUNA CRAFTSMAN

You may not think much of the guy who comes to wire your office or the construction worker whistling at you from the roof of the building next door, but they could care less. They're the ones having the last laugh. Because while most of corporate America is withering away behind a desk, they're working sane hours for good wages. And the jobs aren't going anywhere. They may not be new, or hip, but carpentry and electrics are two of the hottest job fields out there.

GET WIRED: CAREERS IN ELECTRICITY

Americans use electricity like it's going out of style. From air conditioning to refrigerators, lights to computers, we've got juice flowing through the wires twenty-four seven. Somebody's got to know how to get it all working. And that somebody is an electrician.

Compared to other trades, electricians have it pretty good. They usually work indoors, unlike most construction workers. They rarely have to put in late or crazy hours. And the pay is high—the top 10 percent make more than $1,018 a week.

Even starting out, the money isn't bad. Apprentices learn under the watchful eye of a journeyman—an experienced worker who shows them the ropes. And they get a check even before they know what they're doing: Their pay starts at half what the journeyman makes and goes up as they become more useful.

Some apprentices use that money to get a college diploma. The apprenticeship alone is worth forty-seven semester hours of credit—almost enough for an associate's degree. And because most apprenticeship classes meet only once or twice a week, there's plenty of time to take college classes at the same time.

The biggest electrical apprenticeship program, not even a blip on the screen sixty years ago, is now offered at over three hundred different locations across America. The International Brotherhood of Electrical Workers (IBEW) and the National Electrical Contractors Association (NECA) will pick up the tab for the training, investing a total of over $50 million in the program each year. Why are they so generous? They're looking out for themselves. According to A. J. Pearson, the executive director of the NJATC (National Joint Apprenticeship

Training Committee), these guys "expect to need to fill 80,000–100,000 new jobs within the next few years."

This program isn't the only game in town. There are other electrical apprenticeships as well, but they don't have the same kind of clout. IBEW is the biggest electrical union in the world, so it carries a lot of weight. Their apprenticeship is the longest—typically eight thousand hours of on-the-job training and eight hundred classroom hours. Classes cover everything from electrical grounding and theory to basic math and blueprint reading. On the job, apprentices learn how to install conduit, connect and test wiring, put in outlets and switches, drill holes, and a slew of other skills. The apprenticeship takes about four and a half years to complete.

Getting in can take a while. Karmen Lawson, a telecommunications installer technician from Oregon, admits, "I'll be honest with you—it took me two years to get into this program." But she's quick to mention that she didn't have any experience. Lawson took the rejection in stride. "When I first applied I was turned down and thought, 'Well, how can I make myself look better?'" she says. A few attempts, a few years, and a few community college electrical courses later, things turned around. "I guess when I went in the third time they thought, 'Wow. She really means business.'" They accepted her.

Lawson isn't alone. It takes a lot of people a few tries to snag an apprenticeship spot. The admission committees are extremely picky. But once you get through the selection process, you're home free. Absolutely everything is paid for by the IBEW and the NECA.

So what are they looking for? The right attitude, physical strength, dexterity, and math. Yep, math. "If you don't know math, you're lost because you have to do a lot of calculations.

If you don't know the math, you won't be able to troubleshoot," says apprentice Ramon Caban. The IBEW agrees, math is paramount, "especially algebra."

Getting in is tough, but if you can make it through the program, you're golden. According to the Occupational Outlook Handbook, electricians are going to have more work than they know what to do with in the coming years because "demand will outpace supply of workers." The jobs are going to be plentiful and the pay is good, even the first years out. In 1995, the middle half of electrical workers earned between $15.32 and $18.83 an hour—much more than the typical liberal arts graduate.

But the job is not for everyone. And not just anyone can pull it off. R. J. Lance, an apprentice instructor, warns, "It's not just pulling wire through a pipe. It's making everything work in a logical manner. You've got to be able to think. You have to be able to reason. You must be able to take a problem and reach a conclusion that's correct." A. J. Pearson agrees. "Don't be influenced by those who see the electrical construction trade as an occupation requiring only a strong back and a weak mind. The electrical trades are becoming more technical with each passing day."

Electrician

Training: An apprenticeship lasting about 4 1/2 years

Salary: About $468–814 a week, avg.

Outlook: Great. There will be 80,000–100,000 new jobs in the next few years and not enough people to fill them.

Perk: High pay, good working conditions

Contact: The International Brotherhood of Electrical Workers (202) 833-7000

THE BUILDERS

Were you a Lego fanatic? Did you build forts in your basement and igloos in the backyard? Well then, screw the desk job. You can turn your childhood fantasies into a steady paycheck.

Carpenters build stuff. All kinds of stuff—from furniture to cabinets, houses to bridges. A good carpenter has a body strong enough for manual labor and an eye sharp enough for detail work.

Anyplace things are being constructed, carpenters are there. Which basically means carpenters are everywhere. They're the largest trade profession by far, with 992,000 at work. And even though there are a lot of them, there's always room for more. Why? High turnover and lots of injuries: Carpenters work where lots of people wouldn't want to be—in the glaring sun or the freezing cold, perched on ladders or in other precarious positions.

There's no question the career has its drawbacks, but it can also be pretty damn rewarding. For one, you're actually making things. From scratch. And these days, few jobs offer that kind of tangibility.

Should you decide the work's for you, the best known apprenticeship is offered by the United Brotherhood of Carpenters and Joiners of America, in conjunction with the National Association of Home Builders, a contractor's association. It's similar to the electrical internship: free, competitive, and about four years long.

In class, apprentices learn safety and first aid, freehand sketching, construction techniques, and how to read a blueprint. On the job they're taught rough framing, layout, form building, and inside and outside finishing. They learn to use equipment, tools, and machines under the eye and thumb of a journeyman carpenter.

Math rears its ugly head here as well—with quick arithmetic being top on the list for apprenticeship requirements. If you think about it, it makes sense. Carpenters often need to run calculations through their heads on the spot and in a hurry. Other top apprentice qualities are strength, "manual dexterity, aptitude, and a willingness to take direction," according to the apprenticeship training committee. Work experience or a few years in the military or a job corps catch their eye, too.

What's Out There

In a nutshell, there are two types of carpenters: structural and detail. Structural carpenters are the guys you see outside with the hard hats. They do what the name says—build structures. They work from blueprints, usually with contractors, and they build big. Detail carpenters focus on the little stuff—they fix things that go *inside* the structures. Usually that means furniture or cabinets. A detail carpenter might specialize in restoring old furniture, or in creating new furniture from scratch. She might have a business that refaces cabinets or puts together prefabricated components—like hardwood floors or stairs.

Carpenters can make good money, but usually not as much as electricians. The middle half take home between $345 and $660 a week and the top 10 percent make $874. But their average work week is only thirty-five hours and since one out of three work for themselves, the hours are flexible. And the job is hot. Openings for construction contractors and managers are expected to grow by more than 25 percent by 2005.

Five Top Construction Jobs, According to *Jobs Rated* by Les Krantz

construction foreman, carpet installer, surveyor, plasterer, painter

Carpenter

Training: An apprenticeship lasting about four years.
Salary: $345–660 a week, avg.
Outlook: Excellent. Openings are expected to grow by more than 25 percent by 2005.
Perk: Flexibility—one out of three carpenters is self-employed.
Contact: United Brotherhood of Carpenters and Joiners (702) 938-1111; American Furniture Making Association: (336) 884-5000

THE NEXT NOAH: BUILDING BOATS

Buildings aren't the only game in town. If you're good with tools, you may find your calling at the docks, not on a scaffold.

It happened to David Wood. He got into boat-building the way most carpenters do: by chance. "I met a man who had built a sailboat using nothing but hand tools and sailed across vast expanses of ocean. I was hooked," Wood says. Figuring the best way to learn was by doing, he checked out every book he could find on the subject, pulled out some tools, and got to work. Wood started small—first with a dory, then with a larger vessel. "Soon people were asking me to work on their boats," he says.

Learning carpentry through boat-building may not be the

most typical entry, but it's a solid one. Shipwrights need to be masters with hand tools, blueprints, and close woodwork. After all, their work has to do more than look good—it's got to float. Trust me, if you can build a yacht, a cabinet's not going to be a problem. "I found that house carpentry and furniture was easy," Wood says, "because a house was nothing more than a poorly built boat."

Getting up to snuff takes a lot of training. "The Chinese language consists of thousands of idioms that apply to virtually every aspect of life," Wood says. "My favorite is that 'a carpenter must first be sure one's tools are sharp.'" In other words, you need to get the skills before you can get the jobs. Wood recommends lots of trial and error: "Theory, practice, and an apprenticeship to make one aware of gaps in understanding or skill."

Boat-building is definitely a niche market, and with dwindling timber supply and a growing feeling that "cheaper is better," less people are buying handmade wooden boats and more are going for cloned fiberglass or vinyl vessels.

But there will always be sailors who shudder at the thought of buying a Big Mac of boats. So there will always be a need for people to build something beautiful from the ground up. If you're good with tools but an old salt at heart, consider getting your education on the water, and leaving the buildings to someone else.

How to Float Your Boat

Schools to Consider:

These schools will get you shipshape, with classes in everything from woodworking basics to drafting, joinery, rigging, lofting, and bronze casting. In all three you'll build at least one boat from scratch.

The Landing School

Kennebunkport, Maine

You'll build dories and daysailers, or help with a yacht, depending on the program. You'll be grilled in naval architecture, engineering, computer-aided design, and drafting.

Contact: (207) 985-7976; www.landingschool.org

Ten months. $9,150–9,350

Arques School of Traditional Boat-building

Sausalito, California

The focus here is on traditional wooden boat-building. You'll build four boats—two historical, one carvel, and one lapstrake. Past historical projects have included a Kingston Lobster Boat—a pre–Civil War precursor to the yacht—and a Bush Island Double Ender—a replica of a twenty-seven-foot fishing boat built in 1930 for use off Nova Scotia.

Contact: (415) 331-7134; arqueschl@aol.com

One-year apprenticeship: $4,600 plus tools.

Northwest School of Wooden Boat-building

Port Townsend, Washington

Back to the basics—these guys focus on traditional boat-building techniques. Each class offers hands-on training building a twenty- to thirty-five-foot sailing or motorboat. Students also get an earful on restoration and repair.

Contact: (360) 385-4948

Six-month program: $5,600. Nine-month associate's degree: $8,265

Books to Read:

Anything by Howard Chapple, Nat Herreschoff, Charles Borden, Eric Hiscock, or Miles Smeeton.

IF I HAD A HAMMER

If you're having trouble pinning down an apprenticeship or you're not ready to make the three- to four-year commitment, there is another option. You can get all the training you need, and sleep well at night, by signing on with Habitat for Humanity. These guys mean business. Their mission? Oh, nothing big . . . just to single-handedly eliminate poverty housing and homelessness from the face of the earth.

Obviously, they need help. Since 1976, Habitat has built more than 75,000 houses around the world, giving 375,000 people in more than two thousand communities a decent place to live. Most of their workforce is trained volunteers.

You can volunteer for Habitat as much or as little as you want—a weekend here, an afternoon there. But to get knee-deep in the good stuff, you need to make a decent commitment. The easiest way to do that is by joining up with Habitat through Americorps.

Habitat for Humanity has affiliates in twenty-one cities across the country—from Miami to Omaha, Portland to Baltimore. What you'll do and what you'll get depends on where you are. Some places build everything in the house from scratch—others use prefab cabinets or doors. Some farm out plumbing and electricity, others do it in-house. Smaller cities usually provide volunteers with housing. Places like New York City don't. So before you choose a location, figure out what you'll need. If you want to learn how to build furniture, don't go someplace where they furnish new houses with IKEA donations. If you don't have a car, don't go somewhere where you'll need one.

According to Heather Smock, the Americorps coordinator at Habitat's headquarters in Americus, Georgia, "Eighty-five percent of volunteer jobs are in construction." This isn't one of those volunteer positions where you're hoping to make a hands-on difference and end up getting shuffled off to an office somewhere to do filing. If you're looking for carpentry experience, there's no question you're going to get it. And at locations like Americus, volunteers with an interest in specialties like plumbing or electrical work can work under a journeyman doing just that.

If you're interested in pursuing an apprenticeship in carpentry or electrical work, your Habitat months will be worth their weight in gold. Volunteers can usually skip to at least the second year of an apprenticeship program with no problem.

Smock, herself a former Habitat Americorps volunteer, spent seven months of her time learning plumbing. "After that time, I could have probably gone out and got my journeyman status if I'd wanted to. I could have pursued it professionally—I knew enough. But I didn't want to do it forever. I just like to run around my house and fix my pipes," Smock says.

Right now, Habitat is on a hot streak. Millard Fuller, the nonprofit's founder, made a commitment to help "eliminate substandard housing by the year 2000." In places like Americus, volunteers are trying to make his dream a reality—by throwing up house after house, nonstop. Volunteers there will have the chance to work on "thirty to fifty houses a year," according to Smock.

They'll do everything from help families select floor plans and house options, to cut lumber and put up drywall. They'll lay bricks and concrete blocks, paint trim, install pipes, pour concrete, build cabinets, lay electrical wire, and construct roofs. They will do whatever needs to be done to transform a house from blueprint to finished product.

In Americus, a 1,050-square-foot, three-bedroom house, including land, goes for a mere $35,000—plus a lot of sweat. Habitat doesn't want families to feel like they're getting charity. They want them to feel like they worked their asses off to get a place to call home. So families pay only for materials, nothing else. Instead, they are responsible for putting in an average of 350 "sweat equity hours" in labor. In addition to the skills you'll learn, one of the coolest things about Habitat is that volunteers get to meet and work alongside the people whose houses they're building.

"We want them to feel like they own it," Smock says. "Nobody gets a free house from Habitat. People think we give houses away but we don't. It's not a handout. It's a hand up."

That hand up applies to the volunteers as well. "A lot of people come out of college with this degree and they don't know what to do with it. They have no skills. Experience is what people are looking for and as for Habitat, that's what we give you," Smock says.

Making It a Habit(at)

What: Habitat for Humanity builds houses throughout the world for low-income families with no profit added and no interest charged.

How: Get involved. In addition to the skills you'll learn, an 11-month-long Americorps stint pays $8,730 and a

$4,725 educational award, plus health care, child care, and sometimes housing. (There's also an International Partner Program if you've got three years to go global.)

Contact: (800) HABITAT; www.habitat.org

BLUE COLLAR BONANZA

Carpentry and electrical work are only the tip of the iceberg when it comes to blue collar careers. Here's the lowdown on some other cool options:

Plumber

Training: An apprenticeship lasting four to five years

Salary: $413–812 a week, avg.

Pro: Unlike other construction trades, plumbers can live anywhere. Everybody gets stuffed pipes.

Con: Most work is done in cramped or uncomfortable positions.

Contact: United Association of Journeymen and Apprentices of the Plumbing and Pipefitting Industry (202) 628-5823; www.ua.org

Painters and Paperhangers

Training: Most learn informally, on the job.

Salary: $285–517 a week, avg.

Pro: No strict requirements for entry into the profession

Con: Fumes

Contact: International Brotherhood of Painters and Allied Trades (202) 637-0720; www.ibpat.org

Auto Body Repairers

Training: Advances in technology make certification through vocational schools or community college desirable. It lasts two years, but is not required.

Salary: $319–686 a week, plus incentive-based bonuses

Pro: People are bad drivers: There were 225 million repair jobs needed in 1996.

Con: The tools for the job are incredibly noisy.

Contact: National Automotive Technician Education Foundation (703) 713-0100; www.asecert.org

Auto Mechanic

Training: Auto manufacturers and dealers sponsor two-year associate degrees at 213 schools across the country with ASE certified instruction. Certification requires two years experience and a written exam.

Salary: $333–667 a week avg., plus commission. Master mechanics make $70,000–100,000 a year.

Pro: Figuring out what's wrong is challenging.

Con: Pretty greasy

Contact: Automotive Service Association (800) 272-7467; www.asashop.org

The Ford Asset Program (800) 272-7218

The Chrysler Dealer Apprentice Program (800) 626-1523

The GM Automotive Service Education Program (800) 828-6860

Bricklayers and Stonemasons

Training: A three-year apprenticeship or on-the-job training

Salary: $345–624 a week, avg.

Pro: Stone masonry, especially, can be extremely creative.

Con: The materials are heavy.
Contact: The International Union of Bricklayers and Allied Craftsmen (202) 783-3788; www.bacweb.org
The International Masonry Institute (800) IMI-0988; www.imiweb.org

Carpet Installer

Training: Most learn informally, as helpers.
Salary: $345–660 a week, avg.
Pro: Work normal hours in clean, well-lit places.
Con: There's lots of bending, stretching, and lifting. Carpets are heavy. So's furniture.
Contact: Floor Covering Installation Contractors Association (706) 226-5488
United Brotherhood of Carpenters and Joiners (702) 938-1111

CHAPTER 11

Sitting Pretty: *Breaking into Beauty*

> **"Ask a toad what is beauty? . . . A female with two great round eyes coming out of her little head, a large flat mouth, a yellow belly, and a brown back."**
>
> —Voltaire

WHO MADE HILLARY CLINTON LOOK LESS MOUSY when Bill was running for president? Who snipped Liv Tyler's long locks and gave her a fresh little boy's cut? Who makes hung-over models look rested and camera-ready and your average Jane at the Clinique counter look like a million bucks? A cosmetologist, that's who.

It may be a mouthful, but if you were one of those kids who holed up in the bathroom for hours at a time, trying out mom's lipsticks and fiddling with the curling iron, it's worth learning how to slide those syllables off your tongue. Cosmetologists are pretty powerful people. They wave their magic mascara wands and make everybody look beautiful.

If you've never heard of them, that's probably because they go by a lot of different names: hair stylist, manicurist, facialist, electrologist, esthetician. . . . Your eyebrow specialist and the lady who does your spa herbal wrap may seem to have absolutely nothing in common, but assuming they're legal, they both spent some time at cosmetology school.

BEAUTY 101

A cosmetology program lasts anywhere from three to twelve months, depending on what you want to be come graduation. Hairstylists hit the books longer than anyone else in the beauty business. Usually, they put in well over a thousand hours. Manicurists squeak by with around three hundred. Estheticians about twice that. Whatever the program, students get a mix of classroom work, demonstrations, and hands-on experience. They also get to play professional on customers in school clinics.

This may be beauty school, but it's not all nail polish and facial scrubs. Students get an earful on fascinating topics like sanitation. They also take classes in basic anatomy and business skills. The goal of all this grilling is to prep them to take a state licensing exam once school is out.

BEAUTY FROM HEAD TO TOE

There are niches galore within the beauty business—hair, makeup, nails, eyebrows, body waxing . . . And according to a survey done by the NACCAS, the guys in charge of evaluating and accrediting beauty schools across the country, more and

Free Money

The cosmetology field is so desperate for new talent, they've established a grant program that will give you cold, hard cash to attend cosmetology school. The grants, sponsored by the American Association of Cosmetology Schools, the Beauty and Barber Supply Institute, and the Cosmetology Advancement Foundation, are called ACE—Access to Cosmetology Education. To see which schools are on board, call (888) 411-GRANT.

more salons are going wide—offering a slew of services, rather than specializing in just one. With day spas becoming more and more popular, 70 percent of salons are busy branching out into more than just haircuts.

The weird thing is that while the cosmetology field is growing by leaps and bounds, not enough people are entering it. It's a job-seekers dream! In 1998, according to the NACCAS, three out of four salon owners looking for new employees had trouble finding them. The most vacancies fell into two major categories: hair and skin.

GETTING HAIRY

When George Eliades went to high school twenty years ago, becoming a hairdresser wasn't something to brag about. "Everybody moved off into what was called the Arts and Sciences and you were moved off into what was called a Vocation: You could be a hairdresser, you could be a mechanic, you could become an air-conditioning guy," he says. Hairdressing had a kind of stigma. "You weren't considered an artist," according to Eliades, "you were considered a loser."

Well, those times are long gone. In big cities like New

York and L.A., hairdressers rule the roost. They're the kings of Hollywood, charged with keeping The Beautiful People beautiful. These days, a cut or color with a top stylist at a top salon goes for several hundred dollars a pop.

Over the past few years a strange thing has happened: Hairdressing has become an art. And the cool thing is, unlike other artists, hairstylists have an easy time making a living. "It's not like if you have this urge and think, 'Oh, I'm never going to make it!' " Eliades says. Unlike the art world, where you can be more talented than Picasso and never get noticed, "in a salon, you go to work and create your own form of artwork and if you're consistent, you'll have a client base that, quite frankly, won't ever leave you," Eliades says.

In addition to fame, top stylists can pull in big bucks. "You can make fifty, seventy-five, a hundred, a hundred-fifty, two hundred, or three hundred thousand dollars a year. There are hairdressers making that kind of money," Eliades says. And that's not even the ceiling. "There are top colorists in this country that are making five or six hundred thousand dollars a year," according to Eliades. "Now certainly that's an exception—like there are traders that make a million dollars on Wall Street and then there's guys that make a hundred and fifty thousand dollars. But that's not such a bad living!"

Stylists are branching out into much more than just hair. Eliades himself began life training to do haircuts and ended up a VP at the biggest beauty company on the planet, L'Oreal. There are noncorporate options as well: Some stylists are opening day spas. Some are designing hair product lines. Some are pushing the envelope even further. "Look at Frederick Fekkai," Eliades says. "He's making purses, eyeglasses, scarves. I mean, he's like a French Ralph Lauren. Who would have thought twelve years ago, when he came from

Europe, that he would become a household name? I mean, he was on the cover of *Elle Decor* magazine—a hairdresser!"

Hairstylist
Training: About 1,000 hours
Salary: $6 an hour– $100,000+ a year, average
Pro: Creativity is rewarded.
Con: Sore feet from standing all day

There's no question that the hair profession has arrived. But guidance counselors and parents just aren't steering kids toward careers in the beauty field. And because of that, salons are scrounging for people.

Colorists, especially, are in a prime position. Hair color is growing in demand, but hair colorists are scarce. That's because it's a lot more complicated than your typical haircut. You need to know the color spectrum, you need to know application, you need to know chemicals. And most cosmetology grads never take the time to become color experts. They just stick to cuts.

These days, everybody wants their hair dyed. Color has become about much more than covering gray. It's a fashion accessory. "When I talk at beauty schools I say, 'If you know hair color, here's my card. Give me a call and I'll get you a job in any salon you want.' Because when I talk to owners they say, 'We need people, George! There aren't enough people!' " Eliades says.

According to Eliades, "There are salons that turn away a hundred customers a month." They just don't have enough qualified colorists to meet client demand. And "if a salon is turning away a hundred people a month because they don't have

The Dirt on Beauty

According to the NACCAS, people in the beauty profession make about $18.50 an hour, including tips.

Contacts: American Association of Cosmetology Schools (800) 831-1086

Cosmetology Advancement Foundation (212) 388-2771

enough licensed people, even if the average service is only fifty dollars, that's $60,000 a year. That's real money," Eliades says.

Be aware, though, one of the main reasons for the employee shortage is this: Even though salons are dying for people, they're not always willing to shell out the cash they need to get them. There's a black hole between pay for the Beauty Beginner and for the virtual Beauty Queen. Top stylists may make big bucks, but a freshly licensed cosmetologist barely makes minimum wage. And with the economy on a roll, it's hard to get someone to start working for minimum wage. For god's sake, they can make more at McDonald's. . . .

SKIN DEEP

A career in skin care may not seem all that complicated. But trust me, it's a lot more than slapping on a facial treatment or wrapping somebody in seaweed. Everybody's searching for the fountain of youth, and spas that claim to have found it can make a small fortune. The skin care business is all about the next new thing. Estheticians, the official name for skin care gurus, are in charge of doling it out.

From chromalift therapy (where colored light beams are projected on various pressure points across the face) to fruit acid exfoliation followed by a blast of pure oxygen, spas are offering a string of truly bizarre beauty options. Estheticians need to keep up with the latest inventions and analyze a client's skin to see what's best for them. Dry skin? Maybe a little ginseng. Problem skin? Chrysanthemum can work wonders. A vitamin C treatment combats weather-damaged skin and acupressure helps remove sinus congestion.

Before you put an ad in the phone book and run out for a few tubs of facial scrub, know this: School is in your future. Lots of it. It's not enough to live and breathe beauty. Estheticians need to pay their dues at cosmetology school before they can get licensed and hired. And once they're on a spa's payroll, there's usually some *in-house* training, to get them up to speed in their employer's specialty treatments.

At high-clout spas like Burke Williams, the in-house stuff is no joke. Estheticians get three months of grilling before they're allowed to lay a hand on paying customers. Why? "It doesn't matter if you've been doing [skin care] for ten years or two weeks," according to Lana Fernandez, who works for the spa chain, "you have to learn how to do it the Burke Williams way."

And learn it you will. You'll put in about fifteen hours a week in the training area, where they've got wet rooms, beds, oils, lotions . . . basically the whole shebang. New hires are given a group of models to practice on. Then the evaluation begins. "We test them until they know it like the back of their hand," Fernandez says.

Even estheticians with ten or fifteen years' experience behind them need to go through beauty boot camp, just like everybody else. "There's a certain way we like to do things," Fernandez explains, "certain oils we use, certain movements of the hand, certain techniques. . . ." Burke Williams, like most other famous spas, wants their treatments to be distinctive. And drilling in that consistency takes time. "A signature Burke Williams facial is consistent, no matter which practitioner you go to," Fernandez explains.

Esthetician
Training: About 600 hours
Salary: On average, $32,000 a year
Pro: A flexible schedule
Con: Potential for boredom

GETTING AHEAD

Cosmetology is a weird mix of art and therapy. And while it's important to get someone's highlights just right or their brows perfectly plucked, it's at least as important to listen to them vent about their boss or pick apart their latest relationship. Clients have to sit in that chair a pretty long time—and they'd much rather pass that time with a friend.

A little chatter does more than endear you to your customers. It helps you get a sense of what they're like. So when they need their nails done for a wedding or feel dissatisfied with their makeup, you'll know their style and can find just the right thing. A cosmetologist who can get a handle on someone's personality and deliver something perfect, has a client for life.

With over one million people in the profession and the numbers rising every day, there's a lot of competition, but there's also a lot of opportunity. As Eliades says, "If you think back, the beauty profession is something that has been present in all parts of history—as far back as Cleopatra. It's not a profession that's going away."

There are cosmetologists working in fashion, on movie sets, upscale day spas and glamorous salons, and in the tiny corner shack of a barbershop in Nowhere, U.S.A. To make it really big, you'll have to set up shop in a city. That's where the numbers are, that's where the bulk of the media is based, and that's where most of the big trends are born.

Wherever you decide to hang your hairdryer, the jobs will be there. Cosmetologists are basically in the business of making people feel good, and there will always be a market for that. As Eliades puts it, "When you're feeling bad, a fifty-dollar facial might make you feel better. And that's money that will always be available. You may not have the money to buy a Lexus to feel better, but there will always be enough money for a haircut."

Manicurist

Training: About 300 hours.
Salary: $5–10 a customer
Pro: A relaxed working environment, low stress
Con: Fumes

Job Squad: Ten Ways to Break into Beauty

1. Makeup artist
2. Beauty advisor at a cosmetics counter
3. Guest artist or demonstrator for a cosmetics manufacturer
4. Esthetician working with a dermatologist
5. Manicurist
6. Colorist
7. Cosmetics buyer
8. Hairdresser
9. Eyebrow specialist
10. Hair removal and waxing expert

Part 4

School's Out Forever! Amazing Careers With or Without College

CHAPTER 12

Life with Mother Nature: *Jobs in the Great Outdoors*

"As a guide you're constantly evaluating the terrain, conditions, rock quality, stability, dangers. But you're also observing and analyzing how your clients are doing, how their abilities change as the terrain changes. So your role is to not just find a route and go up it, it's also to constantly make these evaluations and to make adjustments to your progress as needed. You may need to speed up, slow down, stop, go back, whatever. And that's part of what makes the job so intriguing—it's teaching, it's people handling, it's a little psychology, it's keen observation and analysis. It really calls on all one's talents. It takes quite a while to become a good guide, and a *long* time to become a great guide. And because there is so much to learn and accomplish, it holds people's attention."

—Dunham Gooding, professional mountain guide

ONE DAY, CAUGHT IN THE HELL ON EARTH KNOWN as L.A. traffic, going barely five miles an hour, I started understanding why people shoot each other on the highway. I began wondering why so many of us actually *choose* to live in some crazy, sprawling metropolis. I started dreaming of making a break for it.

Signing on for a gig with corporate America and a shoebox apartment in L.A., Manhattan, or D.C. might make your parents proud, but I'm here to tell you, it's not the only option. There's still time to give corporate America the boot.

Imagine it. Your office: no walls, no desk, just wide open spaces. Your workday: ever changing, dependent on the whims of nature rather than the rules of the powers that be. Your commute: by foot, horse, raft, or bike, far from the horrors of rush hour. The sun instead of a harsh fluorescent light. Crickets chirping, instead of the whine from some coworker's favorite easy listening station. Campfires, flashlights, air that doesn't scare you. . . .

OK. Reality check. It's not *all* s'mores and ghost stories. Work in the outdoors has its drawbacks. It's physically exhausting, it's seasonal, and it won't make you rich. At best, you're at the mercy of the elements. At worst, you're also at the mercy of whoever's willing to slap down their money. Some will be Patagonia-clad dreams; others may be ill-prepared or spoiled rotten. Either way, it's your job to be eternally cheerful. You need to be able to smile when they're whining, joke through their cursing, hug them when you want to wring their necks. Before you burn your neckties or toss your makeup, listen to some words of wisdom from some people out in the field.

INTO THE WILD

Work in the outdoors offers a little something for nature-lovers of all sorts: the thrill-seekers, the cowboys, the explorers, even the hillbillies. It's up to you to analyze your personality type and pick your career path. Generally, there are three major categories of outdoor occupations: active travel, parks and forests, and farming and ranch work.

ON THE ROAD: ADVENTURE TRAVEL

Want to see the world? Got good legs and half a brain? Adventure travel just might be your ticket. Fact is, there are thousands of people out there willing to shell out some pretty hefty cash to sweat themselves silly. And they need a guide. If you're up to the task, you could be saddling up to a scone in Ireland, checking out the ruins in Turkey, or resting your sleepy little head on a down pillow in a turn-of-the-century B & B.

To get you started on your road to dreamland, I got some words of wisdom from two people doing the hiring: Maribeth Hutson, a recruiter at Backroads, and Larry Niles, owner of Bike Vermont.

First, some perspective. According to Hutson, there's a pretty wide spectrum of opportunities under the name "active travel." There are hard-core outfits like KNOWLES, where you'll be scrounging for nonpoisonous berries and bushwhacking your way through the South American jungle. And then there's the other end of things—trips "where you can choose to be as active as you like but have everything, absolutely everything, taken care of for you. So even if you get a little bit uncomfortable, a little bit too wet or cold on a rainy day and say, 'This is enough. I want to go back to the hotel and crash by the hottub,' that's a possibility." That second option is where Backroads and, to a lesser extent, Bike Vermont fit into the picture.

Where *you'd* fit into the picture, should you become a leader, is somewhere between tour guide, bellboy, and personal trainer. The official word on the ultimate candidate, according to the Backroads website, is this: They're looking for someone who's "a master problem solver, effective public speaker, area expert, chef, translator (on European trips), skilled driver, and meticulous record keeper" all rolled up into one.

You've got to be in good shape, no question, but it's mind as much as muscle. Leaders are the outfit's reps in the field, and they've got to be more than good athletes, they've got to be good company. Niles likes leaders who "know how to keep things lively, keep people happy. They exude confidence and competence. They're interesting and interested."

Hutson agrees. You don't have to be a hiking or biking fool to get a gig with an adventure travel company. "It's much more about being interpersonally oriented and an autonomous, quick problem solver," Hutson says. Some of her hires don't even have any real guiding or teaching experience. "We've got about 210 leaders on staff and they run the age range, they run the experience range. We have individuals who come from corporate backgrounds and people who come straight out of school," she says. What Backroads is looking for is hard to pinpoint, but it basically comes down to working well with a team and being "a warm, nice, engaging person." It's a people industry and you've got to like people. Fact is, technical skills can be learned, but you can't teach personality.

Both companies want "smart people," but they've got to be strong, too. This job is anything but a free ride. Leaders have to hike all day carrying heavy packs full of equipment, or bike like the wind weighed down with a saddlebag full of food and tools. "We don't need triatheletes," Hutson says, but leaders need to be "willing to learn what it feels like to lift thirty pounds of bike over your head on a windy day." That, and the mountains of luggage that guests bring along. It may be a short trip, but you'd never know it from the way some of these people pack. And guess what? You're the one heaving their bags in and out of the van each day.

It may sound rough, but if you're in decent shape, Hutson says, the physical part of the job shouldn't be a problem. Weirdly enough, "active people who are seeking this position sometimes are faced with a situation where they're actually getting *less* cardiovascular work than they would normally get on their own." Because while some trips are pretty challenging—like whitewater rafting in Nepal—many are a cakewalk—like a bike ride through the Loire Valley where guests stop at châteaux along the way.

"Roughing it" with either one of these companies is pretty damn luxurious. While some of the trips have camping, most put clients to bed at a comfy little inn each night—or some grandiose villa. Every little need is taken care of. Be aware though, you'll be the one taking care of it. On a typical day with either outfit, you'll wake up at the crack of dawn, check all the equipment to make sure it's working, put water and snacks in all the packs, whip up some picnic lunches if need be, and get the logistics together—all before breakfast. Then you'll eat with the guests, brief them, load their luggage, and hit the road.

Usually trips have about a dozen people and two coleaders. One's in the field and one's in the van. Every other day, they switch. Oddly enough, the van man's the one breaking a sweat. They need to troll back and forth from sunup to sundown, "making sure that everybody's happy, well fed, safe, and pointed in the right direction," Niles says. They also pack the van, load and unload any equipment, and deliver anything (or anyone) to each day's final destination.

INTERVIEW

Vince Anderson, guide, interviewed by shortwave radio from an Alaskan mountain peak

What made you decide to become a guide in the first place?

I've been hiking, climbing, and skiing since I was four years old. I thought I wanted to be an engineer so I went to college, the University of Colorado at Boulder. There were plenty of recreational opportunities there and I felt myself getting more and more absorbed in that kind of thing.

By the time I finished college I realized that I wasn't going to make much of an engineer, or at least if I was an engineer, I wouldn't be a very happy one. So I started looking at other things I could do. I went to some towns where I used to ski a lot and figured out that the only jobs there that you could actually make some money at were jobs that would take away from my skiing and play time. So I started thinking about guiding people around.

You're the youngest person in North America ever to get full international certification. Most employers don't even know that certification exists. What made you go to all the trouble?

Well, the first place I ever got a guiding job, a real one, was North Alpine Guides in Alaska. And the owner of the company there, Bob Jacobs, was pretty active in the American Alpine Guides Association. He got me motivated to get involved, at least as a member, not necessarily on a certification basis. North Alpine Guides also had a number of people hired to train the staff who were certified guides. And it opened my eyes to how much I didn't know and to all the opportunities they had. They were guiding at places that I had only dreamed of going some day—on challenging mountains like Denali. They were going to the South American Andes, going to the Himalayas. And I was used to going to the Tetons or the Rockies, which was fun, but I would have loved to have taken a *vacation* to the Peruvian Andes, let alone *guide* there. Certification seemed like a potential doorway to some opportunities and guiding skills.

How long did it take?

I think it took me about five to six years. There's three different certifications: rock guiding, alpine guiding (which is more mountaineering kind of stuff), and ski mountaineering. And then for the international certification you have to acquire all three of the individual certifications.

To start the process, you need to have the basic skills of an accomplished climber in that discipline. The next step would be learning the skills as a guide. That comes in a number of ways—either through some kind of guide training instruction or apprenticing, or doing an internship or job with a guide service. As you continue on, you start to get the beginning of some guiding. You actually go out under the supervision of someone else or sometimes, on some easier type guiding, on your own. You continue with the education until you eventually feel that you're ready to take an exam, which happens after at least several years of guiding.

It's a practical exam where any segment—rock, alpine, or skiing—is approximately one week in length. You go out with the examiners who are certified guides trained to do this sort of thing and they pretend like they're clients. They ask you to guide them on things that are challenging in one respect or another all week long, and test your skills as a guide. You'll also have a couple days where they're setting up rescue scenarios that you have to perform in a certain amount of time. I thought it was more stressful than anything I've ever done in my adult life—far more stressful than anything I'd ever done in engineering.

What would you say it costs to get certified?

You're looking at *at least* seven to eight thousand dollars, and it's probably more like ten thousand. It's kind of a catch twenty-two. To get a job as a guide, you've got to have training as a guide, otherwise most people won't hire you. If you can get your foot in the door, which I fortunately was able to do, you can maybe save a step and get training as part of an apprenticeship or something. But it's not always that way.

It's very expensive, but for someone who takes it seriously, the expense is worth it. It's no more than, say, getting a truck driving license, to become a certified truck driver. In any profession, you would expect to have to pay a bit to learn the skills.

How many certified guides are there in the U.S.?

There's maybe a total of a dozen guides fully certified at the international level. I was twenty-eight when I got certified. In the States, I'm still the youngest.

Compare your pre-certification life to your post-certification one.

Well, first of all I have to say that the amount I learned through the certification process was amazing, and I know that I'm a far better guide than I ever was. Looking back, I can't *believe* some of the stuff I used to do. So my skill level has gone up tremendously. I don't feel as worried about "Can I do this?"

And it certainly allowed me more opportunities than I would have had otherwise, because it's easier for somebody like a guide service owner to know what they're getting into. I've had people contact me because of the certification. And now I can charge a decent rate for the amount of work that I do.

What's your dream climb? Where do you really want to guide eventually?

I guess the dream things for me to do would be to guide what I call small ratios—private guiding on beautiful, remote, and slightly technical peaks. That's what I enjoy the most. I just like going to the places a little less visited with people, and sharing a little bit more special experience than, say, the real popular climbs. Everest and Mount McKinley are good bread and butter routes but I prefer to go to, say, Mount Saint Elias in Alaska or Mount Shishipangma, in Tibet. I've had the chance to do that. I give it as an example because a climb like Mount Shishipangma is an eight-thousand-meter peak. You get a similar experience to Everest, but without quite the throng of travelers and popularity. It's a more unique spot, and that's what I like.

What advice would you give people who want to make a go of this?

Get really good at what you want to guide in first. Don't try to shortcut the personal experience. Then seek out qualified instruction. There's a lot of folks that want to try to skip through some of the process. And I think that it's well worth it to try to get the entire experience and not just part of it, even though there's a little extra cost. In the long run, it's not that much more.

Along for the Ride

Adventure travel recruiters are looking for incredibly interesting, smart as a tack, just plain fun leaders. And you'll be working with them. That, and leading some pretty groovy people, believe it or not. Unlike many jobs in the service industry, where you're treated like crap, adventure travel attracts a cool crowd. "It's not just anybody who's going to spend a fair amount of money to spend six days on a bicycle, when they could be on the beach," Niles says. The high-maintenance contingent is sort of self-selected out of the picture, so it's unusual to get a real jerk. Besides, with scenery like this, even the most difficult people chill out. "They're on vacation. I mean, you're not dealing with them when they get a toothache or an appendix out or anything like that," Niles says. "They're accomplishing something they probably thought that they could not achieve. A lot of people get on tour and say, 'I don't know what I'm doing here. I can't ride forty miles.' And then they do and they feel fantastically about themselves. They're on beautiful backroads, they stay at really nice inns, and they're dealing with really nice leaders, so the net result of it is that these are happy, happy people. That's one of the nicest parts of the job."

The seasonality of adventure travel makes it perfect for a short-term gig. But while a lot of leaders come through for one or two years and move on, many companies have had employees stay for ten years or more. Why? Why not. There's good food, low pressure, constant excitement, and a free ticket around the world. "It becomes a lifestyle instead of just a job," Hutson says. So while it may be tough to find an opening, and your friends may bug you about getting a "real job," you'll have the last laugh. Take it from Niles, "It's a fun job. It's a hard job. Combined with other things, it can be a career. In a nutshell, it's a neat lifestyle for people who have a little gypsy in them."

Guide Guidance

Backroads: Job Hotline (510) 527-1889 ext. 560, www.backroads.com

Bike Vermont: (800) 257-2226, www.bikevt.com

Water Works

Got saltwater flowing through your veins? If adventure on the high seas sets your heart aflutter, check out the Seafarers Harry Lundenberg School of Seamanship. Funded by the Seafarers International Union and absolutely free, this place will set you up with all the skills you need to shape up and ship out as a deep sea merchant mariner. Not only is it the largest training program out there, but it guarantees you a job! The only catch? You have to be eighteen to twenty-four years old and willing to join the union. Seafarers Harry Lundenberg School of Seamanship (301) 994-0010

Take a Hike

Get paid to lace up your hiking boots.

1 Contact the American Mountain Guides Association (303) 271-0984.

2 Or pick up *Helping Out in the Outdoors*, a booklet published by the American Hiking Society. It lists over a thousand paid and somewhat paid positions at hundreds of different agencies. Call (301) 565-6704, ext. 115 for a copy.

Seasons Greetings

The biggest drawback to adventure travel is the lean times. "There's a seasonality to the thing that's hard to overcome," according to Dunham Gooding, who's been guiding for almost twenty-four years—from Alaska to Ecuador, British Colombia to Patagonia. "In all outdoor guiding that's true—river rafting or guiding, or horseback riding or whatever. There tends to be a greater volume in the summer than at other times of the year."

When you're shopping your résumé around, try to pick employers with something cooking all year long. Gooding's outfit, for example, plans trips that chase good weather. "In the fall we're domestically doing rock climbing at Red Rock, trekking and climbing. In the winter we're in Ecuador, Argentina, Chile. And in the spring, back to Joshua Tree and Red Rock," Gooding says. The bulk of the work is still in the summer, and until you get some seniority, the bulk of your opportunities will be, too. But trips in the off-season are becoming more popular. Stick to companies that offer some seasonal creativity.

Training

Most adventure travel companies admit official training or guide certification isn't necessary. While they give you a lot of hours of hard-core experience, you could probably piece together most of it on your own. But if you want to make yourself official, these places can help:

1. **North Carolina Outward Bound School**—A 111-day instructor apprenticeship that covers river skills, wilderness first responder, managing a rock site, course design, and being nice to Mother Nature. They pay you once you're able to make yourself useful. All told, you'll shell out about $780, which includes room and board. NCOBS: (800) 841–0186 or www.outwardbound.com
2. **The Wilderness Education Association**—A network of places across the country that take 21–35 days to whip someone into shape and get them certified as an outdoor leader. Skills taught: minimum impact camping, food rationing, health and sanitation, navigation, first aid and emergency procedures, and environmental ethics. "Exists solely to promote the professionalization of outdoor leadership." (615) 531–5174 or www.wildernesseducation.org
3. **American Alpine Institute**—Considered the number one climbing school in America by everyone from *Condé Nast Traveler* to *Outside* magazine. Offers two guide-training programs: a twenty-four day deal for $2,940 or thirty-six days for $5,620 (including an expedition to Mt. Washington). The programs review the fundamentals to make sure everyone's up to snuff, move on to "a complete repertoire of technical skills," and finish off with the art of guiding. (360) 671-1505

❹ **Deep Springs College**—In the middle of nowhere, literally. About an hour from the nearest "town"—population seven. Founded in 1917 by a philosopher named L. L. Nunn, this desert nirvana is a two-year liberal arts college with a 30,000-acre cattle ranch. What happens inside the classroom will blow your mind, but so will what happens outside of it. Students spend about twenty hours a week keeping the ranch running—milking cows, delivering calves, tweaking the irrigation system, putting up fences, cooking, branding, or whatever else needs to be done. Each guy has a job. If you're a woman, you're out of luck. This place is men only, and likely to stay that way. (760) 872–2000 or www.deepsprings.edu

❺ **Wilderness First Responder**—This program is worth its weight in gold—offering medical training for emergencies in remote locations. The core curriculum is usually a mix of American Red Cross Emergency Response, CPR, and first aid skills based on guidelines from the Wilderness Medical Society. You'll learn how to take care of normal things like high altitude illness, asthma, sprains, fractures, and dislocations. You'll be briefed on how to deal with psychological emergencies. Then come seizures, diabetes, and big-ass problems like heart, lung, or abdominal trauma. From CPR to a traumatic injury to the head, spine, or chest, this course has it covered. Of course, all this security doesn't come cheap. Expect to shell out several hundred dollars for about 90 hours of schooling.

WHERE TO PARK IT

In 1872, long before highways and high-rises, smog alerts and urban sprawl, some guy had the idea to start America's first national park. The guy was President Ulysses S. Grant. The park was Yellowstone. People may have called him crazy then, but today, America's national parks are swamped with people hip to the idea. Yosemite, the most popular park, gets over three and a half million visitors *a summer.*

Somebody's got to take their money, clean up their campsites, and clear new trails for them to hike. A lot of somebodys actually. And each year, over a hundred thousand people are hired to keep things chugging along at more than three hundred national sites across North America—parks, forests, wildlife refuges, and wilderness areas. There are admission fees to be collected, forest fires to be put out, history to be explained, maps to be sold, trails to be patrolled, trees to be planted—you name it, somebody somewhere is getting paid to do it. Very little, mind you. But what did you expect. . . .

There are three major agencies in charge of keeping an eye on the wilderness: the U.S. Forest Service, the Bureau of Land Management, and the National Park Service. Problem is, with so many cooks in the kitchen, figuring out where to apply can be a headache. If all you're looking for is a summer job in a national park, you can send a letter directly to the National Park Service. If you want to work any time or anywhere else, you've got your work cut out for you.

National Park Service

Your pre-job job is to get a handle on where you might want to park it. If you've got your heart set on a particular place, your best bet is to contact them directly. You'll become either a seasonal employee or a VIP.

Seasonal employees are exactly what they sound like—short-term hires. They keep the gears well oiled during peak seasons (especially summer) and are gracefully let go when the crowds start to thin out. There are all kinds of positions—from ranger to clerk, lifeguard to landscape architect. In general, seasonal workers get minimum wage, maybe room and board.

VIPs (Volunteers in the Parks) are a bit lower down on the food chain. Because even though the parks couldn't run without them, VIPs usually don't put in enough hours to be given anything significant to do. They might dress up in period costume to give a historical demonstration, work the desk at an information booth, or get to patrol a few trails. But basically, they do what no one else really feels like doing. And they get a little bit of money to do it—sometimes. The truly stingy or extremely famous places may not give them a red cent. Best case scenario for VIPs would be about seven bucks a day to cover meals and a little bit for gas money, with a free campsite or RV hookup if they're *really* lucky.

For seasonal jobs in the parks send a resume to:

Seasonal Employment Unit
National Park Service
PO Box 37127, Mail Stop 2225
Washington, DC 20013–7127
(202) 208-5074

Tell them when you can start, when you're out of there, what you want to do, which two parks are your favorites, and the lowest salary you'll accept. Deadlines are July 15th for winter, January 15th for summer.

Student Conservation Association

If you want something sweeter for your sweat, there's an agency that can swing it for you: the Student Conservation Association. SCA isn't just for students. You can be a slacker and still hit them up for jobs. The great thing about SCA is that, in addition to getting you a paid gig, they finagle free round-trip transportation to wherever you're going—even somewhere like Hawaii. Can you see yourself patrolling Alaska's two-million-acre Kenai National Wildlife Refuge by canoe? Surrounded by 14,000-foot peaks in the Rocky Mountains? Helping out with bat research in Arizona's Petrified Forest National Park? Well, brush up that résumé! Those were some of the jobs SCA had available when this book went to print.

Of course, some jobs are easier to get than others. When candidates apply, SCA asks them to pick "four positions you would be delighted to take." Then they sort through all the applications, send three or four standouts for each position to the appropriate recruiter, and wait for the results. In general, half the people who seek their help end up with a job. These are much better odds than you'd snag with the do-it-yourself method.

SCA positions range from endangered species protection to archaeology. Depending on how much time you're willing to give, you'll either be a Resource Assistant (12–16 weeks) or a Conservation Associate (6 months–1 year). Whatever they call you, you'll do the same kinds of jobs and all your basic expenses, plus room and board, will be taken care of. CAs usually get a little bit more money—maybe $160 a week. They can also get close to $5,000 from Americorps. But more than the money, the main difference between RAs and CAs is the number of openings. About one thousand RA positions open up each year, compared to only seventy-five CA ones. Whichever way you decide to go, you'll beef up your chances by picking someplace less popular—the Curecanti National Recreation area gets a lot less attention than the Grand Canyon.

The Student Conservation Association
Contact: (603) 543-1700; www.sca-inc.org

A Walk in the Park

Which park is for you?

a) Rocky coastline, gorgeous peaks, deep forests, and crystal-clear lakes.
b) Streams running through rugged mountains. Deep woods and over three hundred miles of hiking trails.
c) Forests full of the biggest trees on earth—the Giant Sequoia. Waterfalls and the Sierra Nevadas.
d) A haven for mountaineers—Mount McKinley smack dab in a six-million-acre Alaskan dream of clean air and caribou.
e) The most visited park in the U.S. Seventy miles of Appalachian trail and six hundred miles of streams.
f) Red dust, a raging river, and the most spectacular canyon in the world.
g) Rain forest and a famous goat relocation program. Really.
h) Chilly reminders of the most recent ice age. Glaciers, waterfalls, sparkling lakes, and wildflowers.
i) The granddaddy of American parks. Boasts a slew of geysers and a huge wildlife preserve.
j) Dreamy mounds of rose-colored sand. An incredible collection of fossils—footprints of saber-toothed tigers and skeletons of animals that lived more than twenty-five million years ago. Otherworldly.

a) Arcadia National Park, Maine; b) Rocky Mountain National Park, Colorado; c) Yosemite National Park, California; d) Denali National Park, Alaska; e) Great Smoky Mountains National Park, North Carolina–Tennessee; f) Grand Canyon, Arizona; g) Olympic National Park, Washington; h) Glacier National Park, Montana; i) Yellowstone National Park, Wyoming; j) Badlands National Park, South Dakota

WIDE OPEN SPACES

If you're "city folk," you've probably got no idea what it's like to live hundreds of acres from your nearest neighbor. You don't know the feel of a steady horse beneath you or the smell of clean mountain air. You've never whipped off your cowboy hat in respect for a lady, mucked a barn, or milked a cow. And maybe that's just fine by you.

But if you've always dreamed of getting caught with Billy Crystal in the middle of *City Slickers* or imagined yourself chatting it up with the Ingalls in a little house on the prairie, there are ways to make those dreams a reality.

First things first: truck or tractor? Horse or haystack? Because a ranch and a farm are as different as night and day.

FARMING IT OUT

When I say "farm," I'm not necessarily talking *Grapes of Wrath*. Agriculture covers a pretty broad spectrum—from picking grapes at a vineyard, to harvesting wheat smack-dab in the middle of Kansas. Regardless of where your interests lie, most of these places have work to spare.

Because the range of agricultural opportunities is so vast, it may be tough to find a good fit on your own. Luckily, there's an organization that can help—the New England Small Farm Institute. They run a matchmaking program that hooks up workers and farms willing to take them on. What kind of experience do you need? "Absolutely none," according to NESFI's Kathy Ruhf.

The way it works is this—you send NESFI eight bucks, they send you a list of about seventy organic farms looking for help. Most are on the East Coast, but there are a few places farther flung.

You might end up tending the fields, but not necessarily. There are a wide variety of experiences to be had. Your employer could be "a vegetable farm, it could be a dairy farm, it could be an orchard, or a place with lots of animals," Ruhf says. And what you'll end up doing varies as well. You could be pitching hay or "you might be involved in making teas, planting flowers, selling things at a farmer's market, trellising," who knows, according to Ruhf. It all depends on what needs to get done.

NESFI jobs are officially apprenticeships, though most will give you a place to live and a small stipend. Be aware, "a place to live" means different things to different people. Make sure you get it straight with your new boss before landing on his doorstep. "Someplace to live could be a separate house, it could be a loft in the barn, it could be a small cabin, a tent," Ruhf warns.

Because the options are so varied, "people should be really clear on what they expect from the farm experience," Ruhf says. This is no time to be shy. Make sure you interview the farm as well as let the farm interview you. Find out how much time you'll be expected to put in, and for how long. "Apprentices work five or six long days on average," Ruhf says, "but that's individually negotiated." In other words, come to the table knowing what you want.

The New England Small Farm Institute

What: Apprenticeships at over 70 organic farms, orchards, and gardens around the U.S.

Experience needed: None

Cost: $8 membership fee

Pay: Room, board, and a small stipend
Contact: (413) 323-4531; nesfi@igc.org

RIDE 'EM, COWBOY

Can't get enough of dark jeans and fresh air? Think there's more to life than desks and door locks? Well, pull out your chaps, shine that saddle, and start looking for a home on the range.

Your first stop in your hunt for howdy should be a directory of 100+ places put out by the Dude Rancher's Association. All you need to do is ask, and they'll send it to you for free. And if you tell them what kind of job you're looking for, they'll even post it on their board and tell ranches about you should they call in. "We're not an employment service," says Jim Futterer, the association's executive director, "but we do try to help out."

Dude ranches started humbly, with the first few opening their doors in the late 1800s, to take advantage of the stream of visitors pouring out West. They were pretty cheap. According to the Dude Rancher's Association, "History has it that the first fee was the handsome sum of ten dollars, for a week of accommodations, meals, a good horse to ride, and the pleasant company of the ranch family." Well, ten bucks isn't what it used to be, but the all-in-one ranch vacation package remains today. Only now, guests get a lot more than horseback riding. Today's dude ranches have everything from whitewater rafting to hot air ballooning, private access fishing to photography workshops. In the winter, places like Montana's Lone Mountain Ranch offer snowshoeing and cross-country skiing. Vista Verde Ranch, in Colorado, has ditched chili and burgers for gourmet fare like "grilled venison with a purple potato napoleon" or "boneless rocky mountain rainbow trout with lemon caper sauce." I guess home cookin' means different things to different people. . . .

Some of the ranches are just like they were a hundred years ago. They don't require much staff. But others have become a sort of roughing-it resort. These places can hold up to a hundred guests at a time, so they need more than cowboys. They need cooks, wait staff, housekeepers, maintenance workers, even kids' counselors. Still, this fantasy job wouldn't be a fantasy without horses. No surprise, those are the hardest jobs to get.

You can be a housekeeper anywhere. If your dream is to spend long days in the open air with a steady horse beneath you, you want to sign up as a wrangler. The job will have you leading guests on trail rides. It will have you grooming the horses and looking after them. And on a cattle ranch, you'll be working with the cattle as well. Know this: You need to be much more than a so-so rider to make it as a wrangler. "You better be able to ride like the wind, teach riding, and pick out a sore horse from a herd of fifty while you're driving them in the pitch dark," Futterer says.

Most of the ranches in the Dude Rancher's Association are out West and up North—in Colorado, Wyoming, and Montana. Wranglers are in highest demand during the high season—a four-month period around summertime. But pair that with a gig at a ranch in Arizona, where most places are closed for the summer heat but go strong all winter long, and you just might make a living. It's difficult, but not impossible.

The hours for dude ranch workers are long—typically eight to twelve hours a day, six days a week. But, you'll spend a lot of those hours *getting paid* to do things other people pay to do. Futterer himself was employed by a few ranches before coming onboard at the Dude Rancher's Association. He remembers night shifts where he drove a wagon for hayrides or roasted marshmallows with the guests. "Sometimes it was hard to decide if we were working or having fun," he says

Ranch employment may be hard to get, but once you're on the payroll the money's pretty decent. According to a recent survey by the Association, wranglers rope in an average of $1,200 a month. Which is kind of a lot, considering that "most ranch jobs provide room and board, employees don't have any expenses, and there's no place to spend anything," Futterer says.

Of course some ranches are as far from rustic as Timbuktu is from New York. Many a would-be cowboy has headed off for his first day of work and found himself employed by a place that looked more like a movie set than a working ranch. If you're looking for an upscale Rocky Mountain getaway or a place with its own reconstructed saloon, go for it. But if you'd rather be mending fences than mending a hole in someone's designer jeans, get the facts straight before hitting the homestead.

The Dude Rancher's Association

What: Jobs at over 100 member ranches
Experience needed: Varies
Cost: Free directory there for the asking
Pay: For wranglers: room, board, and about $1,200 a month in pay and tips
Contact: (970) 223-8440; www.duderanch.org

CHAPTER 13

Art Smart: *Art Without Starvation*

> **"The best audience is intelligent, well-educated, and a little drunk."**
> —Alvin Barkley

I REMEMBER WHEN I WAS A KID, I TOLD ONE OF MY teachers that I wanted to be an actor. He looked at me, shook his head, and said, "My cousin's an actor. He's so poor that when he goes to a restaurant he orders a cup of hot water. Then, when the waiter's not looking, he takes the ketchup off the table, pours it in the water, stirs it around, and drinks it. The guy can't even afford a bowl of soup. You'd have to be crazy to want to be an actor."

So much for encouragement. But in a way, my teacher was right. You *do* have to be a little crazy to want to be an actor, or any other kind of artist. If you look at things with a clear head, you'll realize you've got about as much chance of surviving as an ice cube in a campfire.

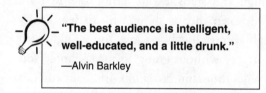

The statistics are definitely against you. Less than 10 percent of all artists make a living above the poverty level. It doesn't take a genius to figure out why. There are too many artists and not enough jobs.

And why not? I mean, who *wouldn't* want to be an artist. If you can make it work, it's one of the greatest jobs in the world—you've got no one to report to, creativity coming out of your ears, and the chance to make a huge impact on the way that people see the world. Long after we're all dead and gone, people will look at the art our generation produced and try to figure us out. In a way, artists are the keepers of the flame.

And even though the statistics are grim, they're only statistics. I've got my own theory about why so few artists make it: Not enough approach it like a job. You wouldn't try to do open heart surgery without going to med school. You wouldn't expect to sell a thousand boxes of Girl Scout cookies without ringing at least two thousand door bells. But many people expect to make it big as artists without any training or self-promotion. Any slob off the street can call themselves an "actor," a "painter," a "musician," but to make a living, you've got to do more than dress in black and act aloof.

You've got to get serious. It's hard as hell to make a living as an artist. You need a strategy. As I see it, there are three major ways to keep your head above water until your fifteen minutes arrive: Get a job, live cheap, or create your own work.

GET A JOB

Ahh, the bane of artistic existence. . . . The butt of many a joke. . . . The only way to get food on the table. . . . The "day job." Also known as the "survival job"—for good reason: This is the stuff artists do to make ends meet.

Day jobs run the gamut and there's hot debate over which

sort is best: brainy or brainless. In the first camp, we have the artists who think it's good to have something meaty to keep you occupied until your ship comes in. In the other camp, we have the artists who think it's a mistake to expend any energy whatsoever on anything but their art—they're only punching in the clock so they can pay their rent, period. Whichever way you look at it, the d-job is a necessary evil. So get used to it and find something good.

FOR PEOPLE WHO THINK A PICTURE'S WORTH A THOUSAND WORDS

Put down the paints for a second. Get out of the darkroom. Stop dreaming in color and *listen.* It may be years until your first museum exhibit. That doesn't mean you have to live in a pit and drown your sorrows in turpentine. If "you've got an eye," exploit it.

According to the Princeton Review Online, 90 percent of visual artists make under a thousand bucks a year on their art.

Cool School

Into *Aladdin*? Nuts for *Mulan*? The American Animation Institute teaches everything you need to know to get your sketches off the page and onto the big screen. Brought to you by the union for writers, artists, and other people involved in the world of animation, the school's main purpose is "to provide a reasonably priced education" taught by industry veterans. How reasonable is reasonable? Most classes are under five bucks an hour. From basic figure drawing and composition to background painting and design, storyboarding to acting classes for animators, these guys have it covered. Contact (818) 766-0621.

But go to the dark side, and you can rake in much more—*part-time* commercial artists make as much as $40,000 a year. Headshot and wedding photographers make several hundred to several thousand bucks a session. Even your lowly public school art teacher has made almost forty grand by the time summer rolls around.

Lots of places need artists and they've probably never even crossed your mind. So use the creativity that got you here in the first place and start thinking out of the box. Any job that's high on form or color needs people who understand those things.

I have a friend who makes jewelry and sells it at craft shows. It may sound like the small leagues, but let me tell you, she pulls in a pretty paycheck. And not only is her work sold in museums, she's been written up in a slew of major newspapers. She spends her days knee-deep in creativity and her nights sleeping easy. What started out as a hobby has turned into a very lucrative career.

Hospitals, nursing homes, correction facilities, rehab centers. . . . All these guys are starving for a way to get their charges to "express their feelings" and art is a safe, relatively cheap way to do it. You may find that art therapy challenges you enough to make it more than a day job. Or you might make ends meet by working part-time as a floral designer, makeup artist, or interior decorator and spend your off hours covered in paint.

The trick to artistic satisfaction is to find something you love to do that can pay the bills. Artsy jobs can come in the most unlikely places. Take your friendly neighborhood police station. They need artists to sketch crime scenes and suspects before they can get things rolling on a hot case. If you can make it work, you'll pull in between twenty and sixty grand a year. And who knows, you may even get out of a few speeding tickets. . . .

Survival Jobs for People with Vision

Junior Interior Designer: $25,000–35,000
Art Therapist: $14,000–50,000
Commercial Artist: up to $40,000 part time
Police Artist: $20,000–60,000
Headshot Photographer: on average, $200–500 a session
Wedding Photographer: on average, $400–1,000 an event
Public School Art Teacher: $20,000–40,000

FOR PEOPLE WHO THINK A WORD IS WORTH A THOUSAND PICTURES

If you're an actor reading this book, the odds are both for and against you. For you, because more than half of all acting jobs go to people under the age of thirty. Against you, because even with the numbers stacked, less than 5 percent of all professional actors manage to make a living. That said, there are lots of jobs out there that can fill in, while you're waiting to hear back from Harold Prince.

Actors talk a good game. So anything that requires the gift of gab is a great match: sales, PR, advertising, DJing, restaurant hosting, telemarketing. . . . There are also your more off-the-wall jobs, like owning a 900 number, becoming a singing messenger, posing as an artist's model, or becoming an audience recruiter for a television show. You could pay your rent by becoming an extra—sitting in the background of a movie scene. You could go undercover as a secret shopper, and evaluate the service you get at a store or restaurant. You could start a business entertaining at parties. You could get certified as a massage therapist, aerobics instructor, fitness trainer. . . .

INTERVIEW

Neal Brennan dropped out of NYU before making it big in Hollywood as a screenwriter for *Half Baked*.

You're a smart guy. Why did you leave college?

Most of what they teach at NYU is really hard-core film theory that respects about fifteen filmmakers and the rest is like, shit. You mostly *talk* about film for two years and then you get to make a film, which you have to pay for on your own. So I would have ended up spending like a hundred and twenty-five grand on an education that I could have gotten on the job, by being a production assistant.

A good friend of mine had dropped out the semester before, to go to L.A. and write a movie, and it just seemed so glamorous and exciting. Meanwhile, he went out there and got walking pneumonia and had the most miserable experience of his life, but in my mind he was living it up.

I saw that a shortcut to getting a movie made was becoming a writer. If I could learn how to write, then that would do the trick. So I dropped out of school and more or less threw myself into the lion's den.

How did you make ends meet?

I essentially didn't know where I was going. I wrote a couple of articles for magazines. I wrote a screenplay with a guy that didn't go anywhere. I was a doorman at a comedy club. I sort of thought I wanted to be a stand-up—but I did it one time, and was really bad at it. So then I sort of figured out how to write jokes. I'd help out my buddies with their acts. I would write sketches with people.

I had a sense of instant nostalgia when I was suffering. Like, as I was eating tuna fish I'd have interviews running through my head of me saying, "Iused to eat tuna fish!" The instant nostalgia of "Boy, I was struggling in 1991!" And meanwhile it *was* 1991. That was my way of coping.

An opportunity that I got from the comedy club was that a friend of mine there was on an MTV show and they needed sketches for it. He asked me to write one with him. I didn't get paid or anything, but they shot the sketch, so it was a sort of a victory in that way.

After the comedy club, I moved to L.A. I was nineteen. I started working for this casting director. She was casting a show for MTV. And they brought me in, but they couldn't hire me. And then the writers for this show quit, so they made me "writer's assistant." They had no writers! They made me a writers "assistant" but there were no writers. *I* was the writer. It was a pilot for this show called "Singled Out"—a dating game thing. I wrote for that—all these dumb categories, everything they said, the whole game essentially.

Even that was a great experience. And then I got a job at Nickelodeon writing for a sketch show called "All That."

Why are you laughing?

I essentially got my ass kicked. I got an education. I learned what TV writing was like—how to do rewrites, to see a sketch in read-thrus with everyone sitting around. It was about twelve hours a day at least, grueling, thankless, sort of humiliating. I was like, "Wow. This is not fun and I'm not really good at this."

They used to call me "The Boy." I was twenty at the time and they referred to me as "The Boy." Not in a good way, like "kid." They might as well have just called me "Boy." Nobody respected me. But it was good. It toughened me up.

So that ended. I wrote a screenplay that was not that good but it got to a woman of some influence at Universal—Julia Dray. I had a meeting with her and was really funny in the meeting. She had me meet her boss and I was funny again. They didn't do anything with the script, but they knew me as "that guy was funny."

I went back to L.A. I worked on another crappy dating game show. And then while I was working on that crappy dating game show, a buddy of mine from the comedy club in New York, who's an actor and comedian, Dave Chappelle, had a meeting with those people at Universal and told them he was writing a pot movie with a friend. They asked who. He said my name, not expecting them to know me, but they said, "Neal Brennan? We just met Neal. We love Neal!" So he called me and said, "If Julia calls you, I just said we were working on a movie together, so just bluff."

Julia calls me and asks, "When are you guys going to come in and pitch this weed movie?" She wanted to set a date. So now me and Dave have to come up with this movie.

I went to visit him and we'd talk about it. But we weren't really getting anything done. We were talking a lot of theory, but we had no plot. We had less than no plot. We had nothing. So the night before the meeting I said, "Listen, we fucking have to do this!" We stayed in this hotel room and we literally outlined two thirds of the movie in about six hours. Then we went across the street to the *Comedy Store* where they were having this after-party for the comedy awards and we hoisted a few as it were. I was a little tipsy. It was three o'clock in the morning. And then we came back and outlined the rest of the movie.

Do you have any regrets about dropping out?

They don't teach anything in school that you won't learn if you get a job in L.A. They really don't. Nobody taught me how to write comedy. The way I think of jokes now is basically the way I thought of jokes when I was in high school. It's just now I know how to structure them and put a plot around them. I've learned how to work ideas from watching other people. Watching comedians, working with Dave, being at Nickelodeon all taught me about comedy writing. It was osmosis. I gave myself an education. I watched everybody.

What do you think a person needs to make it in Hollywood?

I think thirty to forty percent is luck. But there's this old golf adage, "The more I practice the luckier I get," and I think it's true. The rest is skill. The "talent" is how hard can you bust your ass.

There's a place for everyone in L.A. You can meet all kinds of people. You can rub elbows. You can live out some pretty fun stories in Hollywood. You can also work your ass off.

> L.A. is sort of hyper interesting. It's not all good. A lot of it's gross. There's a lot of sex and glamour in Hollywood but there's also a lot of sweating and ugliness, in-fighting and disgusting behavior. At the very least, there's a lot of interesting sociology happening in Hollywood. Even if you hate it, it's interesting. It's fun to surround yourself with hate-able people. And you can learn a tremendous amount.

Survival Jobs for People with Golden Tongues

Singing Messenger: makes $30–50 a telegram
Artist's Model: makes $10–20 an hour at most art schools
Audience Recruiter: makes $5–10 a head
Movie Extra: union actors make about $80 for eight hours, plus meals. Non-union about half that.
Critic: typically earn $15,000–55,000
Copywriter: $30,000–72,000
Stage director: paid about $37,000 for a five week rehearsal period on Broadway, $3,000–14,000 for four weeks at a regional theater, or $600–1,000 for a week at a summer stock theater.
Personal shopper: paid about $10–60 an hour

If you're as good getting words on paper as you are spewing them out, you might consider becoming a freelance copywriter. Sum things up in a heartbeat and you'll have an easy time filling your plate with work for catalogues, brochures, ad agencies, or publishing companies in need of some sassy copy. A few good greeting card verses can reel in up to a hundred bucks a pop, and since, according to Hallmark, the average person gets thirty cards a year, work is plentiful. If you're willing to turn on your friends, you could make a few bucks as a critic. Even crossword puzzle writing can bring in some dough.

Who knows where your day job will take you. Nicole Conrad came to New York to become a singer-songwriter "despite some intense objections from my parents, who believed music and entertainment were full of swindling sleezeballs and drug addicts. I learned that music is a multibillion-dollar industry with very smart, sensible, and creative people working behind the scenes." A little time spent on the *business* end of things brought a career turnaround. The work was challenging. And Conrad realized that she could potentially make even more of an impact backstage than she could on it. So she swerved off

Traveling Light

Want to be all you can be? Prefer costumes to uniforms and a microphone to a rifle? You can join the military, if only for a short while. Since 1951 the Department of Defense has been shipping entertainers all over the world to make military life a little less bleak. In exchange for a few laughs or a little night music, they'll feed you, put you up, and give you a free ticket to ride. There are four major circuits: Alaska & Greenland, the Caribbean, the Mediterranean, and the Pacific. Your three- to eight-week tour could have you sunning yourself in Greece, chowing down in Italy, swimming in Spain, or sightseeing in Japan. Panama, Honduras, Turkey, and the Pacific Islands are some other prime possibilities. If you've got a show you'd like to take on the road, contact:

The Armed Forces Professional Entertainment Office
2461 Eisenhower Avenue
Alexandria, VA 22331

course and started working for one of the most powerful music attorneys in the industry. "It's so important for someone with a background as a musician and performer to work with artists because most music executives, my boss included, have never even picked up an instrument," Conrad says. And while she may get a tweak of jealousy once in a blue moon, "I get so much joy helping musicians gain success," Conrad says. "I switched paths because I found myself getting more and more interested in the business end of things. And every day I feel it was the best decision of my life."

LIVING CHEAP

There are lots of ways to make a living. How *much* of a living you have to make, depends on how you like to live. Live like a miser and you won't have to work too hard. Live lavish and you could be in trouble—you'll be too tired from punching in the clock at your day job to ever get to your art. There's no nice way to say it. An artist has got to be cheap.

Ten Ways to Be Stingy

1. Join grandma for the early bird special.
2. Make Happy Hour a habit.
3. Usher at the events you want to see—you'll watch the show for free.
4. Rent movies, or go to the matinee.
5. Get a few friends together and buy in bulk. Make Costco your new best friend.
6. Buy clothes that won't go out of style—when they go on sale at the end of the season.
7. Use half the amount of recommended laundry detergent—it's been proven that half's all you need.

8. Eat out less, party at home more. Single-handedly bring the potluck dinner back into vogue.
9. Become an apartment manager.
10. Have many roommates. More is always better.

CREATING YOUR OWN WORK

Don't wait around for work to find you. The art world is ruled by the people with the most entrepreneurial spirit. Being an artist is a business, and you need to look at things as a business person. Like it or not, you're a product, plain and simple. And you're competing with all the other products on your shelf. So look at what's out there. Look at what's missing. Scour the horizon for a niche in the market and squeeze yourself into that little foothold.

If you're an actor, that might mean starting a children's theater for inner-city kids. If you're a painter, that might mean creating a traveling art exhibit. Every industry has its holes. Maybe it's doing photographs to fill the pages of some tiny little hometown newspaper or playing calypso music at Scandinavian weddings. Who the hell knows. The point is, there's not enough work to go around. So when you're starting out, no job is too small, no contact is too irrelevant. And whatever doesn't kill you makes you stronger.

GO FOR THE GRANT

Another option is to go for a handout. The idea is simple: You beg for money, someone forks it over. There is absolutely no downside to this equation, other than the obscene amount of competition and the extreme pickiness of the organizations handing out the cash.

Grant-makers are very nervous people. They have a limited amount of money and they don't want to make a mistake. Not to say they have no reason to be skittish. The National Endowment for the Arts once gave a serious chunk of change to an artist who soon after created a sculpture of a miniature Jesus, swimming in a glass of urine. Taxpayers were not pleased.

The corporations, institutions, and government agencies that give out grants aren't big on risk. They don't want the unknown genius sculpting away in his basement. They don't want to be the first ones to take a chance. They like funding people who've already gotten money from somebody else.

Playing the Odds

When money is tight it usually goes to the people who dare to get specific. So when it comes to grant proposals, don't guarantee what you can't deliver, but don't hide behind vague promises, either. Goals are abstract; proposals need *objectives*. Here's an example of the difference:

Goal:

Our after-school program will help children learn to paint.

Objective:

Our after-school program will pair fifty at-risk kids with professional painters. They'll meet twice a week for six months, at which point a communitywide art exhibit of their work will take place. In addition to preparing individual work for the exhibit, each team will also collaborate on one piece to be auctioned off at the end of the evening, with all profits going to next year's program.

You don't have to be famous to get a grant. You just have to be useful. You're more likely to get some money if you're filling a need that others don't.

Take Cornerstone Theater, for example. These guys started out with nothing. They became a grant-giver's dream. How? In the beginning, they worked the Massachusetts school system, bringing theater into the classrooms. Not their eventual goal, maybe, but it brought them their first grant—the hardest barrier to break. Next they piled a dozen actors into a big blue van and traveled throughout the country, bringing theater to people who'd probably never seen a show in their lives. Small towns would put them up in a church, a gym, a deserted school—wherever they could. And Cornerstone would set up shop for a few months and work with local residents on a collaborative theater piece. After almost a decade on the road, Cornerstone settled in California, where they're now one of the most highly respected and consistently funded theater companies around. Most of their budget comes from grants. Why? Because they're good. And because they saw a need and filled it.

Every grant committee is different. There's no one thing that everyone's looking for. *Except in proposals.* When it comes to proposals, it's pretty easy to play the game. That's because there are certain things that every proposal should have:

What Funders Expect in a Proposal

1. Executive Summary: A one-page snapshot of what's to come. The most important ingredient in your big enchilada.
2. Statement of Need: The facts and stats that make your project worthwhile.
3. Objectives: The place for big promises.

4. Methods: The nuts and bolts of how things will be carried out—when (timetable), why (defense of methods), and who (staff and volunteers).
5. Budget: A one-page summary of expected expenses.
6. Evaluation: A plan for measuring if you did your job.
7. Future Funding: How the project will carry on, once the initial funds have run dry.
8. Organizational Info: Your history, mission, audience, and all your other vitals in two pages or less.
9. Conclusion: A summary of what's been covered. A final appeal for funds. A good spot for high drama and emotion.

Let me let you in on a little secret. You're a lot more likely to get a grant if you're out to change the world, not just your income bracket. So if you're serious about getting some funds, shield your selfishness under a veil of good will. Pitch projects that will improve life in your community and help others while you're helping yourself.

Granting Help

New York Foundation for the Arts: (212) 366-6900, ext. 217
Foundation Center: http//fdncenter.org
New York Artist Equity Association: (212) 941-0130

RETREATS

There are places across the country willing to cut you a break so you can stop worrying about money and get something done. They're called colonies, or artist's retreats. They come in all shapes and sizes—some high-brow and some relaxed, some competitive and some welcoming.

Many retreats offer nothing more than studio space and extremely cheap rent. In exchange, they may ask you to put in a few hours giving presentations or helping out. Other retreats are a virtual free-for-all. They'll put you up for a few months and take care of your every whim. They'll give you a studio, bring you supplies, and deliver meals right to your doorstep. Then they'll leave you alone to do whatever it is you do. As I said, there's no typical retreat treatment. It all depends on what kind of funding is keeping things afloat.

Seven Fellowships Where Young Is Good

1. **Nicholl Fellowship:** A screenplay award specifically for someone who's never sold anything. Five awards of $25,000 each, plus a one year fellowship. Contact the Academy of Motion Picture Arts and Sciences: (310) 247-3000
2. **Walt Disney Pictures and Television Fellowship:** Writers wanted! Disney is on the lookout for new talent. Should you be it, you'll get a year with The Mouse, a $30,000 salary, airfare, and a month's accommodations while you look for an apartment. Contact (818) 560-6894 or send a SASE to them at 500 Buena Vista Street, Burbank, CA 91521
3. **Fine Arts Work Center in Provincetown:** Seven months by the sea for writers and visual artists in their early stages. The twenty people lucky enough to snag this fellowship have a woodshop, printshop, and darkroom at their disposal. They get live-in studios, $375 a month, and absolutely no responsibilites. Contact (508) 487-9960 or send a SASE to them at 24 Pearl Street Box 565, Provincetown, MA 02657.

❹ **Jacob's Pillow:** A dancer's mecca offering month-long residencies in the mountains during both spring and fall, and the chance to interact with some of the most famous dancing shoes in the business. Contact (413) 637-1322.

❺ **National Foundation for Advancement in the Arts:** Four months of bliss for emerging visual artists aged 18–40. The chosen will strut their stuff for a never-ending stream of critics, curators, and art dealers. Renewable for up to three years. Contact (305) 377-1147.

❻ **Fund for New American Plays:** Free money from the Kennedy Center for the Performing Arts. So far, the Center's shelled out over two million bucks to help theater companies who want to produce new plays. You could be next. Contact (202) 416-8000.

❼ **Morton Gould Young Composer Award:** For budding Beethovens under the age of thirty. Winning composers split $20,000 between them. Send a SASE to the American Society of Composers, Authors, and Publishers, 1 Lincoln Plaza, New York, NY 10023, or check out www.ascap.com.

IS IT ALL WORTH IT?

So why go through the trauma of unemployment and the uncertainty of ever making it? Because being an artist is incredibly rewarding. It's hard, no doubt about it. But at the end of the day, most artists do it because they wouldn't be happy doing anything else.

CHAPTER 14

How to Be a Player: *Going Hollywood*

> **"A person who wants to make it has to sweat. There are no shortcuts."**
>
> —Bette Davis

HOLLYWOOD. JUST THE NAME ITSELF CONJURES up fabulous images of sunshine and superstars. But don't be fooled. This is not the life of the little people.

Your first years in Tinseltown, you're the lowest of the low. Coffee fetcher, actor chauffeur, gopher, and general whipping boy. You drown your sorrows in brief glimpses of movie stars and stuff your pockets with the endless stream of food coming from the catering truck. The hours are terrible. The pay stinks. Your only comfort is that everyone starts this way. Your only hope is that someone will see your potential and move you up the production ladder.

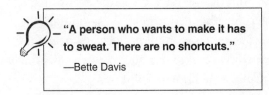

In all areas of Hollywood it's the same. Unless you're rich or related to someone famous, you've got to start at the bottom and work your way up. And I mean the *bottom*—picking up the boss's dry cleaning, making a star's vacation reservations. . . you get the picture. Not only will you be up to your ears in grunt work, but you should expect a certain amount of torture. Because in nowhere but fraternities is hazing approached with such glee.

The problem with Hollywood is everyone wants to work there. People can afford to be mean—there's a line around the block of future movie moguls waiting to turn the other cheek. If you've ever seen the movie *Swimming with Sharks* you know what I'm talking about. If you haven't, rent it and get back to me. The Hollywood bottom is bleak and the sad truth is, unless you're willing to eat whatever anyone decides to dish out, with a smile on your face, you're not going to make it. On the other hand, if you can take it, the rewards are big: money, power, profile.

THE HOLLYWOOD FOOD CHAIN

Hollywood is like a grown-up version of dodgeball. There's a certain amount of skill and a certain amount of luck. The guy who ends up winning isn't the smartest, he's just the one who knows how to stay out of the way when the person in the middle starts throwing things. Hollywood is literally survival of the fittest.

Before you can even think about winning, you have to figure out how to get into the game. Good luck. Hollywood is one of the toughest tickets around. Even the lowliest jobs are fought for tooth and nail. If a fight's going to stop you, you might as well forget it. This town is not for the meek. But if you're up for a struggle, you've got three basic bottom-feeder options: working on the set, getting into the Second Assistant Directors Training Program, or doing a desk job.

ON THE SET

When most people think about working in Hollywood, they think about working on the set. They want the lights, the camera, and most of all, the action. They want to meet the stars, schmooze with the directors, and see their name roll by on the production credits. Well the first step on the road to production glory is the PA.

PA, short for production assistant, is the term slapped on every film and television set's little worker bees. The job description is pretty murky—a PA basically just fills in wherever they're needed. They can be asked to do anything. From holding the boom (a big furry microphone that looks something like roadkill on a stick), to stopping traffic in between shots, to going to get the Frappuccino someone can't work without, PAs give service with a smile. And that can be tough when the workday drags on for sixteen or seventeen hours.

All this for the grand total of about a hundred bucks a day . . . if you're lucky. Smaller films might only be able to sport you fifty. On the upside, commercials usually pay closer to a hundred and fifty dollars a day.

Aside from stargazing, the best perk on a set is the food. Some film executive long ago must have decided that it was too expensive to pay people what they were worth, but it was cheap to keep them well fed. Whatever the reason, sets have an endless supply of snacks and drinks there for the asking. Just when people are about to tear their hair out, someone will come by with a cart full of lattés or a plate piled with hot cookies. And in between these magical moments, there's always "craft service." A throwback to the Good Humor truck you chased down the street as a child, the craft service truck is a permanently parked vehicle dispensing much-needed sugar hits throughout the day.

Don't get me wrong. Life on a set's not all snacking. There are meals. And I'm not talking hamburgers here. These are all-you-can-eat-athons: I've seen everything from steak to lobster, gourmet omelets to homemade apple pie. If you're the kind of

Having (and Making) an Effect

You don't have to be on the set or in the studio to make an impact. Take it from Dean Lion, a visual effects director who's worked on some small films you might have heard of—*Air Force One, Starship Troopers, Armageddon,* and the *X-Files Movie.*

Lion's responsible for sending films off with a bang. Literally. "I'm known for explosions," Lion says. Let's say there's a scene where a car explodes behind Jean Claude Van Damme. "The Special Effects guys can give us a small explosion, just enough to rock the scene a little bit. Then once I get it on the computer I take some fireball that was filmed at another location and put it behind Van Damme's head to make it look like he was in a great deal of peril," Lion explains.

This is a great job for high-tech artists. And if you've got some web design experience, you may already know how to use some of the tools you'll need: Photoshop, Aftereffects, Commotion, Shake. "You can actually buy the same sort of equipment and use the same sort of applications that are currently being used on music videos, TV commercials, and even films," Lion says. "And with all the cable stations now and all the direct-to-video and independent movies being made, there's a lot of opportunity."

If you like playing with people's minds, this is the job for you. It's all about optical tricks—making the planes in *Air Force One* look real even though they were hand-held models or totally computer generated, or making the Taco Bell Chihuahua look like he's talking. "When I tell somebody that I worked on the Taco Bell dog they'll say, 'Oh, that's the cutest dog in the world!'" Lion says. "And I say, 'Yeah. I made him that way.' Because, in reality, he was just some dog. I'm the one who makes his eyelid go up and down, I'm the one who puts the glisten in his eyes, I'm the one that made the girl dog cry when he snubbed her in lieu of the taco."

person who eats when they're bored, beware, because PAing consists of two major things: eating and standing around.

From the Horse's Mouth

The money may not be great, but there are benefits to PAing beyond the food. David Shultz, my neighbor and a PA pro, explains it like this: "If you want to direct or produce, it's good to know pretty much everything. And one of the best ways to learn is by being a PA."

David moved to L.A. almost two years ago, knowing he wanted to be involved in film, but not sure exactly how. "The beauty of being a PA is you can go anywhere from that," David says. "That's where you learn what all the positions do, what you want to do. Then you can move into the camera department, or the grip department, or the production office, whatever."

Choose Your Path

On a film set, there are several career ladders. Post-PA, you'll choose which one to climb.

ELECTRICS: electric (peon) → best boy electric (assistant) → gaffer (boss)

GRIPS: grip (peon) → best boy grip (assistant) → key grip (boss)

PRODUCTION OFFICE: assistant coordinator → coordinator → production manager → supervisor

CAMERA DEPARTMENT: loader (loads the film) → second AC (assistant assistant camera) → first AC (assistant camera) → DP (director of photography) and/or cinematographer

DIRECTING: second AD (assistant assistant director) → first AD (assistant director) → director

The hardest thing about working as a PA is finding work. Television jobs can last for several seasons, but film work is project by project. To eke out a living as a PA, you have to be liked enough to be remembered when another project comes up. "People definitely notice what you're doing," David says. "They're definitely watching you to see how fast you learn. And if you have a good attitude, it makes an impression on them."

Ben Conklin, who's been a PA on and off for about a year, warns, "If you do *too* good a job, your employer will keep calling you back . . . as a PA. It's hard to find a really good PA in this town. Once you find a good one, you're going to keep him." David agrees: "If you're the greatest PA that ever walked the earth, you'll probably just be a PA for the rest of your life. You want to be good as a PA, but you don't want to be too good. There are people on sets I've worked who've been PAs for five or six years now. I'm sure they want to move up in the food chain, but you kind of get pigeonholed after that amount of time."

As a PA, there are lots of slow times, when it seems like no one's hiring. So when the phone rings, it's hard to be choosy, no matter how trashy the film. Every PA has stories of bizarre sets or diva actors. David spent four of the weirdest days of his life on a film called *The Killer Eye*, a feature-length movie about "a beachball-sized eyeball that goes around having sex with women and zombifying men." Ben once worked on a music video for a group of German rap stars called *Funk Leib*. The art director asked Ben to help him out, and, like a good little PA, Ben agreed. "We were stapling this big plastic sheet onto this frame. I had no idea what was going on," Ben says, "Finally I ask him, 'What is this thing?' And he says, 'It's a condom. The band is going to stand in it.'"

Weird moments can lead to some pretty hard-core bonding. David got into the DGA, the director's union, because of his days on *The Killer Eye.* He got hired on a *Killer Eye*-ster's next shoot and was promoted when the second AD unexpectedly quit. On their next job, they brought him in as a second AD. Suddenly, he was eligible for the director's union—one of the toughest nuts to crack in all of Hollywood.

THE SECOND ASSISTANT DIRECTOR'S TRAINING PROGRAM

Speaking of the DGA, they've got a program in place that's the ultimate Hollywood hookup: the Second Assistant Director's Training Program. In action since 1965, the SADTP is a shortcut to the upper rungs of the production ladder. The two-year stint is guaranteed to get you into the union and onto the official list of qualified Second Assistant Directors (no small thing in a town full of hacks).

A Trainee is usually treated like a glorified PA. The hours are similar—a typical workday is twelve to sixteen hours. Many of the responsibilities are the same. But life as a Trainee differs from life as a PA in two major ways: 1) Trainees always get paid, and 2) they're given a series of business seminars, in addition to their experience on the set.

The job is far from glamorous. There's a funny picture on the DGA's website of the twelve pairs of sneakers one guy wore out during his time in the program. The pace on the set is unrelenting, with almost no sitting or down-time. Trainees hand out paperwork, keep the extras under control, make sure people are on time, deliver actors to the set, keep an eye on traffic, maintain quiet on the set, take orders for takeout, and do a slew of other underappreciated tasks for the grand total of $470 a week (for the first one hundred days), and up to $578 (for the last hundred). They also get free health care, plenty of food, and loans if they need them.

Getting into the program isn't easy. You have to be at least twenty-one and send proof that you have either two years of college under your belt or two years (520 actual work days) of paid work experience in the entertainment industry. You'll need to fill out a collegelike application, get recommendations, and take a written test.

Cheat Sheet

The test changes a little bit every year, but the questions usually fall into seven major categories. Some of the sections are similar to what you might get on the SAT. Verbal reasoning tests your vocabulary, spatial reasoning tests your ability to think in two or three dimensions, and general reasoning tests if you have a head for numbers. Here are two past examples:

1) Select the word that has a meaning most like that of the underlined word.

sincere

a) fair b) naïve c) genuine d) guilt-free e) honest

Answer: c

2) Three people dig a trench twenty feet long in three days. How long would it take two people to dig the same ditch?

a) 2 days b) 2.5 days c) 3.6 days d) 4.5 days e) 6.7 days

Answer: d

Other sections are less traditional. The social perception segment asks you to "make judgments about the appropriateness of certain actions involving people," while another section contains creativity tests with sample questions along the lines of "You have two minutes to come up with uses for a brick."

With such bizarre questions, it's easy to get stressed out. The Trainee application effusively states that there are no right or wrong answers and that candidates shouldn't "spend a lot of time thinking about each question." Easier said than done.

Even with all the requirements, competition is fierce. Your chances of being accepted are pretty slim. Each year, after applications have been waded through, about one thousand people are invited to take the written test. Only ten to twenty are accepted.

What a lot of people don't know is that there's a sister program in New York. If you're willing to get the Hollywood experience outside of Hollywood, it might be worth looking into it. New York Trainees get the added bonus (or added burden, depending on how you look at it) of spending a few one-week stints at organizations like the Director's Guild, a film equipment rental house, and the Mayor's Office of Film, Theater and Broadcasting.

In order to graduate from either location, Trainees have to work a minimum of four hundred days. But the film business is flaky. While the program does its best to find Trainees work, it warns candidates to "be prepared to cope with periods of unemployment."

Graduates are eligible to join the Director's Guild as Second Assistant Directors. Some decide to park themselves in that capacity; others use the connections they've made to get a leg up. While the program emphasizes that it's "not a director-in-training program," many of its graduates have gone on to become directors or producers.

Where the Jobs Are on the Set

Assistant Director:

The key word here is assistant, not director. The AD's job is to keep everything running smoothly so the director can focus on his work: The Second AD is a funnel for information—managing everyone on the set and telling them where to go. The First AD is the director's right hand—creating a shooting schedule, intercepting problems, and keeping the director happy.

Transportation Captain:

In charge of all the production vehicles—prop trucks, vans, trailers, equipment vehicles, the honeywagon (a trailer with bathrooms and dressing rooms)—and with getting the crew and the actors from place to place.

Driver:

Has a license to drive almost any vehicle on the road—from a motorcycle, to a city bus, to a double trailer.

Script supervisor:

Because scenes aren't filmed in order, they make sure that all the shots match. If someone was only halfway done with their cigarette in one take, it can't be a stub in another—otherwise the editing won't work. Takes notes and Polaroids of costumes, props, makeup, etc., for each take.

Boom operator:

Holds a microphone on a pole over the actors but out of the frame. Moves it from actor to actor and works with the location sound mixer to gather ambient noise and make sure the lines can be heard.

Set dresser:

In charge of everything on the set that's not a prop—hanging pictures on the walls, putting pots on the kitchen stove, making the place look lived in. Needs to keep time period and each character's income in mind, and create a look that fits.

Animal wrangler:

Keeps the animals in line. When a character is attacked by snakes, or bitten by a spider, or riding on a horse, the wrangler is the guy who makes the snakes, spider, or horse behave. He also teaches the actors how to handle them.

Fight choreographer:

From fencing to punching, they create the fights in the movies, just like someone would choreograph a dance scene. This way, no one gets hurt.

Grips:

They're the muscle on a film set. They set up equipment and move it out of the way if it's in the frame.

Gaffer:

The chief lighting dude. In charge of getting rid of shadows and adjusting the lights to make everyone look good.

Director of Photography:

The cameraman. Also called the DP. Decides on the color, feel, and lighting of the movie. Takes test shots on location and hires the gaffer and camera assistants. Decides which lenses, camera types, and shots will work best.

Assistant camera:

Helps the DP: The Second AC works the clapper, loads the film, and keeps track of how much film is left and which shots the director liked. The First AC cleans the camera and takes care of it. He's also in charge of focus.

Camera operator:

The guy actually sitting behind the camera looking through the lens, not the artist behind the way it will be shot. In charge of keeping the action in the frame and of panning and tilting the camera.

> ***Makeup, Costume, and Hair:***
>
> Just what you'd think. They make everybody look good. Actors should not piss them off.
>
> ***Stunts:***
>
> In charge of all the dangerous stuff. Highly trained to jump off of cliffs, do car chases, run through burning buildings, and other scary things. Not for the amateur.

Second Assistant Directors Training Program

Pro: An "in" to the Hollywood scene
Con: Extremely competitive
Duration: 400 days on the set
Contact: Los Angeles: (818) 386-2545;
New York: (212) 397-0930;
Website: www.dgptp.org/jobdes.html

AT THE OFFICE

What do Mike Ovitz, Jeffrey Katzenberg, and almost every other studio hotshot have in common? They all started in the mailroom. It's true. Before planning multimillion dollar deals, dining at Spago, and holding the fate of hundreds of people in the palm of their hands, most studio royalty were licking stamps and shoving letters into cubbyholes. The mailrooms of Hollywood's biggest talent agencies are the spawning ground of the next decade's powerbrokers.

Problem is, you have to have horseshoes running through your veins just to get the privilege of delivering the mail. These

The Hollywood Five

Creative Artists Agency (CAA): (310) 288-4545

International Creative Management (ICM): (310) 550-4000

William Morris Agency: (310) 859-4000

United Talent Agency (UTA): (310) 273-6700

Endeavor Talent Agency: (310) 248-2000

positions are tougher to land than tickets to the Oscars. Just getting the lowdown on how to *apply* is a lesson in clandestine operations. Agents may make money by running their mouths, but when you call to ask about agent training programs, they become pretty tight-lipped. The best agencies guard the mailroom secret like it's gold in Fort Knox. Don't ask me why. If you're ready to sweat, call one of the big Hollywood Five—CAA, ICM, William Morris, UTA, or Endeavor—and you'll see what I mean. You won't get a word out of anybody until you prove that you're worth the conversation.

If the snobbery proves too much for you, you can start at a smaller agency and try to switch once you've learned the ropes. But since these places run on a tighter budget, it may be difficult to get paid—the backlash from small bank accounts and too many actors willing to work for free in order to get their foot in the door.

What most people don't realize about agencies is this: They're not just a starting point for agents. People who've paid their dues at a hot talent agency have an easy time getting hired almost anywhere in Hollywood. That's because agencies provide a potluck education—a chance to learn a little bit about everything—from casting to contract negotiation, packaging to setting up a studio deal.

One person I know who's been through the process agreed to give me the scoop as long as I promised not to mention his name.

Clawing Your Way to the Top

The basic agency climb goes something like this: After an average of one year in the mailroom, the best trainees get promoted to "assistant," a.k.a. glorified secretary, and spend their days scheduling appointments and answering phones. Next step is junior agent and, if you decide to stay, agent, at which point it becomes your inalienable right to torture all those below you.

If you can get into one of the five top agencies, you should. These are the real Hollywood powerbrokers, and if you want the inside track, you have to get inside. Regardless of which you choose, the hiring process is about the same. "First you have to make it through a human resources person—that's the first line of defense," my source says. "They basically check to see if you have three ears or one eye in the center of your head." If you make it past that person, you'll be in for a typing test and a stream of endless interviews. CAA, for example, has been known to put candidates through up to eight rounds of interviews, lasting up to six weeks.

Should you dazzle them, you'll be in for three to five years of virtual slavedom. You'll start your tour of duty in the mailroom, which is exactly what it sounds like—delivering mail. Some agencies make you *such* a delivery boy that you'll see about as much of the building as the FedEx guy. Maybe less. You'll spend your days speeding around town, trying to avoid an accident.

Agents want their stuff there fast, and there's pressure to deliver it with superhuman speed. Crashes are more common than you think. In fact, there've been so many car accidents at the top agencies that most are starting to use professional messenger services, to cut down on any liability potential.

Other than shuffling mail, the mailroom will have you making photocopies, sending faxes, and doing errands. The whole point of the mailroom is to make the most of it. Don't just photocopy like a zombie—take a look at what's going through your hands. Don't just send a fax—sneak a peak at what it says. You need to be a human vacuum cleaner—sucking up whatever information you can, tucking it in the back of your brain for later use. But do it quietly. "You don't want to stand out in the mailroom. You want to stay below the radar. The only way somebody gets noticed in the mailroom is if they've done something bad—like if they've ticked off a

Only Temporary

One of the best kept secrets of Hollywood is the sneaky way in the door—as a temp. Many a studio employee has tiptoed their way in as a fill-in and been so damn delightful answering phones and typing letters that they were hired on the spot—no pesky résumé to write or interview to sweat over. Regardless of whether it leads to a job, temping is a great way to dip your toes in the water and see if a job's for you.

The three key agencies specializing in Hollywood temps are:

The Freidman Agency (310) 550-1002

Blaine and Associates (310) 785-0560

The Job Factory (310) 475-9521

client delivering something," my sources tell me. Keep your head down and "just bust your ass."

Other than that, look busy. Move quickly. "You should always be moving quickly and if you have nothing to do, move quicker. Just run down the halls like you're doing something. There's one guy in the mailroom who literally sprints down the hallways and everybody says, "Wow. Look how hard that guy works!" an agent told me. This business is all about perception. It has nothing to do with reality. Because you could just be someone in the mailroom who moves quickly and they'll say, "Oh, he's brilliant! He's a go-getter. He knows what he's doing."

If you're good at running yourself into the ground, you'll move up a notch—to assistant. The mailroom should have schooled you in the basics—what's going on at the agency, who works there, where the major studios are and who works at them. . . . You don't really start learning how to be an agent, though, until you land yourself a desk.

When you're at a desk, you have become the agent to your agent. That is your only client and your entire job is to make that one client happy. For most people in this town, that is probably the most difficult client that you will ever encounter in your whole career. You will do absolutely everything for this person. From typing their letters to answering their phones, setting up their meetings to running their personal lives. You know more of what is going on with their families than they do. You end up doing prescription orders for someone's mother or making dinner reservations for someone's wife—things that have nothing to do with your boss. You are a slave. And that's just the process. They've all done it. There's no other way around it.

Not only is the treatment often abusive, but it's downright unhealthy. Assistants are kept so busy that "there's literally no time to go to the bathroom." Your boss will be on the phone from the moment she wakes up in the morning. "The only time you lose contact with them is the few seconds they're in an elevator." They leave their house with cell phone in hand, reach the car and switch to the car phone, come up to the office with the cell on again, and sit down at their desk and pull on a headset so they can talk away and keep their hands free. In addition to connecting all their calls and juggling the people on hold, you're listening in on most conversations, taking notes for them about what was said. All this while fending off a steady stream of cursing and abuse.

"It's funny," a source tells me. "When I saw *Swimming with Sharks* before I came out here I was like, this is ridiculous, this can't even be close. It is unbelievably accurate, aside from somebody getting murdered, which I'm kind of surprised has never happened, believe it or not. Because people get spit out in this business so quickly. I mean there are horror stories."

Having entered the mailroom at minimum wage plus overtime, by now you'll have gotten at least a small boost in salary—usually fifty bucks a week more for every six months you manage to stick it out. Assistants who've been there two to three years are usually taking home thirty grand, forty or fifty if they're putting in a lot of overtime. If you make it past the hazing, keep a low profile, and manage to bite your tongue for three to five years, you'll eventually become a junior agent.

You'll be one of the few. By all accounts, climbing the ranks at an agency is "really demeaning." Most people can't hack it. They're not willing to put up with the bullshit. "The

Film School

There's an age-old debate as to whether film school's worth the money you'll need to pay to go there. If you're hell-bent on spending two or three years working toward a diploma, the top schools are generally considered to be NYU, USC, and UCLA. Only problem is, it's their *grad* schools that carry water. In other words, you need a college degree before you can apply. For people looking to spend less time, or less dough, here are two of the best bangs for the buck:

The New York Film Academy

Hands-on workshops where students write, produce, direct, and edit their own film. Come knowing absolutely nothing. NYFA will whip you into shape with classes in everything from lighting to sound design, and send you out the door eight weeks later with a 16mm original of your film in hand. The difference between this school and the longer programs is you'll learn by doing, not by sitting in a classroom. They also have the highest ratio of cameras to students of any film school in the world.

Cost: $3,500–4,000, full-time or evenings

Where: New York, Los Angeles, Princeton, New Haven, England, Italy, and France

Contact: (212) 674-4300; www.nyfa.com

Los Angeles City College

It may not have the clout of some of its more expensive competitors—but it's got all the basics and more: a fully equipped sound stage, two TV studios, sixteen editing rooms, three screening rooms, extensive audio and video post-production systems, and great instructors. You'll learn to master everything from lenses to film stocks, lights to microphones. And for California residents, a typical class will only set you back thirty-six dollars.

Cost: $12 a unit for California residents, $137 a unit for everyone else

Where: L.A.

Contact: (213) 953-4545; citywww.lacc.cc.ca.us

burnout rate is incredibly high," one agent tells me. "I would estimate that it's over 90 percent." It's hard to keep your head up when you're working sixteen-hour days for minimum wage, just to spend your weekends running your boss's garage sale.

OTHER OFFICES

Agencies are at the heart of everything, but they're not the only game in town. There are studios, production companies, casting agencies . . . you name it. Wherever you land, you'll probably start out as an assistant or an office PA. It's important to realize that, even at this level, it's all about who you know. If you want to get ahead in Hollywood, you have to treat it like a full-time job, from the time you get up to the time you lay your pretty little head back down on the pillow. Even as an assistant or PA, you should make an effort to meet people.

When you deliver something, play nice. When you're on the phone with other people's assistants, get to know them. They'll be moving up the ranks just like you. Today's assistant is tomorrow's low-level executive. Meet each other while you're nobodies. You can help each other out when you're somebodies.

Where the Jobs Are off the Set

Personal Assistant:

From walking their dogs to typing their letters, these people keep the rich and famous happy. They run their lives. According to the Association of Celebrity Personal Assistants, there are about five thousand personal assistants currently working in Hollywood. They make between $400 and $1,500 a week. Most are hired by word of mouth, but a few temp agencies (like The Job Factory) place them.

Office Assistant:

They do in the office what the personal assistant does in the home—keep Hollywood executives' lives ticking. They're usually smart people, willing to put in a few years doing errands and secretarial work, in the hope of getting promoted to low-level execs. They exist everywhere in Hollywood—studios, networks, agencies, production offices, casting . . .

Casting director:

Takes the script and figures out which actors need to be hired. Finds them, auditions them, and, for the larger roles, creates a short list of favorites to show the director and producer. Meanwhile, they cast most of the small roles themselves. Then, once all the decisions are made, CDs negotiate the contracts with each actor's agent.

Foley artist:

Creates everything from footsteps to sound effects—any real-world noises not recorded directly on the set. Feet come first: dancing, running, skipping. (They watch the action on a big screen monitor and mimic what's happening.) Then everything from refrigerators, to guns, to water running or doors opening is created and recorded. A feature film usually takes three weeks—five days a week, eight hours a day. For their work, foley artists make about $400 a day.

Location scout:

Finds places to film all the scenes not slated to be shot on a soundstage or studio set (usually outdoor ones). To do well as a scout you need a camera, and a brain that thinks like a camera, so when a director says "We need a waterfall," your mind pulls up all the places you've seen one.

Location manager:

The casting director of locations. Not only finds the sights but negotiates for them. In charge of all the scouts. Narrows down their photos and shows the best and most practical to the director. Negotiates for rental prices, permits, and insurance.

Researcher:

Does the writer's homework. Tracks down photos, historical documents, and information, fast. For example, for a 1920s film, they might find out what everybody was reading or wearing or what music was most popular at the time.

Editor:

An artist in his or her own right. Looks at all the footage options and chooses the best takes of each shot. Puts the film into sequence.

CHAPTER 15

Yes, Sir!: *Careers in Uniform*

> **"Be all that you can be."**
> —Army slogan

I'VE NEVER BEEN A BIG FAN OF THE MILITARY. Actually, that's an understatement. I have always considered the amount spent on the U.S. Armed Forces nothing short of obscene. What kind of country spends more on one B-2 bomber than they're willing to drop on the entire budget for the National Endowment for the Arts?

That said, you'd be crazy not to take them for all they're worth. The U.S. military is like one big (albeit bureaucratic) learning free-for-all. They'll pay you to train, take care of your loans, and teach you any profession you choose. Think of it this way: if the Navy can pay 3.1 billion dollars for a Super Hornet tactical fighter, it can certainly foot the bill to teach you how to fly it.

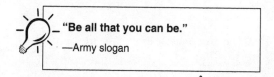

OK. So you're probably thinking what I was thinking before I got my butt on over to the recruitment office, "That's fine if you want to be a pilot, or a soldier, or a sailor, but what about the rest of us?" Here's the thing. Did you know that the military will also pay for you to learn photography? Journalism? Japanese? Believe it.

THE GOOD, THE BAD, AND THE UGLY

GOOD

The U.S. Armed Forces is the biggest employer in the nation. If you decide to join, it's almost impossible that you will be turned down. In fact, as far as I can tell, it is impossible. My friend, these are good employment odds.

The military offers training and work experience in almost two thousand different occupations, most with counterparts in the civilian world. Assuming you show some potential, they'll let you pick whatever career you choose—from aircraft mechanic to dental technician—and train you from scratch, no experience necessary. Not only will they pay you to learn, but the experience itself can save you big bucks. (Would-be pilots, for example, can save the $20,000 they'd have shelled out for a commercial pilot's license and the thousands of dollars they'd have paid to log the required flight time. Eighty percent of Southwest Airlines pilots are former military.) Whatever field you choose, there's plenty of room to climb within the military. After your stint is over you can also take your set of skills off the base and into the boardroom.

BAD

Of course the armed forces don't provide these perks out of the goodness of their hearts. You will be trading a small chunk of your life for the privilege of donning that uniform. A military contract is generally a four- to six-year commitment. And once the clock starts ticking, it's hard to leave.

The military is extremely regimented. The food isn't great. The housing, while free, is often far from luxurious. And autonomy is hard to come by—usually you have to agree to go wherever the job takes you.

UGLY

Basic training. Need I say more? You've seen the movies, you've read the press. Basic training is the main reason most people I know would never consider the armed forces. We're talking eight uninterrupted weeks of self-inflicted pain—sit-ups, push-ups, windsprints, rifle practice, hand-to-hand combat . . . I don't think even Dante could have made this stuff up.

The good news is—once it's over, it's over. Unless you've signed yourself up for grunt work, you will never have to go through this again. There is no "refresher" course. The bad news is, even if you want to be trained as a radio dispatcher, you have to make it through basic training.

THE COLLEGE CONNECTION

College is the carrot your military recruiter will relentlessly wag in front of your nose. In exchange for four years of active duty, the military will give you $19,008 to attend college or vocational school. Serve part-time in the Reserves and you'll earn a little

Basic Training: A Day in the Life

What's it like to be in boot camp? Here's a bird's-eye view, care of the Marine Corps:

From day one, it's good-bye familiarity. The night you get there, you'll strip down to your birthday suit and pack up all your personal possessions. In exchange, you'll get three camouflage uniforms, six sets of socks and underwear, and a few basic hygiene items.

You'll be assigned to a platoon. Size depends on the season, with summer the most crowded. Drill instructors "will usually have no less than three and no more than five recruits."

Hope you're a morning person! A Marine's day starts at 5:30 A.M. and goes nonstop until about 2130 hours (9:30 P.M.).

The military's got it all figured out for you—even portions.

A Typical Marine Breakfast:

Scrambled eggs made with egg whites

Either: 3 slices of bacon, a 4-ounce slice of ham, or 1 sausage patty

8 ounces of grits, farina, or oatmeal

1 hash-brown patty

2 pancakes or slices of French toast

Yogurt and fruit

1 doughnut or muffin

Milk, juice, or sports drink

To get into boot camp you'll have to:

Run 1.5 miles in less than 13:30

Do a minimum of 2 pull-ups and 44 crunches in 2 minutes

To get out of boot camp you'll have to:

Run 3 miles in less than 28 minutes

Do a minimum of 3 pull-ups and 50 crunches in 2 minutes

Before their twelve weeks are up, the typical recruit has fired 603 rounds with an M16A2 rifle, received 54 letters in the mail, consumed 336,000 calories, and spent 1,387 hours awake.

over $9,000 for about four months of service spread out over the space of six years (two weeks a year and one weekend a month). Not a bad deal. Plus, when recruits get too scarce, most branches offer special enlistment bonuses or "College Funds," to make themselves more attractive, bringing the grand possible total of college assistance up to as much as $50,000.

Once you're enlisted, the Armed Forces also offer various education centers and learning programs for free. Some soldiers decide to get a lump of credits out of the way while Uncle Sam's picking up the tab, in order to get a jump-start on college later on. The Navy, for example, offers what can only be described as floating college. Through flesh and blood instructors or the magic of computers, sailors can take courses in hundreds of areas from the middle of the ocean. The only thing they pay for is textbooks.

Then there's the SOC—the Service Members Opportunity for College program. Think of it as college for carpetbaggers. Here's how it works. Let's say you're stationed in San Diego. You enroll in SOC and start taking classes at San Diego State. Two years later you've got a whole bunch of credits taken care of, but you're transferred to Hawaii and enroll in a university there. If your new college is part of the SOC program (and they probably are), they have to accept all of your credits—no matter what their usual transfer policy. "It's like being under an umbrella," one recruiter told me. "You can go to any network of these schools in any order and they must accept all of your credits."

TESTING, ONE, TWO, THREE

"Azvab" may sound like a German punk band or a strange tropical disease, but it's much worse than that. It is the test that will determine your fate in the military. Because, while there are thousands of jobs available, you have to earn the chance to train for the one you want.

This is done through an evil little test called ASVB, the Armed Services Vocational Battery, pronounced "azvab." Once you've passed the military's physical requirements, they sit you in a room with this thing to figure out how your mind ticks. The test is like an SAT that acts as a career dating game. It tests your strengths and weaknesses and then suggests a few possible partnerships. For example, it might say that you'd thrive in communications—great if you want to train as a journalist, but not so helpful if you had your heart set on nuclear propulsion. Once the test has spit out an assessment of your strengths, your recruiter will give you a list of areas to choose from and the commitment involved for each.

A word of warning. Choose carefully. Some forces, like the Army, will hold you to your decision. Sure, they'll train you in whatever job you want if you qualify through the ASVB, but if you drop out of your selected position, it's at the "Army's discretion" to transfer you into whatever job they see fit. In other words, you could leave your slot as an engineer and end up a line cook.

This Is a Military Job?

Bassoon Player, Linguist, Broadcast Journalist, Optical Laboratory Specialist, Psychiatric Specialist, Multimedia Illustrator, DJ, Firefighter, Dental Specialist, Accountant, Pharmacy Specialist, Multiple Launch Rocket System Repairer, Cook, Computer Programmer, Weather Observer, Telephone Technician, TV Producer, Animal Care Specialist, Cartographer

YOU GET WHAT THEY PAY FOR

The military's basic benefits package is pretty impressive, but there are some easy ways to sweeten the deal. Work the system. If you take a few college courses, you'll start at a higher pay level. Recruits with two years of college under their belt, community or otherwise, begin at a salary of $1,172 a month. Four years will get you $1,243 to start. Any college classes at all will bump you from the base of $1,005.80 to $1,127.30 a month.

None of this is big money, but considering that you will have next to no out-of-pocket expenses during your years in uniform, it's not too bad. Plus, you'll get your first pay raise after a mere four months of service. And even in your first year, you get a whopping thirty days of vacation. Free housing, free food, an allowance to pay for your uniforms, free health care, free dental, and almost free travel to anywhere in the world . . . The military does a lot to flesh out the package. And should you decide to make the military your life's work instead of bailing out when your contract's up, you can retire with a tidy monthly pension by age forty! No joke. Twenty years of service and you're off to the Bahamas, baby.

TRAVELING LIGHT

One of the benefits of being at the military's beck and call is where they send you. Being shipped all over the place may leave you rootless, but you'll get the chance to see what all those exotic locales are like—and hopefully not from the inside of a tank. Talmadge Jones, who's just celebrated ten years in uniform, says, "One of the things that made me join the Navy was the chance to travel around the world. I've been

INTERVIEW

INTERVIEW: Roger, a boot camp survivor

It was the summer of 1994, and I had three years of college behind me. I felt like taking a long trip to someplace remote and wild: Like in those movies where a plane crash-lands in the mountains, or the desert, or the jungle, and the survivors have to hike back to civilization, battling starvation and killer animals and what-not along the way.

I suppose I could have just hiked the Appalachian Trail or something like that, but then it seemed to me that I should have more by way of woodsmanship. (After all, I'd only been in the Boy Scouts for a year.) And growing up in suburbia I'd never learned to shoot a rifle. So, to sum up, I joined the Army, and chose the infantry in particular, to get a practical outdoorsy education, the kind of thing you don't get sitting in a classroom.

I enlisted because I was in a hurry. I could've been an officer, since you only need two years of college. But the application is a big mess. Enlisting is much simpler. You walk into a recruiter's office. He's glad to see you. He sits you down with a cup of coffee or a soda to watch some cool videos, all with a "Be all you can be" theme that gets you pumped up. He asks you what you want out of life and right away he tells you that Uncle Sam's got just the thing for you. And then he waves the dollar signs and the college money.

A few days later, you take one of those fill-in-the-bubble-with-a-number-two-pencil tests so they can see what kind of jobs you're smart enough for. You get a physical. You go meet the guy who draws up your enlistment contract. And then you sign.

Basic Training is supposed to be the same for everybody— men, women, infantry, cooks, whoever. It's not. The Army's got a lot of jobs for people who sit in air-conditioned offices; I'd be surprised to learn that they ever had to march twenty miles carrying eighty pounds of gear. We got up every day at 0400 hours, or 4 A.M., and hardly ever got to bed before 2200 hours. The Army loves sleep deprivation for some reason.

Your only contact with the outside world during boot camp is letters from home. No books, newspapers, TV. No candy, soda, coffee, smokes, or chew. Officially, you do a little more than an hour's worth of physical training, or PT, first thing in the morning. But you'll do lots more PT in the course of the day, because that's how Drill Sergeants assign punishment. Whenever you do the slightest thing wrong, or slow, a Drill Sergeant is there to make you do push-ups.

I've got to tell you, though, Basic Training can be a lot of fun too. You get to play with cool toys. You make new friends. And the Drill Sergeants can seem like the funniest comedians you ever saw. When you think about it, they get a fresh source of comic material every time a new class of recruits comes along. There's nothing funnier than a recruit: awkward, clumsy, and ugly as sin because his head's shaved. And then there's always at least one kid who, you'd swear, sprang from the carnal union of close kin.

If you join the Army for the sake of self-improvement, like I did, then almost everything after boot camp is a letdown. When you get to your regular unit, training the individual (you) is no longer the primary mission. The training is mainly focused on getting everyone acting together effectively as a *unit.* Rambo has no place in today's army. Everything on the battlefield has to be coordinated, planned out, and rehearsed. If you ask me, this takes the fun and spontaneity out of war. But no one ever asks a private.

The Army has schools for everything, from digging latrines to jumping out of perfectly good airplanes. Some of them (like Ranger School) are tough and elite, some of them (like Airborne School) only pretend to be, and some just aren't concerned with all that hooah. ("Hooah," by the way, is the Army's favorite word. It connotes every meaning that a die-hard soldier could want. Whenever you can't think of anything to say, just say "hooah" and people will start to like and respect you.) The only surefire way to go to one of these schools is to have it in your enlistment contract.

As for me, I served my enlistment, three years and some change, then went straight back to college to finish up. I kicked butt in all my classes, and a lot of that had to do with maturity. I wasn't smarter, just more motivated to do my best. A year and a half later, I'm about to start a new job in the civilian world.

The discipline and sense of purpose I learned in the military have stayed with me. I mean, I don't jump out of bed at oh-dark-thirty and run four miles rain, snow, or shine. There's no reason to do that. But I have the discipline to choose worthwhile goals and then do everything it takes to meet them.

Next time you're curled up nice and snug sipping tea and it's a miserable day outside, just remember that on some Army post in the middle of Bumblef——, there's a platoon of wet, tired, and cold grunts slogging through the woods. As my old CO used to tell us, somebody's got to be out there "paying the price for our freedom." It's like they say in *A Few Good Men*—every night without fail, somebody's got to stand on the wall that faces toward the enemy. That person on guard is always and has always been a volunteer. And even though it was hard, I'm proud to have been one of them.

to Japan, Hawaii, all through Mexico and Central America, Panama, Costa Rica, Ecuador and into South America, Thailand, Canada. I've been to Vietnam. And I can honestly say that ninety percent of America would never go there."

In addition to the places you'll visit because of short-term assignments, the military maintains bases in some pretty kick-ass locations—Greece, Italy, Bermuda, Guam—and luck of the draw may land you in one. But while the military's recruiters will be sure to mention this to the travel-hungry, when it comes down to it, they aren't making any promises. One recruiter warns, "If you come to me and say, 'I want to join the Navy if you can station me in Bermuda,' I'll tell you no. I can't guarantee your location. There are certain places that we need you at specific times." When it comes to reenlistment, though, it's a whole 'nother ball of wax. To keep you on board, some of the services will give you the opportunity to pick exactly where you want to be stationed.

GETTING PICKY

People in the military are clannish. They're trained to be. Get one of these guys going as to why his branch is the best and they'll talk your ear off. It's like getting a basketball fan yapping about his team during the last game of the playoffs. Forget about it.

But other than the color of the uniforms, or the length of the training, it's hard to figure out what one of these branches has over the other when you're sitting in the recruiter's office after just one more spiel. To make things easier, I asked four people in the trenches what made them choose their fate over another.

THE NAVY

"What makes the Navy different than the others? Versatility, bottom line. In the Navy, you've got a little bit of everything. The only thing the Navy doesn't have is tanks. That's the only thing we don't have. If you're dead-set on being a tank driver, go to the Army. We have aviation, we have ground, we have subsurface, we have surface—just straight versatility all the way around.

"We're all a team. To get a ship underway, to get a submarine going, to get a bird in the air, you need to think like a team. If you decide to do something else on that team, we allow you that versatility. A lot of other branches won't offer you that.

"I've read statistics that say as many as 60 percent of college graduates aren't able to find work in what they studied. They have no skills. Now am I anti-college? No. Was I ready for college when I was 18? *No.* But I wasn't happy punching in the clock at the grocery store either. When somebody called me at ten o'clock at night and said, 'Can you come in at eight tomorrow morning?' it was hard for me to say, 'Great! I'll be there!' My wage at that time was like $4.25 an hour. I found my answer in the Navy."

—Talmadge Jones, Jr.

THE COAST GUARD

"One of the unique things about the Coast Guard is that we work for the Department of Transportation, so we're out there saving people's lives, doing maritime law enforcement, and environmental response. We don't practice or train to shoot a bunker or take a hill or anything like that, or kill people even. What we're doing is saving people. On the average, every twenty-four hours we're saving fourteen people's lives, preventing over nine million dollars' worth of narcotics from hitting the streets, conducting a hundred and eighty search-and-rescue missions, and responding to thirty-two oil or hazardous chemical spills. These are our main objectives.

"We don't have missiles or any sort of weapons. We do have handguns and other guns, so when we do boardings as we call them (jumping on someone else's boat to check for drugs or other violations), we're able to defend ourselves.

"Every time there's some kind of action going on like in Yugoslavia, as far as I know, there hasn't been a single Coast Guard person over there. We had a few port security units and a few reservists during Desert Storm, but I believe there was only one active duty Coast Guard vessel in the area (of several hundred). Only a few dozen can even endure the long trip over there."

—Lee Weldon, Petty Officer First Class

ARMY

"Each service has its own mission. Depending on what an individual wants, he may not want to go into a specific branch. I would never say, 'The Army's best because. . . ,'—there's just no such thing. I *can* say that it's the oldest service, that there's more money, more bonuses. It's got a larger number of jobs you can enlist into, so your options are greater: The Army has over two hundred and fifty different jobs. The Navy and Air Force more like seventy-five.

"Probably all the forces have almost all the same jobs, except for medical. The difference is, the Army breaks it down so you know exactly what you'll be doing when you enlist. You enlist for a *specific* job, you're not a general 'mechanic,' like in the Air Force. In the Army you're told, 'You will be a mechanic on this specific type of equipment.'

Currently, for people enlisting, we have a guaranteed MOS, a guaranteed job up front. Some of the services, you come in, you enlist, you have additional testing and basic training to accurately identify the specific job you can do for that branch. Whereas in the Army, the specific job's already determined up front. Based on your ASVAB, your physical, and the current vacancies that the Army has, we say, 'OK, this is the list of jobs that you'd qualify for.' And then the individual can pick from that, *prior* to enlisting. If they don't like what's available, well then they don't join."

—Sgt. Everheart

MARINES

"The Marines are the smallest branch of service of the armed forces. All the branches offer the same benefits. They pay the same. But the thing that makes us so different is the Marine Corps's values: honor, courage, and commitment. For over two hundred and some years, we've practiced this.

"Have you ever read the Fortune 500? Thirty-five percent of these people are former Marines. We did a survey and determined what types of traits make people so successful. And we found it was pride of belonging, leadership and management, discipline. And so these are the things that we train you in.

"I see us as the Ivy League of the armed forces, I really do. Because not to exaggerate about the Marines, but it's *really* tough. If you don't like it, I can't take you. Because we can handpick who we want to bring in the Marines. We don't want people to come in and dirty what's been passed on from generation to generation. And so when we are talking to people we thoroughly screen them. We test them. We take (people who've scored) fifty and higher (on the ASVAB). Passing is thirty-one. If they pass the screening morally, physically, and mentally, then they're ready for boot camp.

"If they don't score that well we pass them over to the Army, the Navy. . . . We've worked with many kids who spend twelve months with us, taking the test, taking the test. . . . But they cannot make it. So instead of wasting their time, so they can get somewhere in their lives we say, 'Come on man, why don't you check out the others.'"

—Sgt. Fredricko Suzunu

AIR FORCE

"I think one of the things that makes the Air Force special is that we deal more with education and technology than any other force. We do physical fitness six times a week, but an individual only runs three times a week and the maximum they would run in the Air Force is two miles. We don't have backpacks on, we don't do mud and all that good stuff. I appreciate what people like the Marines or the Army do, I really do, but we have a different mission. Ours is more technical and theirs is more physical. They tend to laugh at us a lot and call us a bunch of wimps but I just grin and go about my business. I think the greatest weapon in the world is the mind.

"We're not combat-trained in the Air Force. We don't do a lot of maneuvers or exercises or deployments like the other services do. A lot of times with the other services, people have to leave the local area for training or they get sent overseas to different bases and stay gone for weeks or months at a time. We tend to stay very stable. You can stay on the same base for your entire tour. This gives our people greater access to the local colleges and universities that are around the base. We're generally three times more likely to complete our degrees in a timely manner than people in the other military forces, because we're so stable. Also, our lifestyle is very relaxed, it's not as rigid as the other forces. And the camaraderie tends to be a lot greater.

"Congress gives each military service a budget. And the first thing we do is spend money on quality-of-life issues. And *then* we spend the rest on our weapons programs. The other military services do it in reverse. And when each of us runs

How Long You in For?

Most military stints are four years long. But that's not always the case. On the short side of the stick, you have the two-year commitment. (As far as I can tell, only the Army and Navy offer this option.) These are jobs that require very little training—an example might be working as a deckhand on a Navy ship. On the long side, you have the six-year commitment. This is a job like advanced electronics or nuclear propulsion—something that requires a big investment in training and money. Keep in mind, even the two-year stints will entitle you to the GI bill, if not more.

out of money, generally Congress is willing to give us more money to finish a weapons system, but they're a little bit reluctant to give them more money for quality-of-life issues, because it has nothing to do with national security.

"Because we spend a lot on it, our quality of life is very similar to what you would live yourself. The housing that the Air Force has is second to none. If you were ever to look at any of our base housing, you'd be very surprised. You're not giving up anything. An Air Force base is like a little Middletown, U.S.A., it really is. I think our food is excellent. Most people who are in the other services, they know that our food is the best.

"A lot of people think that all we do is fly planes. Actually less than 4 percent of the individuals in the Air Force actually fly. The rest of us do everyday nine-to-five jobs—programming, accounting, plumbing, electrical work. . . . We have our own hospitals with our own doctors and nurses in them, we have our own lawyers, fitness instructors, people who manage hotels (which we call billeting, but it's hotel management), restaurants. Any job that you could think of that you would

The Extremes

The Fearful

Some people are chickens. There's no way in hell they'd sign up for the military, knowing they might be shipped off to war. If the thought of combat leaves you shivering in your boots, don't worry. That's okay. You can still hit the government up for cash and training. Join the Coast Guard!

In case of war, not only are they the last to go, but they haven't gone for a while. It all comes down to wording. "The last real *war* we were engaged in was World War II. All these other things with Bosnia and Saudi Arabia, were *police action*," explains recruiter Lee Weldon. "But if we were *engaged in war*, then the Coast Guard would work with the Department of the Navy," he says.

To put things in perspective, consider this: During basic training, most Coast Guard recruits don't even learn to shoot a gun. The U.S. would have to be pretty damn desperate to call these guys in to help with a war effort.

The Fearless

On the opposite end of things, there's the Marines. You know how I told you before that you just had to get yourself through basic training, and then you can let yourself go to pot? I lied. If you're a Marine, you have to prove yourself every year, twice a year, with a fitness test that will kick your ass.

Marines are the first ones in when war's declared. They guard the president when he visits Camp David and stand watch at embassies and consulates around the world. But for a real sense of what the branch is about, take a look at their brochures: "Although nobody likes to fight, somebody has to know how . . . Marines are asked to accomplish the impossible and to distinguish themselves from all others. Anything easier would make you less than a Marine."

have in the civilian community, we have in the Air Force. The only difference between my job and a civilian job is that I wear a uniform to work and most civilians don't, every four or five years I might move to a different city or country, and I can't readily quit my job until I fulfill my contract.

"Each recruiter speaks about their branch like it's the greatest. I'm in the Air Force, and I honestly think that ours is, but at the same time, I still believe that each one of us has something good to offer. And I still think that everybody needs to search out and find what's best for them."

—Sgt. Robert Choice

THE CHOICE IS YOURS

Whichever force you pick, you've got a trump card. Truth is, the military is desperate. According to a recent report on *20/20*, the armed forces are scrambling for recruits. In 1998 the Navy came up 17,000 short. The Army missed their goal by a whopping 17 percent.

So when you head off to that recruiter's office, be strong. Go in knowing that you've got some bargaining room. Because now more than ever, when Uncle Sam says, "We want YOU!" he means it.

Careers Without College

The military's dishing out money for school, but you don't have to take them up on it. There are plenty of careers in the service that don't require any college at all.

Media:

- photo specialist
- broadcast technician
- graphic designer

Medicine:

- physical and occupational therapist
- dental specialist
- X-ray technician

Technical:

- computer programmer
- aircraft mechanic
- meteorological specialist

People Persons:

- recruiter
- drug and alcohol counselor
- court reporter

Specialist:

- air traffic controller
- environmental health and safety specialist
- diver

CHAPTER 16

Getting High (Tech): *How to Make It in a Brave New World*

> **"The reasonable man adapts himself to the world; the unreasonable one persists in trying to adapt the world to himself. Therefore all progress depends on the unreasonable man."**
>
> —George Bernard Shaw

WOULDN'T IT BE NICE IF YOU COULD WEAR shorts to work? Take a break for a game of ultimate Frisbee whenever you felt you needed one? Be the youngest person at your company and still have the nicest office?

There's a little slice of work-world heaven where these things can happen, even when you're awake—the high-tech industry. The hours are long, the pressure is high, but people in this business wouldn't have it any other way. You'd be hard pressed to find another niche in corporate America where even the secretaries get a chunk of stock, where the average

CEO can't grow a full beard, where it's very possible to retire before you hit thirty.

"I think twentysomethings, myself included, are just in this incredibly, incredibly advantageous position," says Chamara Russo, who works at EC2, a new media incubator. "I remember entering college freshman year and saying, 'Oh, god. Everything's been done. What could I possibly add to the existing industry? It's such a machine.' I thought I was going to become just another drone, and here this entire revolution has taken place. And we're in the middle of it."

It's true—we're smack dab in the middle of a renaissance. And you could be the next Michelangelo. "It's total chaos right now, but somebody's got to set the rules," Russo says, "The older generation isn't going to set the rules—they don't even know what we're all talking about. So just get in and establish yourself now."

Don't let inexperience stop you. People couldn't give a hoot how you look on paper, as long as you can deliver. Even recruiters are beginning to realize that high-tech wizards aren't born, they're made. Sure, you've got your exceptions—little geniuses who've been that way since the crib, but in general, technical skills can be learned.

What *can't* be learned is a set of personality traits that most high-tech mavens share—guts, curiosity, intuition, and decisiveness. In a recent article in *Wired* magazine, Silicon Valley recruiter Jon Carter was quoted as saying, "Succeeding in technology is like being a 911 operator or a doctor in a triage unit. People who can assimilate large amounts of data, in a very analytical way, and can synthesize it, and then step back and let their intuition kick in" have what it takes to make it.

Being in high tech is like standing at the plate and having

Turning Pro

Some words of wisdom from high-tech recruiter Terri Potts:

Q: I'd imagine as a recruiter, some people are easier to find than others. Which high-tech positions are the toughest to fill?

A: Software and database developers. Design *technicians*—people who understand design but are a little bit more technical. These guys are much harder to find and they have a much easier time negotiating higher salaries.

Q: You specialize in start-ups and the Internet. What's hot?

A: On the techie, programming, applications development side, there's a product called Cold Fusion that's getting popular with companies. Folks that are really good at that system are going to be in high demand. On the other hand, lots of companies choose Microsoft, just because they're Microsoft. So it's a safe bet to learn NT, because NT-based products are always going to be in demand: Java, Visual Basic, active server pages, Visual Studio, Active X . . . Software development and Internet technologies are always safe. The hardest thing to find in the last year, and I think all my competitors would agree, is UNIX development skills. Now I don't know whether that will stay around forever, but I don't see it going away in the near future.

Q: What else should people get good at?

A: Develop your people skills! Knowing how to talk and work with people is just as important as technical prowess. Because most start-ups are so small, everybody's got to know how to talk to the client.

Q: Anything else?

A: Get experience. We just hired a guy. He got his job offer on his eighteenth birthday. But he was already consulting for a few years at $35 an hour, and he was more qualified than a lot of college graduates because he had actual, physical work experience. Even if you work somewhere a few hours a day, even if you volunteer your time, get experience. Put it on your résumé. Nobody has to know how much you were making!

ten balls thrown at you at the same time. You've got to know when to hit, when to catch, when to duck. You've got to decide in an instant which pitches are important and which you can let whiz by. You can't let the sheer volume of distractions keep you from smacking one into the stands.

HOW TO GO HIGH TECH

To get hired in high tech, you don't need to be a computer guru. You don't even need a college degree. But you do "need to be a believer," says Dan Roddy, a CFO for Internet hotshot Rare Medium. The L.A. branch he runs has grown from three employees to over sixty in less than a year. "It's hard for us to find as many people as we need with actual Internet experience. So more and more we're just looking for great quality people with a passion and an interest in what we're doing," Roddy says.

Passion is a word that pops up with Morgan Cole, a recruiter for Microsoft, as well. "We take a really long-term view in that we don't really need to hire someone with the specific skills, because the specific skills, frankly, are going to be obsolete in two or three years. We're looking for someone who has a demonstrated passion for technology. So when I look at their résumé or I talk to them for five minutes it's quite clear that they think about computers. They think about the way that technology might change the world and have been actively trying to do something about it," Cole says.

The right mindset is more important than the right paperwork. "One of the things we tell our campus interviewers and all our recruiters, is, you've got to get behind the résumé and really figure out what they like to do. Sometimes these people don't put the projects that they've been working on on their résumé and when you talk to them, suddenly you realize, this kid, he's written tons of lines of code or he's taken apart or built his own computer. That's all relevant experience to us," Cole says. What about someone with no college at all, and no "official" training, who's sitting in the basement hacking away? "Give them my e-mail address!" Cole says.

Pedigrees are pretty meaningless in high tech. But college can't hurt. "There's such a sucking sound for people with talent that *I* don't look for college degrees. I mean if somebody's got design talent, they've got experience, they've built sites, you know, sure, I will absolutely hire them," Roddy says. "But it's like being a star basketball player in high school and getting seduced into the NBA or something. I mean, sure, you can probably make it work as long as your skills are valued and you haven't broken any bones. But what happens next?" Not every college dropout is going to be the next Steve Jobs.

WHERE THE ACTION IS

Silicon Valley gets the most press, with good reason. There are over seven thousand high-tech firms smushed between Palo Alto and San Jose. But a career in high-tech doesn't chain you to Northern California. The industry is thriving in Seattle (home of Amazon, RealNetworks, and Microsoft), Texas's Silicon Gulch (where Dell, Compaq, and Trilogy hang their hats), and Manhattan (home turf for Silicon Alley, the mecca for Internet content). Unlikely places like Idaho and North Carolina are also taking up the torch. And Atlanta, wired to the gills for the 1996 Olympics, could be next. It's got more fiber-optic cable running through its streets than any other city on the planet.

Surf's Up!

Web surfing may be the ultimate waste of valuable time, but you can get paid for it. Sign on to scour the net for Yahoo Net Events, a virtual guide to online programming. You're mission? Review live chats, interviews, performances, and special events and set your modem smoking in search of cool sites. If you've got your finger on the pulse of pop culture, a nose for current events, and a passion for the web, this may be the best couch potato gig going.

Send your résumé to: jobs-surfing@yahoo-inc.com or fax it to "Attention Net Events" at (408) 731-3301

Outside U.S. borders, Israel and India are next in line for high-tech honors. There are also plenty of jobs to be had in Asia—Singapore especially. If you've got your heart set on traveling, high tech might be your ticket. And for once, being American can help you. The U.S. is in the lead, and other countries are clamoring to hire Americans to help them catch up.

HIGH-TECH TRAINING

The high-tech world is a strange place. It's hard to know what you need to do to prepare. Three of the richest men in America—Bill Gates, Ted Waitt, and Michael Dell—are college dropouts who started high-tech companies with practically nothing. It's obvious that you don't *need* a degree to succeed in this business. But what if you want a jump start?

According to the *San Jose Mercury News*, the top paper in Silicon Valley, you enroll at Cogswell Polytechnical College in Sunnyvale. Sure, it's nothing much to look at, but looks can be deceiving. "A degree from Cogswell is almost as good as a letter of introduction from one of the two Stevens—Speilberg or Jobs—the school is to digital entertainment what Stanford University is to business administration," the paper says.

Lots of Cogswell students turn down ivy-covered campuses for well-equipped workstations. The computer-student ratio at Cogswell is one to one. It's the only college in the United States where you can get a B.A. in computer and video imaging. And it's pretty cheap—about $3,900 a trimester.

Most Cogswell graduates go on to become 3-D modelers, web designers, animators, video game designers, and multimedia authors. The school is at the top of the recruiting list for places like Pixar, Lucas's Industrial Light and Magic, and a slew of Silicon Valley companies. Grads typically enter the workforce at $50,000 a year. They've gone on to do everything from animate M&Ms or the Pillsbury doughboy for TV commercials, to work on movies like *A Bug's Life, Toy Story,* and *Ants.*

Cogswell Polytechnical College

What: Training grounds for future 3D modelers, animators, multimedia-ites, and video game or web designers

Cost: About $3,900 a trimester

Contact: (800) 264-7955

WHAT TO DO

Where do you fit in? Depends on what you want to do. In general, tech companies come in five major flavors: hardware, software, semiconductors, networking, and Internet. Hardware refers to the machines themselves. Software is what makes them do things. Semiconductors are the brains of the operation. Networking lets computers talk to each other within an office.

Tech-y Tidbits

About 67,000 *new* people get online everyday.

The information technology industry already employs over 5 percent of America.

And the Internet connects individual computers with the big wide world.

Regardless of what area you pick, if you know what you're doing, finding a job should be easy. Twenty-five years ago, no one would dream of having a computer in their home. By all accounts, in the very near future the world will buy more computers than they do TVs.

High tech is growing faster than the speed of light. Each technological advancement creates a storm of new job descriptions and a huge need for new hires. Positions are being created faster than most companies can fill them. Evidence? Take the posters that blanket the walls at Netscape, an Internet giant: "Who is the best person you've ever worked with? How can we hire him/her?" Take the bonus that most high-tech employees are guaranteed, anywhere from $1,000 to $2,000, for every person they recommend who's eventually hired. Take the obscene amounts of stock companies have to offer in order to keep people onboard.

Growth of the computer industry is getting more frantic than a Memorial Day sale, and there just aren't enough people to fill the ranks. Since 1986, computer science majors are down by 43 percent. Good people in general are hard to find. So companies are doing whatever they need to do to get them and whatever they need to do to keep them—however outrageous.

Take Mirronex Technologies, an information technology consulting firm in Skillman, New Jersey. When traditional recruiting tricks turned up next to nothing, the company decided to do something dramatic. They decided to give away cars. BMW Z3 roadsters, to be exact. Crazy? Maybe. But they hooked some great fish.

Even if your recruiter doesn't go to such drastic measures, expect high salaries and good perks. Freelance contractors can make $50–100 dollars an hour. And in busy times, they can clock in as much as sixty or seventy hours a week. According to *U.S. News Online*, entry-level programmers typically reel in $45,300; a network administrator $48,700; an online research analyst $56,400. A website designer at it for a few years can pull in $60,000–70,000.

There are other perks. Free or cheap gourmet meals, weekly parties, company basketball or volleyball courts, hot tubs, gym memberships, vacations, inexpensive housing. At Netscape, overworked employees too busy to buy a gift or arrange a dinner can have someone do it for them. They can also have their teeth checked at the dental van camped out in the parking lot.

And don't forget the stock. High tech's a crazy thing and stock's been known to rise by 100 percent a year, a week, a day—thanks to a quote in the *Wall Street Journal* or a casual comment from an analyst. Pick the right company and you could be a millionaire before you know what's hit you. I know a girl who made $100,000 in one month—her first month with a new company that happened to get bought. Her only previous work experience was an internship.

If you're a recruiter, you're going to be pretty wary about the whole money issue, especially with kids looking for their first job. You want someone who's going in for the right reasons, not just some joker looking to get rich quick. "Sometimes people can get lost when they're looking at the stock and they're looking at what they're being paid," Morgan Cole says. "They need to look at the impact they're going to have. That's one of the things that's so attractive about a place like Microsoft. Whatever you write, or whatever you work on, there's an opportunity that thirty to fifty million people are going to use it. Let's just take as an example this guy I recently hired. He's going to be working on Windows CE, designing part of an operating system that's going to go on every kind of device that you can think of—you could be interfacing with it in your refrigerator, in your copier, in your stove, in your car . . . So some of the stuff this guy's going to be working on is going to directly impact the way you do your life. That's a huge thing that people need to look at: Is the opportunity at the company I'm looking at going to impact the way that people do things?"

Bringing Home the Bacon

When people think of high tech salaries they think of all the employees who've gotten rich quick. Keep in mind, though, that most of those millionaires got wealthy through cashed in stock options, not sky-high paychecks. Still, salaries in the industry are nothing to sneeze at. Here's an idea of what the average Joe makes.

Database administrator: $61,000–88,000 (plus 5–30% for Oracle, SQL Server, Sybase, PeopleSoft, and/or other skills)

Software Engineer: $55,000–80,000 (plus 5–15% for C++, Visual Basic, Delphi, and/or other skills)

Internet Programmer: $48,750–68,250 (plus 5–15% for Java, HTML, Visual Basic, Perl, and/or other skills)

Web Developer: $47,000–65,500 (plus 5–15% for Java, HTML, Visual Basic, Perl, and/or other skills)
Technical Help Desk Specialist: $45,000–54,000
Network or UNIX Administrator: $42,750–69,250
Webmaster: $51,500–73,000
Internet Designer: $48,909 (average)
Software Developer: $72,503 (average)
Marketing and Business Development Person: $65,391 (average)
High-Tech Temps Who Know How to Program: up to $80,000–100,000 a year

—according to the *Wall Street Journal Online*, http://careers.wsj.com

COMPUTER CAREERS FOR THE CREATIVE SOUL

High tech is pretty heady stuff. But you don't have to be a technical whiz to find a job. There's plenty of room for low-tech people who may not know all the latest technologies, but don't approach a computer with panic in their eyes. Companies need artists to create brochures, invent logos, design layouts. They need writers to come up with spiffy catalogue copy or make their instruction manuals halfway intelligible. They need publicists to schmooze the media and marketing people to snag celebrity endorsements. They even need your run-of-the-mill assistants, secretaries, receptionists, and general errand boys. Difference is, if you show your smarts in an entry-level position here, your age won't stop you from catapulting up the corporate ladder. Because in this business, you can never be too young.

Artists for the New Millenium

Are you a New Media artist looking to be farmed out? Consider signing on with one of these high-tech agencies. They place digital talent with companies that need them, temporarily or otherwise.

United Digital Artists, New York (212) 777-7200

Artisan, Los Angeles (310) 312-2062

Digital Talent, offices in San Francisco (415) 731-9900 and New York (212) 581-1990

"There's a tremendous amount of opportunity for people with creative impulses," according to Steve Schardt, who does business development for a very popular e-commerce site. "There's web design, multimedia composition, writing for online publications, and music making," Schardt says. Just because a job is corporate, doesn't mean it's evil. In fact, artists may find that they can make a bigger impact in the high-tech arena than they ever would in the art world—not everything's been done yet. "The Internet industry is in its embryonic stages and there's much room for experimentation and risk taking. New ideas are valuable," Schardt says. And despite artists' fears about the horrors of a desk job, Schardt is quick to point out that both options have their pros and cons. "'Business' does not equal static boredom; 'The Arts' do not equal pure pleasure and effortless creation," Schardt says. It's a lot more complicated than that.

INTERVIEW

How I Got into High Tech by Sarah Ellerman, Managing Editor, *Next Generation* magazine

I never thought that I would work in any kind of technology field. I'm twenty-six; I still call myself a *girl.* I like to read books and draw pictures and play guitar. But improbably enough, I work in the video game industry. All I hear all day long is "s-video this" and "gold disc that," and I sit here drinking Mountain Dew and editing copy about a hobby that I don't even participate in.

I have to say, it's almost mind-bogglingly fun.

You may wonder how an artsy chick like me ended up editing technical manuals. A video game, of all things, changed the course of my life. It was called *King's Quest*; a neighbor kid gave me a pirated copy on five-and-a-quarter-inch disks back in 1986. And it was then, when I was fourteen, that I suddenly understood why we'd even bought a Tandy. Until then, I had found nothing remotely worth doing on the computer. But *King's Quest* was so absorbing that I became determined to learn how our computer worked—and I wrested control of it away from my dad and brother and became the family authority on getting the thing to work.

Look. I'm here to tell you that if a fourteen-year-old girl can use that forbidding piece of equipment, you can approach the user-friendly computers of 1999. Understanding technology starts with simply turning it on. You start pressing buttons, and making mistakes, and finding things out. Later on, you start to optimize it, and speak in the jargon, and insist that your friends get hooked up, too.

At age twenty, I wound up withdrawing from college because of a disastrous personal relationship. I was labeled a dropout. And it quickly became clear that certain options were closed off to someone like me. At school, I had majored in Rhetoric, which taught me how to write persuasively. So I made learning about the Net my hobby, and writing my skill. I knew that I was smart enough and competent enough to somehow make a life out of all this.

My break came when I was chatting with the editor of an Internet magazine. I don't know why, but I brazenly told her that I was a writer—and she believed me. I wasn't lying, of course, I just failed to point out that I was strictly an amateur writer. But a cover story had fallen through, and she was so desperate to fill a gap in her lineup, that she assigned it to me on the spot. And get this—she was grateful to *me* for taking the assignment.

I really made the most of that clip. I parlayed it into other free-lance jobs, I milked her for contacts, the whole nine yards. And my enormous break came when I saw that a publishing company in my hometown was launching a magazine about the Net. Even though the ad was for an editor-in-chief and I had zero editorial experience, I rabidly pursued this job. I figured that they *had* to need a lackey and I was fanatically determined that the lackey would be me.

Eventually I got an interview. And the key phrase that I believe got me the job was "like a dog." I used the phrase many times in the interview. "I will work like a dog," I said. "I expect to get *paid* like a dog." I smiled extremely sweetly when I said it, and I was hired. I went from $27,000 as a secretary to $22,000 as an editorial assistant, but I was thrilled.

I'm now the managing editor for a video game magazine called *Next Generation*. I don't write for it. I supervise the entire birthing of the magazine every month. I edit it and fact-check it. I help manage deadlines and the other editors' time. The fact that I used to read the dictionary for fun in my spare time (honestly, I did) helps a lot. So does the fact that I am comfortable with computers and tech jargon. And so does the fact that I have a likable laid-back personality and can function well as a liaison between all the different departments that have to coordinate to get a magazine put together on time: editorial, art and design, production, ad sales, and management.

The atmosphere here is like a dorm room full of geeks who have finally come into their own. There are toys everywhere, and the people are really smart and funny and just plain cool. For me, the joy of the work is in the people, and in producing a magazine that readers are just absolutely fanatical about.

I can testify that there is a place for low-tech people in the game industry, and there is a place for low-tech people in publishing. The game industry needs artists, and musicians, and people to market games and produce them. Tech publishing also has plenty of non-tech positions for people who are layout whizzes or editing geniuses or production-minded people, either in print stuff or Web stuff. And once you get into the atmosphere, doing the thing that you love, you just naturally start to soak up some of the jargon and passion and energy for technology. Because it's really a very cool thing, a thing that is not going away.

So much of breaking into "cool" jobs is simply in the doing. If you want to write, write. If you want to draw, draw. And if you want to program, program. The Quake levels you make, or the fanzine you start, or the score you compose on your synthesizer, are all parts of your portfolio and your skill-set.

My very best practical tip in terms of getting a job is to write a good cover letter. The cover letter is a hundred times more important, and gets a hundred times more attention, than your résumé. A bad cover letter gets mocked and read aloud, even by the nicest people, so don't use jargon and don't be arrogant; remember to describe your relevant experience, even if it's unpaid; and make the letter have some feel for your personality. Be personable and nice and smart and fun; be someone that the hiring manager wouldn't mind sitting next to nine hours a day, because that's what it usually comes down to.

And if you need some kind of introductory class for technology? I advise you to get in the company of a little kid and ask her to play a video game with you. You'll have a lot of fun. And you might even learn something worth putting on your résumé.

A PERFECT FIT

The thing about high tech is, it's a niche-based business. And there's a place for people with all kinds of backgrounds. Schardt himself got into the field "having had no exposure to the Internet other than a twice-used e-mail account." His baby steps into New Media came post-college, when he began working at an Internet café in New York "advising patrons on cyberculture and food choice." A few months later, looking his "massive college debt" square in the face and acknowledging that his current position "offered a pittance for wages and no stock options," he high-tailed it to Wall Street and started knocking on doors. Schardt landed a job, was there for a bit, met an Internet entrepreneur, and packed his bags for the West Coast. He's now in charge of forging relationships with music websites for his employer. Random? Maybe. But Schardt had drive. He had a great head on his shoulders. And most of all, he knew music.

Jill Goldberg, too, never thought her hobbies would lead where she is today. But when you look at what she loved to do, it's not that surprising. She was a sports fanatic who loved to play video games. Today she's in the sports marketing division of the video game company Electronic Arts. Did she ever think she'd end up there? "Never. Never!" Goldberg says. "But I really believe that the most important thing I ever did for my career is I never forgot what it is I love to do. I mean, I don't love to work. I don't think anybody loves to work," Goldberg says, "but I love golf, I love video games, and I love sports. And I was determined that at the end of the day, somehow those things were going to play a role."

They do. Goldberg has her share of days behind a desk, but she also spends a good chunk of her time on the green, with golfers on the PGA tour. The job's got its perks. Take the week Goldberg went down to Tiger Wood's house to show him his new video game. "It was the first year of the game and we wanted to set him up with a computer and see what he thought," Goldberg says. "So I went down to see him, we're playing the game, and he's going nuts, because I'm beating him. All of a sudden he throws down the mouse and says, 'All right! I've had it! Let's go outside. We're playing real golf!' So I played three rounds of golf with him," Goldberg says.

LAST WORD

High tech isn't a place for people who like to find a warm place, kick up their feet, and get comfortable. There's only one real reason to join this industry. And contrary to popular belief, it's not the money. It's the high. You have to want to "be a part of where things are changing, and where they're less stable and less secure," according to Roddy. You have to want to be a part of creating something. "It's a state of mind," Roddy says.

High-tech companies employ some of the most innovative people around. And if you're one of those people, according to Morgan Cole, there's no other place to be. "We're changing the world and you'll have a direct impact. Any adjustment you make on anything that you do is going to have a direct impact on the way people gather, collect, interpret, and analyze information . . . I can't tell you how many times in my four and a half years at Microsoft I've heard that 'Everything's already been done.' Well, it hasn't all been done. We've barely scratched the surface."

CHAPTER 17

Who's the Boss?: *Starting Your Own Business*

> **"The trouble with the rat race is that, even if you win, you're still a rat."**
>
> —Lily Tomlin

PAUL ORFALAE DIDN'T WANT TO LEAVE HIS COLLEGE stomping grounds. On the cusp of graduating from the University of California at Santa Barbara, he racked his brain to come up with some way to stay in town. Upon graduating, with a $5,000 bank loan in his pocket and a newly rented one-hundred-square-foot garage, he opened a tiny stationery and copy store, which eventually grew so beyond his expectations that copy machines had to be moved onto the sidewalk to accommodate the crowds. He named his little start-up Kinko's: the company is now worth 1.8 billion dollars and has over 900 locations in places as far-flung as the Netherlands and South Korea.

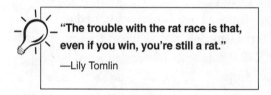

The cosmetic phenomenon Hard Candy was launched when a shoe saleswoman fell in love with the baby-blue tint of twenty-two-year-old Dineh Mohajer's toenails. After a customer offered to buy as many bottles as she had on her, at almost twenty dollars a pop, Mohajer decided to take a crack at marketing the stuff she'd been mixing in her sink.

Some people know how to play the corporate game. Others decide to jump off the board and start another game entirely. If you have the guts to strike out on your own, the rewards can be huge—no matter what your age, experience, or college background. So before you squelch your entrepreneurial instincts, nodding your head when people tell you, "You're too young," consider this: 60 percent of all new businesses started in the second half of 1997 were helmed by people under the age of forty. Likewise, in 1994, 272,000 businesses were launched by people in their twenties. Clearly, age is not the issue. You can start a kick-ass business before ever showing wrinkles. In a way, your age is your best advantage. You probably have no family to support, no home loan to worry about, no pension fund to lose if you strike out on your own. On the flip side, you probably have almost no money, no experience, no business contacts. This doesn't have to stop you. Ambition is a powerful thing.

CALLING ALL CONTROL FREAKS

Maybe you're not cut out for taking orders. If the thought of reporting to someone else, of punching in the clock, of the same paycheck every week, sends you screeching into the night, owning your own business might be the way to go.

But not everyone's cut out to be the boss. And while there's no magic formula, most successful entrepreneurs have a few things in common:

1) **They're not afraid of hard work.** Striking out on your own may mean no more nine-to-five grind, but it usually means even longer hours—sometimes seventy to seventy-five a week.
2) **They have vision.** They can see the end result, even from the very beginning of a long road.
3) **They're risk takers.** It takes balls to hang yourself out there in the wind, knowing you could lose everything.
4) **They're adaptable.** Running a business takes creativity. You need to expect the unexpected and deal with it.
5) **They have drive.** There are a hundred reasons why a new business "can't" work. There will be a hundred times you'll want to quit. If striking out on your own was easy, everybody would do it.

Test Your Entrepreneurial Potential

Eighty percent of all start-ups fail. Time to figure out if you've got what it takes to make it:

How risky are you?

a) I won't bet based on luck but I'll bet based on my abilities.
b) I only bet on the small stuff.
c) I like to bet on the underdog.
d) I've got Vegas written all over me.

How hard do you work?

a) I'm known as a hard worker.
b) I work hard, but I have a life too.
c) I'll work as many hours as needed, but I prefer not to do too much overtime.
d) I'll work whatever hours are asked of me.

Describe yourself:

a) I'm like the energizer bunny.
b) I like to have breaks every few hours.
c) When I need energy I can always find it.
d) Sometimes I get tired for no reason, sometimes I'm on fire.

My major goal is:

a) To have a job where every day is an adventure.
b) To make enough money to live comfortably.
c) To be respected for what I do.
d) To have time for family and a social life.

What kind of smart are you?

a) Street-smart.
b) Brainy.
c) Intuitive.
d) Smart about people.

I like jobs where:

a) I get to be creative and try out my ideas.
b) What's expected is absolutely clear.
c) The boss leaves me alone.
d) There's potential for advancement.

When problems arise:

a) I'm the one with a clear head.
b) I make decisions quickly.
c) I'm not too proud to ask for help.
d) I get annoyed when people aren't pulling their weight.

How do you work with others?

a) I like to be in charge.
b) I'm a loner.
c) People tend to look to me for advice.
d) I work well as a team player.

I am:

a) A do-er—I'd rather try things out than talk about them.
b) A believer—I have faith that things will work themselves out.
c) A planner—I plot things well in advance.
d) A listener—When I need help I bring in an expert.

How do you feel about funding your business?

a) I'm good at raising money.
b) I'm going to use my nest-egg or save until I have one.
c) I can start small and build as needed.
d) I can survive without paying myself for awhile.

How do your friends and family feel about you starting this?

a) They're helping me.
b) They don't know.
c) They're nervous but they're getting used to it.
d) They think it's a bad idea.

How certain are you?

a) Nothing can stop me.
b) Who knows if I'll be good at this—we'll see.
c) I'm willing to take a risk. Then at least I'll know I tried.
d) Sometimes I think I might be making a mistake.

What's your management style?

a) I have most of the skills I need and I'll get the right people to fill in the blanks.
b) I'm planning on doing everything important myself.
c) I'm looking for employees for the long haul.
d) I'm going to hire cheap labor at the beginning, then find good people as I can afford them.

What is your biggest strength?

a) I know this business inside out.
b) I'm a people person—I can get along with anyone.

c) I'm a problem solver—if something goes wrong I can always fix it.
d) I'm innovative—I'm brimming with new ideas.

How much experience do you have?

a) I've worked in this business.
b) I've worked in a similar business.
c) I'm a business person by nature, whatever the business
d) I'm new to this business.

How do you feel about starting this business?

a) I'm so excited I can barely sit still.
b) I think this could be very profitable.
c) As I learn more and more about this, I like it more and more.
d) If this business doesn't work, I have other ideas.

Answers

Give yourself two points for every time you answered "a" and one point for every "c." If you scored:

24–30: Don't just sit there—start planning. You're a born entrepreneur.

16–23: You might have the goods, but they need a little polish. Get a mentor and a strong team behind you.

0–16: Tread lightly. This isn't your calling. Think twice before borrowing from people you know.

GETTING STARTED

Still hot on starting something? Then let's lay down the basics. For any new business to succeed, there are a few indespensables: an idea, a plan, a work space, a wad of cash. Do not underestimate the necessity of any of the above.

Assuming you're not a Rockefeller or the next Bill Gates, let's start from the beginning. To get the ball rolling, you're going to need some help. Let me introduce you to your new best friend: the Small Business Association, a service funded by our very own U.S. government.

Strung from coast to coast, SBA offices are the pot of gold at the end of the start-up rainbow. These guys will spoon-feed you everything you could possibly want to know. Why? The SBA's sole purpose in life is to help new entrepreneurs get up to speed. They offer free classes, free advice, handouts, checklists, research, resources: everything you'll need under one roof. They'll help you come up with a plan of attack for launching your business. They'll hook you up with a mentor in your industry. They'll help you get a loan. In short, they will do everything in their power to get your business up and running.

And that's not the half of it. The SBA works hand in hand with an organization called SCORE—the Service Corps of Retired Executives. These guys are the Yodas of the business world: a group of retired CEOs, executives, and small business gurus looking to pass on the torch to the next generation. They'll dole out advice, help you fill out a loan application, even coach you on the dreaded "business plan." All you have to do is ask, and they'll give you enough free handouts to wallpaper your apartment.

ARMED AND READY

So you've raided SCORE and the local SBA for information. You've brainstormed until your head hurt. You've spent so many nights awake thinking about ideas, that you're singlehandedly keeping Starbuck's afloat. What next?

I have two words for you, my friend: market research. It may sound dryer than a summer in Death Valley, but it's a deal breaker. Market research can tell you, before you've borrowed ten grand from grandma, whether your business is destined to go down in flames.

The bad news is, it's time consuming. Market research will tell you whether there's demand for your business, where the holes are in the marketplace, which locations people find convenient, how much customers are likely to pay for what you can give them . . . all the information you need to have an edge from the get-go. But to get all of that information, you need to convince at least a hundred people to talk to you. Not your uncle Morrie and his branch of the Elks Club. People you don't know. Easy? I think not. Consider how many times you've hung up on someone calling to "ask you a few questions." Think of how many times you've ignored the guy standing in front of the grocery store with the clipboard. If you live in an obnoxiously friendly place, expect to have three people give you the kiss-off for every one who agrees to talk to you. If you live in your typical American city, you'll be lucky to get one in ten.

The good news is, this information can give your business an edge, and it's free for the asking—you just may have to ask a lot. If you're feeling rich, or just a little lazy, you can probably find some starving student willing to do the polling for you. This can save you some time and the trauma of being constantly abused by people you don't know.

If you're high on moxie but low on cash, you can do the asking yourself. Deposit yourself in the neighborhood where you're thinking of setting up shop and pass out surveys—at the post office, in front of the 7-Eleven, in the mall, wherever. There's no room for pride here. Go ahead and beg if you feel the need—the sooner you get those hundred surveys filled out, the sooner you're out of there. Bribery goes a long way. Set up a plate of Girl Scout cookies, bring a pitcher of lemonade, whatever you need to do to make it worth people's five minutes.

And make sure you ask the right questions. It's bad enough to go through this once; don't set yourself up for a sequel. Think about what you need to know. For example:

- ✔ Is there already a lot of competition in this area?
- ✔ Who do customers see as the top contenders?
- ✔ What is the competition doing right?
- ✔ What are they doing wrong?
- ✔ What's missing in the marketplace?
- ✔ Will what you offer fill in a gap?
- ✔ How's your price?

Give people a few possible variations of your business to choose from. Ask them which one floats their boat and why. Find out what's most important to them: price, name, quality, service, location, novelty. . . .

If you're up for extra credit, head over to your local Chamber of Commerce for some demographics. They can give you the skinny on potential customers in your area. Most important, they've got census data—the magic numbers you need to estimate the market for your brilliant idea.

THE BUSINESS PLAN

Once you've got your market research out of the way, it's time for the next step: the business plan. The business plan is the holy grail of entrepreneurship. Think of it as a monetary wish list, a plan of attack, a dream journal, a mission statement, a press release, and an investor magnet all tied up into one. Trying to start a business without a business plan is like trying to film a movie without a script. Frustration is inevitable.

The business plan serves as your roadmap to success. It needs to lay out in detail exactly what your business will be and all the steps you'll take to get it there. It needs to include an accurate estimate of the money you'll need to get on your feet and stay there until the cash starts coming in. It needs to hit readers with market research and explain why you're bound to succeed. But aside from all the dry stuff, the business plan needs to have electricity. It's the unofficial invitation to your party. It's what potential investors will see before deciding whether or not to get on board. It has to grab these people by the you-know-what and leave them begging you to take their money.

This brings us to the crucial juncture, the biggest sticking point for most fledgling businesses—the funds. We'll get down to the nitty gritty later, but basically, there are three major ways to fund any business: beg, borrow, or steal.

BEG

Before you rule out this option, consider this: Other than loan sharks, your friends and family are the easiest people to hit up for cash. First of all, they already know you. Second, they wish you well. Third, guilt works wonders on them. Contrast this with a bank: They don't know you from Adam, they think of you as an account number, and guilt is useless. For businesses that require under $50,000 in start-up capital, begging should not be overlooked.

Keep in mind that this method of money-grubbing has its

Did you Know?

Relatives can give you up to $10,000 as a "gift" without paying taxes on it.

downside. Once they've given you their money, your loved ones will also want to give you their advice. Constantly. And before asking grandpa for a loan, think about how you'll feel if your business doesn't do so well. When you get a loan from people you know, it's hard not to feel pressure to pay them back immediately. Don't assume this will be easy, or even possible. If your business bombs you might lose more than money, you might lose your place at the dinner table.

BORROW

Borrowing falls into two major categories: loans and partnerships. Loans place you smack-dab in the wonderful world of debt. Partnerships can leave you wondering if you let the devil sign your dance card.

Loans

Let's begin our journey with your friendly neighborhood bank. Banks are a good option for people looking for a loan of between fifty thousand and one million dollars. Of course, this will take some convincing. Banks want to know that you're capable of paying them back. Because of that, they'll want collateral. In other words, what can they take from you if you're unable to pay—your car, your house, your first born?

When you're just starting out, you're unlikely to have any

of the above to offer. (If you were that set up, you wouldn't be going to a bank in the first place.) But any loan officer worth his name tag will want you to commit yourself in some way. In general, this means expecting you to foot at least one-fifth of the bill. Why? This makes banking people feel like you have a stake in things—you're more likely to push to make things happen if your own money's on the line.

The SBA is also an option. They have a bunch of loans to help people starting out. One, the "General Guaranteed Loan, 7a," is specifically for people the bank rejects! This program is kind of like a first lease, when landlords ask parents to cosign for their kid's apartment: The bank agrees to lend you money and the SBA acts as a guarantor, agreeing to cover between 75 and 90 percent of the loan (up to $750,000) if you turn out to be a deadbeat.

Partnership

If going it alone is starting to sound overwhelming, consider a partnership—shared risks + shared workload = shared profits, should there be any. Assuming we're talking about a *professional* partnership, you have a choice to make: angel or VC.

Angels are the benevolent players in the partnership game. They're usually successful business owners or rich guys with money burning a hole in their pockets. Regardless of where they made their moolah, they're people on the lookout for an upstart business they can invest in, in the hope of reeling in a 15–20 percent return on their money in five years. According to the Colorado Capital Alliance, there are twenty million prospective angels flitting about America. In 1998 alone, angels invested over twenty billion dollars in businesses.

Angels have all kinds of reasons for getting into the game.

They may want to sit on your board and breathe down your neck, or they may just want to write a check and live vicariously through the bumps in your road. Your angel could be a rich benefactor *à la* Rockefeller, or she might be a twenty-nine-year-old entrepreneur who's just sold her start-up for a cold thirty million.

The biggest problem with angels is that they're difficult to find. There's no magic place where you can go and shout, "I'm looking for somebody rich!" The best way to find an angel is to tell everyone you know that you're looking.

If you're willing to give a little to get a little, you may be able to find some funds through an "Angel Network," a company that tries to match givers with takers . . . for a fee. For a small investment on your part, usually ranging anywhere from forty to four hundred dollars, you can get into the clubhouse. Just remember that your money doesn't guarantee you a pitch, it just gets you onto the bench.

Angels are a godsend for entrepreneurs looking for between one to five million dollars. Even better than the money they invest are the introductions and contacts they can give you. Just remember, this money isn't free. However angelic your angel may be, you will have to give up a chunk of your company in order to get the chunk of change you need to fund it. You may also have to give investors a say in decisions. Don't be so desperate for cash that you give up too much control for not enough in return.

Angel Networks

The Angel Capital Electronic Network

www.ace-net.sr.unh.edu

Brought to you by your friendly neighborhood SBA.

The Capital Network, Austin, TX
794-9398
www.thecapitalnetwork.com
Tight with the Austin Technology Incubator.

Environmental Capital Network, Ann Arbor, MI
(734) 996-8387
www.bizserve.com/ecn
Green for the green—helps environmentally friendly start-ups find funding.

Investor's Circle, San Francisco, CA
(415) 929-4900
www.icircle.org
Forty-four percent of entrepreneurs who present at their meetings get funds within six months.

Private Investors Network, Vienna, VA
(703) 255-4930
www.mava.org/pin.html
Gives loot to businesses based in the mid-Atlantic states.

Technology Capital Network, Cambridge, MA
(617) 253-2337
www.tcnmit.org
Should be high on the list of any high-tech start-up.

Start-ups that need a *lot* of money may have to forego the angel all together for what many view as the devil incarnate—the venture capitalist. Unlike angels, who often have benevolent reasons for funding start-ups, VCs are in it solely for the money. They want to earn five or six times their initial investment within five years.

Advice from Roger McNamee, VC Extraordinaire

What Roger would tell every entrepreneur, if he had five minutes alone with them:

Big ideas are a lot better than small ones:

Start with an idea that at least has the *potential* to be huge. We describe this as "having a dare to be great strategy."

Execution is everything:

Most entrepreneurs get enamored with an idea and they don't spend nearly enough time thinking through the execution. They're too busy thinking about the money.

Anticipating all the issues that will come up takes a lot of planning:

You have to think of a way to make this thing, whatever it is, economically viable. You have to have systems in place, not only so you can deliver customer value, but so you can collect for it.

Two business plans are better than one:

Most entrepreneurs focus entirely on the business plan related to raising the money and not nearly enough on how they'll make the thing happen. That's where so many plans fail. It's important to create two types of business plans:

> Business Plan I: Focuses on the recipe and the list of ingredients a.k.a. your idea and how you'll deliver it.
>
> Business Plan II: Focuses on how much money you'll need and when you'll need it.

There's money and then there's smart money:

For any entrepreneurial project raising money is absolutely critical, raising *lots* of money. And where that money comes from matters; entrepreneurs can always be leveraged by smart investors. Venture capitalists are really good at business development, recruiting management teams, adding discipline to business plans, and raising capital. VCs offer more than cash. They offer smarts.

Venture capitalists are more than moneybags, they're partners. They may demand a good chunk of your company, but they provide a lot in return. Most VCs are incredibly connected and can introduce you to some pretty valuable people.

VCs take some of the autonomy out of running your own business. They expect to have their opinions heard—whether it's on marketing, employees, image. . . . On the other hand, that's because their opinions are worth something—unlike the typical entrepreneur, these guys know what they're doing.

STEAL

You're on your own here. . . .

A ROOM OF ONE'S OWN

Once you've got the idea and have scrounged up the money, you need to find a space. Some start-ups require more than others. If your business is a paper route, you obviously don't need an office. If it's manufacturing Frisbees, you probably can't do it in your kitchen.

Assuming you need an actual physical space to do your business, there are several things to consider before scoping out real estate. Does the place need to be accessible to customers? Is it big enough to house your business if it becomes a whopping success? Is there too much competition near by?

There's a beautiful phenomenon called the "small business incubator." Strung out across the country, these little hatching grounds provide a safe haven for little chicks like you until you've grown enough to leave the nest. There are more than five hundred in the U.S. and Canada—most created and

The Home Front

Thirty two million American households have at least one member working from home.

—The American Association of Home Based Business

funded by universities, the government, or nonprofit organizations. And statistics show that new incubators are opening at the rate of four or five a month. They've each got their own little chick specialty: high tech, manufacturing, service—you get the picture.

So what's in it for you? Cheap rent for one. Incubators provide a place to house your business at a very nice price. Other perks? How about shared secretaries, utilities, conference rooms, office equipment . . . You'll also have a posse of lawyers, consultants, accountants, and others willing to work with you on the cheap, sometimes even for free. And since incubators are often buddy-buddy with venture capitalists and banks, they can help you get some money behind you.

The only downside, if there is one, is that you're expected to move out and move on once your business is turning a profit. And office space, while it won't cost you a fortune, may be small.

No big inconvenience when you consider the numbers in a recent *Los Angeles Times* article: start-ups that begin their days in an incubator have an 80 percent success rate—a big boost over the rate of success for start-ups in general, a slim 20 percent.

ADVICE FROM INSIDE

All business incubators are not created equal. Take it from Chamara Russo, of L.A.'s EC2. "Incubator has a benevolent ring to it," she warns, "but it's sometimes just a way for the people running it to make money. The benevolence shouldn't be accepted wholeheartedly." Incubators are started for all kinds of reasons, some more lofty than others. Some are formed as government projects, others to redevelop real estate that's not bringing in any money. EC2 was launched with a $120-million-dollar gift; they're not in it for the bucks.

Russo warns would-be tenants to look at the lease carefully. "Make sure you're not locked in, because God forbid the company doesn't do so well, you don't want to owe a year of rent. You have no money, it's an impossibility, and yet some people will sue you for it." Other tactics to weed out the good from the bad? Visit. "Make a mental note of which companies are there and then just give a call. It takes all of five seconds. Ask them if they're happy there. They'll be honest with you."

Keep in mind, you're not the only one scoping things out. The incubator is looking you over, too. What kinds of things catch their eye at EC2? "The idea and the people are paramount," Russo says. "We look for the novelty of the idea, for innovators—people who might not be financially successful, because it's such a good idea it's almost *too* good. We're looking for pioneers, people who could quite possibly change some very basic and accepted things in our lives."

Russo admits that cheap rent is one of the biggest reasons people join an incubator, but says it's not necessarily the best reason. Incubators can open doors. "It's advantageous for a start-up to be here because they get things that they wouldn't get otherwise," she says. Like connections. "There's definitely a mentoring program in place. We have partnerships with national, global companies, and the people that we work with are at the highest levels. They'll meet with them for free. Plus we have roundtables with experts every six to eight weeks, these people specialize in looking at companies and giving advice."

Sometimes that advice can save start-ups big money. "I've had a partner at a top law firm tell members, 'Don't call me. Just go to this website, look up the annual reports for publicly held companies, look at the legal contracts, and copy them. Just change the words appropriately,'" Russo says, "And for a start-up run by engineers or film school grads, who are not experts in legalese, it wouldn't occur to them to do contracts themselves, for free."

An incubator is an incredible way to get your baby business on its feet. Russo calls it "a sort of parent" but notes,

Top Ten Metro Areas for Starting a Small Business

1. Portland/Vancouver, OR/WA
2. St. Louis, MO/IL
3. Seattle/Bellevue/Everett, WA
4. Greensboro/Winston-Salem/High Point, NC
5. Charlotte/Gastonia, NC, and Rock Hill, SC
6. Denver, CO
7. Minneapolis/St. Paul, MN/WI
8. Las Vegas, NV/AZ
9. Salt Lake City/Ogden, UT
10. Kansas City, MO/KS

—*Entrepreneur Magazine*, Oct. 1997

"These are not children, so we have to have that hands-off approach to raising them." While incubators can help your business along, they're not going to run it for you. "Start-ups need to become self-sufficient," Russo says. "If they're having a major problem, we'll definitely help them work it out. If it's a little thing, they need to do it, so when it's time for them to go out into the real world, they're ready."

ALL IN THE FAMILY: LIFE IN THE FRANCHISE

If you want to start a business, but not completely from scratch, consider the franchise option. A franchise smoothes the road to entrepreneurship, which, make no mistake, can be pretty damn bumpy. Joining is like paying a little extra for travel insurance: You cough up cash for a safety net which you may or may not actually need. A franchise gives your business an immediate stamp of approval because it makes it instantly familiar to the general public—by slapping on a name everyone's heard of. A McDonald's may be new, but it's a McDonald's—people know what to expect.

The downside of joining a franchise is this: With safety comes dictatorship. You can't paint your burger joint electric blue if the whole chain has painted their restaurants yellow. You can't design your own logo if they already have one. In a nutshell, you can't be as creative as you could be if it was all up to you. You're the kid here and you have to do what the parent company says.

On the other hand, sometimes daddy knows best. Franchises may make you do things their way, but that's because their way is tried and true. Fern Sheinmel, who

The Fab Five

These five francise had the highest level of franchisee satisfaction, according to a recent *Success* magazine survey (April 1999)

1 Maid to Perfection/Wild Birds Unlimited (**tied score**)

3 Dr. Vinyl

4 American Leak Detection

5 McDonald's

started a Moto Photo a few years ago in Raritan, New Jersey, liked the guidance that joining a franchise gave her. Moto Photo helped her and her partner (now husband) Barry scout out locations, purchase equipment, even develop a marketing strategy. They offered them a four-week training course at the company's headquarters that "covered every little detail, every single aspect of the business—from setting up employee schedules, to ordering supplies," Barry says. Once that was over, they had two to three weeks of hands-on training in an actual store. And when their own store was ready for business, Moto Photo sent someone from the corporate office to help them get it off the ground. The duo started pulling in a profit after only three months in business. In a few short years, their store has become so successful that they've had the funds to take some dream vacations—to Egypt, the Caribbean, Africa. And because they're in charge, they can. When asked if he's ever regretted his franchise decision, Barry says, "Never. I'd do it again in a heartbeat. All of my weaknesses they seem to help with. There's a lot of support there. And, I mean, these guys have over 450 stores. They've made mistakes and learned from them, which means I don't have to."

FROM THE SOURCE

Whether you are looking into a franchise, or hatching your own business scheme, there is an organization just for you. The Young Entrepreneur Organization is a club specifically for entrepreneurs under forty, and their entire purpose is to give young business owners the chance to pick each other's brains. Problem is, you have to already be a success to join the ranks. While there's no secret handshake to get in the door, your company has to be pulling in at least a million bucks a year. Until that day arrives, here's a jump start: advice from YEO's Executive Director, Brien Biondi.

Biondi came to YEO after starting and running two businesses of his own, so he knows what he's talking about. I asked him why he thought people discouraged young would-be entrepreneurs from starting their own businesses. "I think that the past generations tend to be more conservative," he said. "They want kids to be safe and pursue more traditional means of employment because they don't want them risking what they already have. But youth is actually a huge advantage. There are more people than ever today who want to become entrepreneurs but they're married, they have kids, and it's harder to go ahead and give up the lifestyle and the income they're used to. Younger people are just starting out, so it's not like they've already accumulated a lot of wealth and are investing it in the company."

How young is too young, and how inexperienced is too inexperienced? What is it that separates the next Michael Dell from the guy with big dreams, filing for bankruptcy. . . . "You can't teach people the key characteristics I seem to find in every true entrepreneur," Biondi insists. "I think that entrepreneurial spirit is a product of your environment and your teaching as you grow up, not so much of 'Hey, I've graduated from college and now I'm going to get an MBA in some entrepreneurial program.'" Biondi is convinced that you can teach people business skills, or show them "how to go about it," but that there's a core group of personality traits you need to make it and you either have them or you don't.

What are those magic qualities? Well, the adjectives vary, but the same set of traits seems to turn up on everyone's list, from the SBA to the YEO: drive, enthusiasm, vision, focus, courage, determination . . . you know the drill. As for formal

Starting Your Own Business: Ten Ways to Make a Buck

1. Start a pet photography business
2. Become a professional errand runner for busy executives
3. Launch a drive-thru coffee place—hook up with the franchise Xpresso Drive Through Café (303) 215-0373
4. Rent a food cart and ply your snacks: at concerts, sports games, office buildings, when movies get out or in between college classes
5. Start a car detailing service in a busy office parking lot
6. Offer your services as a professional thank-you card writer—handwritten thank you's for big parties with guests that don't know the host's handwriting (weddings, charities, etc.)
7. Sell your services as a computer set-up pro—on call for the technically phobic
8. Start a travel company for adventurous students on a budget
9. Become a theme party planner
10. Launch a professional gift shopper business—save people time by finding the perfect gifts for their friends and family

education, Biondi says, "I know for a fact that you can make it without a degree. A number of members in our organization have. I think that there's so much change going on out there right now in the business world that really all you need to be is a bright kid. If you're a bright kid, you don't need to have a college education. But to grow that business from a hundred thousand to one million to five million a year, you need some kind of knowledge base. That's where education or prior business experience comes in. You can't run a company half blind."

For those already bringing in the big bucks, that's where YEO comes in. For the underdogs among us, Biondi suggests finding a mentor, someone who's got some serious experience under their belt. "Surprisingly, there are a lot of people out there who will serve as mentors because they've made it and they want to give a little back," he says. Once you find someone willing to take you under their wing, Biondi suggests meeting with them at least once a month. "Entrepreneurs can become blind-sighted. They're so passionate, so committed, that they don't recognize the point at which it becomes clear that the business idea is not a good one. Your mentor is the person you can trust to tell you, 'You know what? You've gone too far now. Call it quits. Let's start the next business. This one's not going to work.'"

The truth is, many businesses fail. And many successful entrepreneurs didn't hit one over the fence their first time up at bat. When you look at them, "You never think of all the failures they've had," Biondi says. "But they're on their third or fourth business because the first three didn't make it. So my advice to anybody that's got the energy and the enthusiasm and the spirit and the vision is this: Don't give up. Because eventually you're gonna hit it."

RESOURCES:

Small Business Association: (800) 827-5722
www.sbaa.net
National Business Incubation Association: www.nbia.org
The International Franchise Association: (202) 628-8000;
www.franchise.org

Afterword

Well, that's it. No more. Finito. We've come to the end of the line, my friend.

For you, though, we've come to the beginning. So stop reading and start doing! Hopefully this book has opened your eyes to some interesting possibilities and fired you up to go after them.

Drop me a line and let me know how it goes!

dkwood1@excite.com

Or check out the website:

www.uncollegealternative.com

APPENDIX

Homework for Life

There are certain things that every adult should learn how to do: drive a car, balance a checkbook, make a passable martini . . . There are also certain books that every adult should try to read—whether they go to college or not. Of course, what those books are depends on who you ask. Here are fifty to get you started on your road to enlightenment:

Aeschylus: *The Oresteia*
Aristophanes: *Lysistrata*
Aristotle: *Nicomachean Ethics*
Euripides: *Electra*
Herodotus: *Histories*
Homer: *The Odyssey*
Plato: *The Republic*
Sophocles: *Antigone* or *Oedipus Rex*
The Bible: The Old Testament
Vyasa: *The Mahabharata*
The Koran
Chaucer: *The Canterbury Tales*
Dante: *The Divine Comedy*

Machiavelli: *The Prince*
Shakespeare: *The Complete Works*
Jane Austin: *Emma*
Cervantes: *Don Quixote*
Galileo: *The Dialogue Concerning the Two Chief World Systems*
Hawthorne: *The Scarlet Letter*
Huxley: *Brave New World*
Ibsen: *The Master Builder*
Thoreau: *Walden*
Milton: *Paradise Lost*
Molière: *The Misanthrope* or *Tartuffe*
Hawking: *A Brief History of Time*
Rousseau: *Social Contract*
Swift: *Gulliver's Travels* or *A Moral Dilemna*
Tocqueville: *Democracy in America*
Beauvoir: *The Second Sex*
Dostoyevsky: *The Brothers Karamazov*
Einstein: *Ideas and Opinions*
Douglas: *The Life and Times of Frederick Douglas*
Faulkner: *Light in August*
Freud: *The Interpretation of Dreams*
Goethe: *Faust*
Hamilton, Madison, and Jay: *The Federalist Papers*
Rushdie: Midnight's Children
Joyce: *Ulysses* (Very hard but very important!)
Kafka: *The Metamorphosis*
Marx: *The Communist Manifesto*
Nietzsche: *Beyond Good and Evil*
Twain: *The Adventures of Huckleberry Finn*
Tolstoy: *War and Peace*
Beckett: *Endgame*

Steinbeck: *The Grapes of Wrath*
Chekhov: *The Seagull* or *The Three Sisters*
García Márquez: *One Hundred Years of Solitude*
Ellison: *The Invisible Man*
Warren: *All the King's Men*
The Autobiography of Malcolm X

A lot of these texts can be downloaded for free off the Internet. Try:

The Internet Classics Archive: classics.mit.edu
Etext Library at Virginia: etext.lib.virginia.edu
Project Gutenberg: www.promo.net/pg

And for help understanding them, check out:

The New Lifetime Reading Plan by Clifton Fadiman and John S. Major
The Complete Idiot's Guide to American Literature by Laurie E. Razakis
www.greatbooks.org (for guidebooks or help starting a classics reading group)